gondolin press

Fr. Ernesto Zucchini

HEAVEN IN A ROOM

The Life of Maria Valtorta

gondolin press

HEAVEN IN A ROOM – *Fr. Ernesto Zucchini*

Original title: *Il cielo in una stanza* (2019)

Translation: Apostoli Cristina – Marabello Helen – Loft Catherine

© **gondolin press**

1915 Aster Rd.
60178 Sycamore IL

www.gondolinpress.com
info@gondolinpress.com

2023 © Gondolin Institute LLC

ISBN 978-1-945658-34-1 *(soft cover)*

All the literary and artistic rights are reserved. The rights for translation, electronic storage, copy and total or partial adaptation, by any equipment, (including microfilm and photostats) are reserved for all countries. The Editor remains at disposition for eventual holders of rights who have not been traced.

First U.S. edition: First edition October 2023

*With very special thanks
to Chiara and Massimo Martinucci
for welcomimg me in the name of Christ
on so many occasions*

*and to Lucia Martinucci
a real godsend for her manifold help*

Contents

Contents 7

Notes on the English translation 10

Foreword 11

Preface 14

Introduction 16

PART ONE 18
The field and the flower 18
The exiled flower 24
Continual confinement to boarding schools 27
A ray of light 31
Florence 35
Harmony apparently destroyed 40
The Gospel of Luke 43
Viareggio, her home 44
The spiritual key 47
A complete woman 49
A new goal: sacrifice 51
Her last Holy Mass in a church 55
The Doctors 56
The arrival of Marta Diciotti 60
The death of her father Giuseppe 60
The persecution by Iside and a thirst for writing 62
A humorous strictness 64
Just before Heaven opened up 65
Father Romualdo Migliorini, spiritual director 67

PART TWO 69
And Heaven entered her room 69
God's pen 71
1943: Her yes to open Heaven 76
The war in Viareggio 79
Dictations and visions 81

Ecstasy	84
1944: Her "fullness of time"	85
Father Migliorini was not able to follow her in flight	88
The evacuation	89
The dark night of the soul	92
Giuseppe Belfanti	96
Everybody back at home	103
Up to her neck in writing	103
The Devil's countenance	104
Heaven in the blood of Jesus	108
The enemy shall not pass!	110
Spokesperson and word for everyone	111
The pagan sky and Christian Heaven	112
The Archangels in her room	113
1946 and the post-war period	114
Azariah, the guardian angel	116
Unlimited immolation	119
The books in the Valtorta household	119
The great and small clergy of Viareggio	126
Father Migliorini between mystic and paramystic	130
Why is Father Migliorini in Rome?	134
The pieces left behind	139
Mother Teresa Maria, the Carmelite	141
A new arrival	143
Father Corrado Maria Berti	144
Light and shadow in Father Berti	146
Father Berti in a trap	149
Preparation for printing	152
The two autobiographies	154
The breakup with the Friar Servants of Mary	156
Comparisons	157
Rejected	161
The Gospel is completed	164
Not only *The Gospel*	167
So much written work!	172
The tortures of Maria Valtorta	176
On the political barricade	180
Marta Diciotti's recollections	185

The radio 187
The telephone, the dog and the hen 189
Radiesthesia 192
The cold 193
A new Evangelization 194
Paranormal? 195
The supernatural 199
Foresight 202
What is typical about Maria Valtorta? 205
Saints understand each other: Msgr. Carinci 208
Èroma Antonini, one of the family 213
Anna Maria Antonini 215
The parish priest 218
The politician 219
An old and dear friendship 221
The creative artist 225
The tribulations of canonical approval 229
Still, the approval is necessary 233
A fifth gospel? 235
Writing and transcribing 237
Broadening the mind 241
The spiritist deviation 242
The real burial place of St. Peter 245
Looking for attestations 248
Pius XII receives 255
America too 259
The publisher 261
A meteor: Luciana 262
Maria Valtorta and the clergy 263
Mystical absence? 268
The envisaged tragedy 270
Entrance into Heaven 273
Father Berti in search of a miracle 277
Maria dressed in heavenly white 278
Conclusion 279
Bibliography 281
About the author 286

Notes on the English translation

The quotations and notes in the text come from the officially translated English editions. Quotations cited that do not have an official edition in English have been translated by the publisher.

The titles of the cited texts and those in the bibliography are the English editions where an official text exists. However, where Italian editions have not yet been translated into English, both the original Italian title and an English translation of that title are given in square brackets the first time they are mentioned.

For the convenience of readers in the event that they may have a different edition to the English texts referred to in this book, footnotes list the dated entry wherever possible.

Foreword

by Catherine Loft

When I was given the translated work, *Heaven in a Room*, I was hesitant, even reluctant to read it because a first-hand and detailed account of Maria Valtorta had already been given in her *Autobiography* – and handwritten by the woman herself. Furthermore, she had been ordered to write her life story by her spiritual director. Therefore, Maria Valtorta had looked retrospectively to reveal the whole truth with an honesty beyond measure because she thought her only audience would be her spiritual director. As such, Maria had already presented a *true* chronicle of her life.

So what *more* could Father Ernesto Zucchini possibly offer English-speaking readers?

As an academic who is extremely well read and as a priest who had encountered something spiritually and mentally profound through these writings, it is evident that Father Zucchini was offering something far beyond a mere commentary or a third-person recount of her life. After reading *Heaven in a Room*, Father Zucchini was true to his purpose. Through his literary expertise and commitment to promote Maria Valtorta and her extraordinary Work, Father Zucchini delivers an exceptional text, stamped with his unparalleled insight and in-depth study of all material available written *by* Valtorta and *about* Valtorta. He enables the reader "to see what she had given to God and received from God, what she had given to men and received from men" (*Notebooks 1943,* p.112).

Father Zucchini reveals that the Mosaic of Maria's life does not merely consist of the particular stones or glass tiles that Valtorta provided in her narrative, but the epoxy resin that held it all in place which he himself provides, is essential in order to explain the unexplained.

In this book, carefully selected excerpts are presented from Maria's *Autobiography* and the *Notebooks*, to which Father Zucchini adds factual information not communicated by Maria herself in the last five years of her life during which she was mentally absent. It also records the intense and sometimes underhanded route the battle plan of the clergy attempted to take, even after the death of Maria Valtorta.

Father Zucchini authoritatively uses an abundance of extracts from numerous publications not available in English. He refers to the books by Maria's live-in carer and friend, and the other women who knew her; letters contained in four volumes that Maria wrote to her spiritual director, a monsignor and to her religious friend and confidante, along with their replies to her. There are written documents from the publishing house, from the clergy and from the Holy Office who at times tried to support her, while at other times, exploited or vilified her. Furthermore, the intellectual Father Zucchini has not only researched publications and books written in Italian, but those published in Latin, French and Spanish – anything that will explain and enlighten the reader even more. He leaves no stone unturned. He helps makes sense of her life – what she gave to God and what she gave to man - and the conflict she experienced that was caused by so many others. There are many notations that are not only significant, but are of importance and magnitude, and also explain the future path of Maria Valtorta and this Work.

While Maria's recount was subjective, this book is objective. While Maria tells her story of what happened within her mind, within her bedroom and within her immediate environment, this book also presents clarity from people and events from the outside and brings it into Maria's room. On several occasions, clarity is even given on matters of which Maria herself was unaware.

Father Zucchini also answers questions that have left people wondering for so long:

Why was Maria's father in Purgatory longer than Maria's mother?

In what ways did both Fr. Migliorini and Fr. Berti damage the cause?

How was Maria's anonymity exposed when Jesus had ordered it to be kept secret?

What impeded the publication so often?

Why is Maria not able to be declared Venerable yet?

Why is her process for beatification and canonization still at a standstill and will be for some time to come?

Where is St. Peter really buried?

Father Ernesto Zucchini has sourced every piece of material available on Valtorta, and he has meticulously compiled all the information in this one book, *Heaven in a Room,* in order to create a full and complete study on Maria Valtorta – the person and the Work, which I highly recommend.

Coordinator of the Maria Valtorta Readers' Group
Good Friday, 7 April 2023

Preface

'Heaven in a Room' is an expression used to indicate an account of facts, which is not just the unfolding of a life, but I would dare to say, it is also the interweaving of something unique in history. Indeed, the life of Maria Valtorta is not only characterized by personal conversations, visions and dictations, but it actually shows the unfolding story of Jesus' life. Several times, the film industry has depicted the life story of a person, of a family, or an epic of what was accomplished over many centuries. With Maria Valtorta, it is possible to go over those same facts, which took place two thousand years ago, with the addition of some further remarks. Whoever approaches *The Gospel as Revealed to Me,* quite often finds out who the author is only later. The dazzling nature of the story of a living Jesus – and not a cardboard cutout or literary one – fascinates and transports us into a world which is not magical but real, even certified by Galileo's science, full of sinners of every sort. It allows us to contemplate Jesus in everyday situations as a real and living man: an itinerant preacher teaching until He was exhausted, never tamed nor resigned. Usually, at some later point, the reader discovers the *medium*: Maria Valtorta. And that is when the question becomes: how did she do it? How could she bring this wonder to pass? This book talks about this unique prodigy in the history of mysticism. An act of love made of blood, sweat and tears that lasted a lifetime and was particularly painful for 27 years. There was nothing spectacular in her life: no 3D-cinema special effects, no remarkable adventures; on the contrary, there was the boring monotony of life day after day, followed by night after night, with no end in sight, except for very brief periods of intensified drama during World War II. This dullness would have prevailed had it not been for the numerous sufferings in her life that never failed to carry out their horrible work. Pain was a constant companion to Maria: constant, yet welcomed and desired. The gifts received from Heaven were not complete until her last five years, when her union with her Lord and God had become so strong that the whole world vanished. Completely enclosed in God, Maria Valtorta was only waiting for Him to decide, at His will, to let her enter His Kingdom forever. Recounting Maria Valtorta's life has been a great honor and I am grateful to the Lord who has granted me this unsought and unwanted gift. May it help all the readers get a better understanding of the one who has led us to a renewed enthusiasm towards Jesus and his Mystical Body, the Church.

Introduction

Time-space coordinates are essential to seriously understand an event or a character, as they often reveal why some events happened and the reasons why other events did not. Especially in the life of Maria Valtorta, events, though minute, were turbulent and varied, and they certainly had an influence on the perception of things and situations, on psychological sensitivities and the management of feelings, on the judgment of people and behavior, on the ability to discern, and on life choices. Therefore, it is essential to start from real events to understand what happened and what the consequences were.

Maria Valtorta's life on earth unfolded between 14 March 1897 and 12 October 1961: 64 years lived in various parts of Italy, but 34 years spent in Viareggio, near Lucca, in Versilia, an area not far from the Tyrrhenian Sea, populated by the Italian lower middle-class in the first half of the 1900s. Her life spanned a time which began with the *Belle Époque*, she then experienced the violent years of WWI, the nationalist and autarchic dictatorship of fascism, the tragedy of WWII, bombings from the sky and from the sea, the Gothic Line and the civil war attached, the crucial Italian political choices of the late 1940s, and the beginning of the Italian economic boom.

From a social point of view, this was the time that marked the shift from a democracy based on wealth to a democracy for all, that went through the rise and fall of an authoritarian regime, and that eventually saw the gradual access of women to all sectors of society, women at last became equal to men in terms of dignity. All this, thanks to technological and social changes that were hard to believe for those who were born in the 1800s: the world advanced from horse-drawn carts to cars and to jet aircrafts; from the humble letter to the radio and to the television; from the early movies to colour cinemascope; from the rifle to the frightful H-bomb, in a crescendo of technological innovations in every field, with a seemingly unlimited horizon in terms of development.

From a religious point of view, Maria Valtorta's life was all enveloped in Catholicism; even if, at times, she perceived the strong presence of sworn enemies, nonetheless her world can be defined as 'socially ecclesial'. The post-1968 crisis had not been felt yet, new religions and new piety were still in their infancy – micro realities that developed only later[1] – and the life of the Church still affected the great majority of Italians. Some noticed the prelude to what was about to happen, but superficially; almost everything appeared to be working as usual. Maria Valtorta lived from the papacy of Leo XIII until that of St. John XXIII, although she had already 'been called away' from this world before Pius XII's death. However, the various theological schools of thought – modernism and progressivism – although present in Italy at the time, did not affect her story directly. To Maria Valtorta, Catholicism was an obvious, natural, and foregone conclusion. To be 'always with the Pope until death'[2] was a choice she suckled along with the milk from her wet-nurse from Caserta. Yet, her life lapped against the spreading of esoteric doctrines through the writings of theosophists and similar characters; not because of her interest – she had no interest in that – but rather because of the interest of her cousin Giuseppe Belfanti. That is why spiritism, so fashionable among the lower and upper middle-classes of the time, ended up knocking at her door, despite her radical rejection.

Without a doubt, her spirituality, indeed her theoretic and tangible mystical experience, focused on atonement, on immolation, on offering herself to Divine Justice as a victim soul for the eternal salvation of mankind. Therefore, she welcomed and experienced all the sacrifices and the various serious sufferings in that sense. She was self-taught until 1942, guided by the catechism of the schools she attended, and by the books that she instinctively read. We can simply say that the Catholic Church and its hierarchy were her guidance until the arrival of her first spiritual director in 1942. Thereafter, she decidedly chose never to depart from it. No scandal ever perturbed her; no slur on her own personal character ever stuck. Her being a Catholic was paramount, absolute and non-negotiable.

---

[1] For further information on this issue cf. Massimo Introvigne–PierLuigi Zoccatelli (under the direction of) Centro Studi sulle Nuove Religioni, *Enciclopedia delle religioni in Italia*, [Encyclopedia of religions in Italy] Elledici, Torino 2013.

[2] From a song by the Italian *Catholic Action* Circle from 1950.

PART ONE

The field and the flower[3]

Maria Valtorta was 'accidentally' born in Caserta on 14 March 1897. Death, according to the doctors, was going to claim her at birth but she survived[4] and, had it not been for the religious choices she made in life, she would have certainly lived longer. Her father Giuseppe, originally from Mantua in Lombardy (born 21 August 1862, the son of Carlo Valtorta and Maria Citella[5]), was Chief

---

[3] The primary source for the first part of Maria Valtorta's life is her own autobiography: cf. Maria Valtorta, *Autobiography* Centro Editoriale Valtortiano, Isola del Liri (FR) 1991. In order to understand the spirit, the veracity and the truth of the autobiography, it is to be noted that Maria wrote it after giving into the insistence of her spiritual director, stating that it would "expose my conscience" (Albo Centoni, *Ricordi di donne che conobbero Maria Valtorta* [Memories of women who knew Maria Valtorta], Centro Editoriale Valtortiano, Isola del Liri (FR) 1998, p. 217).

[4] According to Marta Diciotti, it seems that the Valtortas had three children, but the question remains debated. The first child, a boy, died suffocated in his own blood. Then came Maria, who was saved only because the doctors believing her to be dead, threw her on the bed in the operating room without any further assistance, which 'accidentally' brought up all the blood from her lungs and she thus survived. The doctors had continued to assist her mother. The third child did not even see the light of day: Maria's mother Iside lost the child because she lifted a heavy double bed due to the excessive anger [she felt at that moment] (cf. Albo Centoni, *Una vita con Maria Valtorta. Testimonianze di Marta Diciotti* [A life with Maria Valtorta. The Testimonies of Marta Diciotti], Centro Editoriale Valtortiano, Isola del Liri (FR) 1987, pp. 154, 466). However, in her autobiography, Maria Valtorta wrote as if her mother had only had one other child apart from her. This could only be a trivial simplification (cf. Maria Valtorta, *Autobiography*, op. cit., p. 183).

[5] cf. Corrado M. Berti O.S.M., "Bollettino Valtortiano. Semestrale di informazione e cultura valtortiana" [Valtortian Bulletin. Bi-annual newsletter on Valtortian information and culture], Centro Editoriale Valtortiano, Isola del Liri (FR), n. 1 – May 1970, p. 1; cf. also: Maria Valtorta, *Autobiography*, op. cit., p. 110, footnote. [Footnote not in the English edition].

Warrant Officer in charge of the arms of the XIX Light Cavalryman Regiment of the Army[6] and he had been transferred to Caserta for operational reasons; that is why Maria was born there. However, she did not acquire anything from Caserta because her stay there was too short to have any influence on her. Even though she attributed her tendency to be passionate to her wet-nurse's milk, it is more likely that Caserta was just a transit area for the innocent baby. On the contrary, orderlies, soldiers, petty officers and senior officers had probably helped her grow up and shape her personality. As a matter of fact, Maria loved her father's military world and she thought highly of his colleagues despite noticing some inconsistencies. For example, she described the Colonel, her father's direct superior, as a "saint"[7]. Her father, a generous person[8] is described as a "gentle man, accommodating and very fond of his only daughter"[9], who ensured that Maria's education greatly improved through his own personal teachings, often based on direct observations and descriptions of nature. On Sunday afternoons spent with his daughter, he educated her during their long strolls, and it is not hard to see where Maria's

---

[6] cf. Corrado M. Berti O.S.M., Preface to Maria Valtorta [Preface not in the English edition or subsequent Italian editions], *Autobiografia*, Tipografia Editrice M. Pisani, Isola del Liri (FR) 1969, pp. V-XV. Father Berti made the first brief authoritative description of the life of Maria Valtorta. This preface was removed in subsequent editions. This text remains an important reference given that the author was a culturally well-prepared observer of Maria Valtorta with whom she collaborated from 1946 onwards [From this point forward, this edition of the *Autobiography* will be referred to in this text as *Autobiografia prima* [the First Italian Autobiography].

[7] Maria Valtorta, *Autobiography*, op. cit., p. 47. It should be noted that Maria Valtorta wrote this in 1943 to reveal it only to her spiritual director. This attitude is well described in the rule of Saint Benedict in chapter 7, the sixth degree of humility: "to manifest with a humble confession to one's abbot, all the bad thoughts that arise in the soul and the faults committed in secret" (*La regola di San Benedetto* [The Rule of St. Benedict], Shalom Editrice, Camerata Picena 2016, pp. 44-5).

[8] cf. Maria Valtorta, *Autobiography*, op. cit., p. 77.

[9] ibid., p.16. Corrado M. Berti O.S.M., "Bollettino Valtortiano", op. cit., p. 1. He wed on 20 November 1893 (cf. Maria Valtorta, *Autobiography*, op. cit., p. 77).

knowledge – of flowers, plants, celestial constellations etc.[10] – which she showed in her later writings[11], came from. So, the remote cause was the rich teachings of her father, Giuseppe. And Maria admitted that even her expression: "God is a Father", was derived from her love for the fatherly figure[12]. However, this man, naturally good and very fond of his only daughter, had to face three tragedies which had an impact on this life and on his afterlife. Chief Warrant Officer Valtorta was also an inventor: he could design new mechanical systems capable of improving the army-issued weapons. One of these inventions was extraordinary: it was worth obtaining a patent for it, which would have also greatly benefitted his family's finances. But the hierarchical system meant that he had to present his invention to his superior first, who should have examined it and returned it to him. However, his superior in rank must have been by no means a saint because he 'stole' the patent and took credit for the invention. The betrayed Giuseppe Valtorta could have then sold the patent to some foreign power (Austria, for instance), but he did not, out of patriotism and for the sake of peace, and for the same reason he did not expose his superior. The result at home was terrible: there were huge arguments with his wife, and a subsequent depression developed that ended up undermining his health for good. He resigned from the army in 1912[13] by going into retirement and died on 30 June 1935. Thinking back to those days, his daughter described her father's situation as follows: "…His heart [was] trampled upon, his feelings wounded, his affection scorned, his health destroyed, his intelligence damaged, and his dignity as a man[14] mortified until the final hour…". Maria Valtorta was perfectly aware of this tragedy and in her autobiography of 1943, she wrote very harsh words: "You (Father Migliorini) know what I mean by forgive. (…). To me, forgive means 'to forget the evil received'. Out of love for God, I have now come to forget the evil which *I* have received. […]. But I cannot – I have no right - to forget the evil that my father received. And, in not

---

[10] For example, cf. Maria Valtorta, *Autobiography,* op. cit., p. 56.
[11] This is in reference to all the writings and letters composed by her.
[12] cf. ibid., p. 25.
[13] cf. ibid., p. 118.
[14] ibid., pp. 68-9. On this topic, the pages in the *Autobiography* speak for themselves.

forgetting it, I do not forgive. All I can do is reprove the one who did it and disregard her having been responsible, continuining to respect her as if she had been the perfect companion"[15]. And that is what the daughter did with her mother. The non-forgiveness (to forgive was her father's responsibility, not hers) remained so hidden in her real life that, had she not written about it so frankly in her autobiography, no one would have known.

Her mother, Iside Fioravanzi, also from Lombardy, born in Cremona (11 September 1861)[16], was quite well-read and had been a French teacher. All those who had met her described her as selfish and quarrelsome[17] and she ended up suffocating her severely ill husband and her daughter with unreasonable harshness[18]. In describing her character, Maria Valtorta used very strong words without, however, crossing the line. "A bit of liver trouble and, after this improved, a great deal of the *famous* female malady [...] of *irritability*, had made her a torment, a family calamity"[19]. All witnesses agree on the terrible harshness of Signora Iside, and they differ only in the terminology used by people who remember her words and actions. According to Marta Diciotti[20]: "Signora Iside (...) made life

---

[15] ibid.

[16] Born to Eliodoro Ficravanzi and Giuseppina Belfanti. cf. *Autobiografia*, p. 68 [This footnote in the Italian edition is not included on p. 77 in the English edition of the *Autobiography*].

[17] "Alien from any manifestation of maternal love or word of praise" (Corrado M. Berti O.S.M., *Preface* to Maria Valtorta, *Autobiografia prima* [first Italian *Autobiography*], op. cit., p. VII). [Preface not in the English or subsequent Italian editions]

[18] Corrado M. Berti O.S.M., *Preface* to Maria Valtorta *Autobiografia prima*, op. cit., p. 1.

[19] Maria Valtorta, *Autobiography*, op. cit., p. 61.

[20] Born in Lucca on 2 December 1910, she served in the Valtorta household from 24 May 1935 until Maria's death on 12 October 1961, becoming over time and according to her potential: a helper, nurse, confidante and witness; inheriting everything, and then staying in the house in via Antonio Fratti 257 (at No. 143, then at No.113 and finally at the present house number) until January 1997, when she ended up in a rest home due to a broken femur and where she died on 5 February 2001 (cf. Albo Centoni, *Una vita con Maria Valtorta. Testimonianze di Marta Diciotti*, op. cit., pp. 34, 208, 517-20). For a short biography of Marta Diciotti, cf. also

difficult for everybody because she was touchy, distrustful, unpredictable and moody… yes, all that was needed to poison the lives of those who were around her"[21]. "How she suffered, poor Maria, with such a mother! One cannot even imagine what she had to endure. One cannot believe that a woman who has an only daughter (and what a daughter!) can be as harassing as she was"[22]. "Unbearable"[23]. "Any endeavour to have a peaceful, frank and open relationship with her proved to be totally useless"[24]. "That woman was just selfish; she didn't love anybody but herself"[25]. Sister Antonia Lucchesi added: "She had an indomitable dislike towards nuns, and I think also towards any clergyman, be it a monk or a Parish Priest… she was far from nice! (…) Let's be frank here… she was unpleasant, difficult and off-putting"[26]. Sister Giovanna Antonelli went on: "Her mother instead was brusque, not friendly at all"[27]. Dr Emilio Pisani pointed out, in summary, that the mother "will die (…) without having ever ceased to vex her daughter"[28]. Paola Belfanti, the wife of Iside's cousin, described her "never being particularly affectionate

---

Emilio Pisani, *Pro e contro Maria Valtorta* [For and Against Maria Valtorta], Centro Editoriale Valtortiano, Isola del Liri (FR) 2017[6], pp. 291-301.

[21] Albo Centoni, *Una vita con Maria Valtorta. Testimonianze di Marta Diciotti*, op. cit., p. 36.

[22] ibid., p. 203.

[23] ibid., pp. 45, 211.

[24] ibid., p. 272.

[25] Albo Centoni, *Ricordi di donne che conobbero Maria Valtorta*, op. cit., p. 215. Maria's mother Iside loved to repeat: "Ah! If I were free! Ah! If only this story would come to an end! Away with Marta, away with everyone! Leave me alone to do as I please" (Maria Valtorta, *Autobiography*, op. cit., p. 392).

[26] Albo Centoni, *Ricordi di donne che conobbero Maria Valtorta* op. cit., p. 18. Also noteworthy are some acquaintances of Signora Iside Valtorta, whom her daughter remembered well: "In 1921, when I was struggling with Mother over Mario, my mother went to an occultist. I don't know what they cooked up … He sent me a talisman which I took great care not to wear. But just receiving it, just going to that half-devil (to me, some people are close relations of the devil), brought on me what it did." (Maria Valtorta, *Autobiography*, op. cit., p. 276).

[27] Albo Centoni, *Ricordi di donne che conobbero Maria Valtorta*, op. cit., p. 59.

[28] ibid., p. 8.

towards her infirm daughter"[29]. And there is an episode that exemplifies everything, told by Sister Antonia Lucchini. "I looked for Monsignor Rocchiccioli, (the Parish Priest of San Paolino, and Maria's parish church) and I talked to him about it. He listened in silence, was pensive for a long time and finally, he said (…) 'Will you promise to keep this to yourself?' I said, 'I promise.' 'Listen, last month I went to give Maria Holy Communion. Her mother took me to one side and told me, "Don't come back before… at least 40 days. Maria will take Communion but not as often. Only every 40 days". 'That's why I cannot go there'"[30]. Cruel behavior to say the least. However, every now and then, at least in her old age, she consoled herself like this: "One day, in the darkness of the cupboard under the staircase, I remember – says Marta Diciotti – that she took the wrong bottle, and she drank from a bottle of olive oil. I can still see her grimacing in disgust"[31]. We can even smile at this. But there is an episode with Maria Valtorta, the mystic writer, that shows how God's judgement is quite different from our own and that it is essentially wrong to think that He should comply with our point of view. Maria had a vision of Purgatory in which she saw her mother Iside about to enter Paradise[32]. She had already seen that a year after her (mother's) death: "…the face […] ashen grey – […] it seemed to have just emerged from a sad, nebulous place which had weighed down its robe and color. […]. The attitude was […] a serious, almost sad appearance, and yet peaceful and serene. A humble and yet solemn

---

[29] ibid., p. 88.

[30] ibid., pp. 43-4.

[31] ibid., p. 273.

[32] Twice Maria spoke of the visions of her mother in purgatory, although it can be deduced that she saw her much more than twice. cf. Maria Valtorta, *Notebooks 1944*, Centro Editoriale Valtortiano, Isola del Liri (FR) 2001, dated 1 November 1944, pp. 605-7); Maria Valtorta, *Notebooks 1945- 1950*, Centro Editoriale Valtortiano, Isola del Liri (FR) 2002, dated 4 October 1949, pp. 540-2; Maria Valtorta, *The Little Notebooks*, Centro Editoriale Valtortiano, Isola del Liri (FR) 2022, pp. 77-8. (It is the vision of 6 December 1945 in which her mother, Iside invoked Maria, in the typical way by a soul in purgatory, who simply shows herself to ask for prayers. The last two lines are an apotheosis of Maria's forgiveness towards the mother who had always harassed her).

appearance"[33]. On 4 October 1949 at 3.45pm, six years after her (mother's) death, Maria had a vision: she spoke to her mother who was ready to enter Paradise despite being, astonishingly, partially immersed in the flames of Purgatory; and, as in 1944, she also looked for her father and, failing to see him, she asked about him. This is the dialogue: "And Dad? Where is Dad?" "In Purgatory". "Still? And yet he was good. He died a Christian with resignation". "More than I. But he is here. God judges differently from the way we do. A way entirely His own…"[34]. The vision was actually described in much more detail, but we can still see not just how different God's judgement is from ours, but also we can imagine how much Chief Warrant Officer Valtorta must have suffered for the theft of the patent by his superior in rank, and how it must have been so difficult for him to forgive as a Christian should, that he had to spend some time in Purgatory in order to be cleansed.

The exiled flower

However, despite her relatives' personalities and despite the time that she spent in various colleges as a child, her parents' influence was huge. In any case, it is necessary to judge from the facts; what Maria Valtorta's human and spiritual reply to her mother Iside was. Towards her father, she felt a deep and reverential love, as she herself pointed out, and others. For instance: "Almost eight years have passed but my pain is the same - and I cannot hear someone call out 'Father' or see a child in his father's arms without feeling my heart being crushed under the weight of longing for my father…"[35]. Obviously, the relationship with her mother was extraordinarily more difficult. "In spite of her fearful 'woes', 'I loved and love my mother intensely, and I have always been a beggar at the door of her heart awaiting caresses…"[36]. She endlessly noted: "What did I lack in reality? Everything."[37] And she ended up bearing a grudge: "Until

---

[33] Maria Valtorta, *Notebooks 1944*, op. cit., dated 1 November, p. 606.

[34] Maria Valtorta, *Notebooks 1945-1950*, op. cit., dated 4 October 1949, p. 541.

[35] Maria Valtorta, *Autobiography,* op. cit., p. 382.

[36] ibid., p. 27.

[37] ibid., p. 55.

then, I was afraid of my mother but I also felt esteem. Afterwards, I no longer did because I saw her as unjust and insincere"[38]. "My father's tears... no, I will not forgive"[39]. Nonetheless, after so much strife, she learned to forgive, and she explained how: "Who worked this miracle of removing from my heart that leaven of ill-will towards my mother? My God, my Father who is in Heaven, my Jesus"[40]. "I have forgiven, I have forgiven a lot, I have forgiven those who have pierced my life [...], I forgive my fears as a child [...]"[41]. Marta Diciotti attested: "One of the tasks that she never really liked but that she always carried out and never tried to avoid was to comb her mother's hair. It was an old-fashioned, 19-century hairstyle, very long and elaborate, with many hairpieces and toupees [sic.]"[42]. This is a good example of how Maria reacted to her mother Iside's provocation in a calm and charitable manner. "Christ's charity had won her over"[43].

Maria Valtorta was baptized on 24 March 1897 in the church of St. Elena, Caserta, but she stayed in this town for just eighteen months. Her father was transferred to Faenza[44] with the whole regiment and consequently, all his family went with him. This took place in September 1898. Maria, who by the age of two was already gifted with an amazing memory, noticed the change in climate and temperature: "From the Southern sun to the ice of Romagna!"[45] In September 1901 they moved again, this time to cold and wet Milan. This was also cause for affliction and something that Maria remembered even forty-two years later, despite being only four and a half at the time[46].

Up to this point, her spiritual life apparently did not differ from that of all the other girls. But it was then that the first signs of a great

---

[38] ibid., p. 83.
[39] ibid., p. 68. Note that the date is from 1943.
[40] ibid., p. 144.
[41] ibid., p. 65.
[42] Albo Centoni, *Una vita con Maria Valtorta. Testimonianze di Marta Diciotti*, op. cit., p. 119.
[43] cf. 2 Cor 5:14a.
[44] cf. Maria Valtorta, *Autobiography,* op. cit., p. 21ff.
[45] Maria Valtorta, *Autobiography,* op. cit., p. 21.
[46] ibid., p. 26.

diversity started to show. On 2 October, she entered the nursery school of the Ursuline nuns in Via Lanzone, Milan. She immediately stood out for her ability to read the entire alphabet and write vowels and consonants much better than those pupils who had already been attending school longer. Her parents' influence was obvious: "The sisters then were beautiful and good. But the school was ugly, dismal and old", Maria noticed. But she went through all this, thanks to the loving atmosphere in which the nuns educated the girls. And here we have a new affirmation in her memory: "At school I found God (...), I found God's face and His love at school. The first real and indelible encounter"[47]. In the school playground, there is a large grotto with an angel carrying a sword, which left an indelible impression on her; but what really remained engraved in her mind was a statue inside the chapel which represented the Deposition of Christ. Her schoolmates trembled with fear, she trembled with compassion[48]. She would have liked to kiss Him, but the glass case was closed. This spiritual experience was so important that forty-two years later she wrote: "I have never understood Jesus except in the crimson robe of His blood, and I have always been anxious to console Him by becoming like Him in sorrow, voluntarily suffered out of love"[49]. In 1948, she still remembered this event which took place when she was four-years-old. "That was it. I believe that not even if I were to be plunged into an eternal carnival, would that have made me change my spiritual direction. I drew a veil over it because I saw Him troubled, and I tried, externally, to resemble any other girl, teenager and woman. But in my relationship with God and in my moral and spiritual actions, I

---

[47] ibid., pp. 27-8.

[48] ibid., p. 29.

[49] ibid., p. 30. Later readings will also help her in this determination, and in particular, John van Ruysbroeck (Ruysbroeck, 1293 – Groenendael, 1381). Known as the Admirable Doctor, he was a Flemish author of works of mysticism and spirituality, founder of the monastery and the congregation of the regular canons of Groenendael (Belgium), and proclaimed Blessed in 1908 by Pope Saint Pius X. Sister Benigna Consolata Ferrero (Turin, 1885 – Como, 1916) was born to a wealthy and very religious family, a Visitation Sister in Como, and a lover of the Divine Love, whose inner wonders were known only to her superior and her spiritual director. She died at the young age of 31.

was as I had decided to be in front of my Saviour who had died for me too"[50]. At this point of her life, she showed symptoms of whooping cough which forced her parents to remove her from the Ursuline school to nurse her back to health, and after a holiday in Tuscany (maybe at Viareggio), she went back to Milan. As there were no antibiotics yet, the disease went on for months and, after the summer in October 1904, she was enrolled in the college of the Marcelline nuns of via Quadronno, Milan.

Continual confinement to boarding schools

Her mother Iside had always resented her only daughter Maria and, to be free to live like a well-to-do lady of the house, she sent her back to boarding school[51]. Maria Valtorta attended primary school in Milan which was owned and run by the Marcelline Sisters on via XX Settembre. At this school, the girl blossomed "as bright as a May dawn"[52] and she soon became the star pupil. She was also the most educated because her parents had passed on a huge amount of learning. Her family education, however, remained very strict. She had a lot of sweets and toys – she later remembered – but *"I was never supposed to ask for anything at all"*[53]. This caused her some trauma. She was taken to the 'Oh lovely, Oh lovely' market in Milan and she yearned for a simple toy, but she was not allowed to ask for it or her mother would not buy it. In the end, she burst into tears. This was seen as a tantrum and she was dragged to the main entrance of the Catholic University where she was soundly smacked[54]. On 13 December 1904, her paternal grandmother passed away. The grief was huge but "I smothered my sorrow because Father urged me to, so as not to upset my mother further. [...] It was the first time that I mortified myself with inner weeping, the most bitter and least

---

[50] From an unpublished and typed questionnaire asked by Mr. Arturo Bottai to which Maria Valtorta replied on 28 October 1948, p. 7.

[51] "She was well-educated, if we take into consideration the customs in use in 1907 for young ladies of wealthy families" (Maria Valtorta, *Autobiografia prima*, op. cit., p. V).

[52] Maria Valtorta, *Autobiography*, op. cit., p. 31.

[53] ibid., p. 33.

[54] cf. ibid., pp. 34-6.

understood"[55]. According to the pastoral practise of that era, on 30 May 1905 aged 8, she received the Sacrament of Confirmation from the future Blessed Andrea Ferrari, Cardinal Archbishop of Milan. At the time, she had a curious experience: she wrote down that for the third time, by chance, her dress and veil burst literally into flames. She got really scared but nothing more: "Fire has always respected me"[56], she later wrote. She remembered two types of people during that period: her father's orderlies who cuddled her a little, and about whom she wrote nice things; and the domestic staff who, on the contrary, did not receive her praise. She remembers that one of them even taught her how to steal things at home, and of another whose chit-chat was "not suitable for my age"[57]. In other words, that she alluded to sex explicitly. "[They] could have harmed me a great deal if Jesus had permitted it"[58]. However, it was through the Italian dictionary – "never left it in peace"[59] – and the *Divine Comedy* that she learned about "the real *animal* of life"[60], that is, about human sexuality and a few moral perversions. Later, at the age of twelve, she said that reading in school about the Nun of Monza, from *I promessi sposi* [The Betrothed by Alessandro Manzoni], caused a huge upheaval in class, and a seventeen-year-old girl was greatly upset, while on the contrary, Maria herself was left totally indifferent[61].

In September 1907, her father's regiment was transferred to Voghera and she had to follow as well. She left the Marcelline Nuns' boarding school and all her friends, and ended up in a state school at Voghera. She felt that the town was "ugly and poor"[62], but she described her strolls with her father along the stream in search of flowers and violets, as "How lovely! What beauty!"[63] Not far from Voghera lies the small town of Casteggio where some French nuns had been displaced following the 1904 anti-clerical and anti-Christian

---

[55] ibid., pp. 40-1.
[56] ibid., p. 43.
[57] ibid., p. 51.
[58] ibid.
[59] ibid.
[60] ibid.
[61] ibid.
[62] ibid., p. 70.
[63] ibid.

laws by French President Emile Combes. Her mother Iside, a French teacher, decided to send her daughter there for some French lessons. Maria was ten and had already learnt French quite well from her mother, but she probably improved a lot during this period. It was there, in the small chapel of the Perpetual Adorers of the Most Holy Sacrament where she went for her lessons, that during a month-long stay evidently wanted by her mother Iside, Maria had her first Holy Communion with neither of her parents present because it was useless. She did not have a near-mystical experience[64] but two things are worth mentioning. Among the various acts of tenderness bestowed by those persecuted nuns, Maria remembered that "if I did not reach ecstasy, it really depended entirely on me who had been numbed with spiritual lethargy for years, and not on them"[65]. The night before she went back home, thanks to the nuns, she was consecrated to the Holy Virgin: "at whose feet I deposited my garland of roses"[66].

That summer, something unfortunate took place in the Valtorta family: a maternal uncle[67] who had made unfortunate choices for his family, forced his brother-in-law, Maria's father, to help him pay his debts and also pay for his own daughter's education in order to save her from the clutches of a sex-obsessed mother. Even though he was her brother, Iside got even angrier than usual and managed to send her daughter Maria to a new boarding school by blackmailing her husband. This was a very selfish act[68]. On 4 March 1909, Maria

---

[64] What is meant by this is, extraordinary events, even physical ones, which usually, but not necessarily, accompany mystical experience.

[65] ibid., p. 73.

[66] ibid., p. 75. At that time, entrusting children to the Virgin Mary or to the Sacred Heart was a practice deeply felt by nuns of all Orders.

[67] ibid., pp. 77-8.

[68] This was the atmosphere at home: "I would turn to the right - a scolding; to the left - derision. I wept and was punished. I kept silent and was scolded. I spoke and was rebuked at home [and] out of the house. It was always like that. My mother was uneasy with the headmistress who, striking me with bad grades, indirectly struck my teacher, Iside Valtorta. But she was vexed about the insult made to her, Iside Valtorta, and not about the wrong done to me. Indeed, she set about increasing the wrong

entered the Bianconi School in Monza, owned by the Sisters of Charity of the Most Holy Child Mary of Blessed Capitanio. It was a very sad day for Maria who wrote: "I felt another bond snapping between my mother and myself, and the door open between *the one who begot me and gave me life without having understood me*"[69]. The boarding school was large and beautiful. Despite being far from home, Maria was happy there. She became at once the star pupil thanks to her knowledge of French and to her ability to write essays and short stories in Italian[70] for which she won over the nuns' trust and affection. Even the Mother Superior told her years later, that: "she had grasped that Valtortino[71] – the nickname used by the Blessed Cardinal Ferrari on Maria's confirmation day – though small, shy, morally common in appearance, and physically fragile was, however, really of good substance, made up of generosity, firmness, fortitude and fidelity"[72]. Three sentences in her autobiography show how she felt about living in that boarding school: "I was just fine there"[73], "I was very loved very much"[74], and "My classmates also adored me and were proud of me on account of my intelligence"[75]. She spent most of her youth at Bianconi College from 4 March 1909 to 23 February 1913[76]. They were among the most fruitful years of her life, years

---

[that was commited]. A hellish life" (Maria Valtorta, *Autobiography*, op. cit., pp. 79-80).

[69] ibid., p. 83.

[70] "In Italian, I had an inexhaustible vein of imagination and a naturally good writing style. For this reason, [I could] do the same essay up to eight times, developing it in eight different ways [which] was a game for me" (ibid., p. 32).

[71] cf. Albo Centoni, *Una vita con Maria Valtorta. Testimonianze di Marta Diciotti*, op. cit., pp. 80, 210. Maria Valtorta, *Autobiography*, op. cit., p. 80.

[72] ibid., p. 91.

[73] ibid.

[74] ibid., p. 94.

[75] ibid.

[76] "She was at the top of her class in Italian, French and many other subjects, apart from mathematics. Her talent in carrying out the written assignments went so far as to allow her to write eight different drafts on the same topic - one for herself and the others for seven lazy or less- gifted companions. Considered an eagle and sometimes consulted as an oracle, she was often commissioned to write the essays to be read in public and at

during which Maria became conscious of her possibilities and she displayed them without haughtiness or vanity[77]. However, skill and intelligence were not enough for her mother Iside: she expected much more from Maria. In 1910, her father Giuseppe suffered from a nervous breakdown which, within two years, would lead him to retirement[78]. Consequently, her mother had a free hand regarding her daughter's education. She wanted her to become a teacher, but she was advised against it because Maria was not good at drawing. So she chose a Technical Institute and it was a predictable failure. Maria pleaded with her mother because despite her huge effort, she couldn't even understand what was being taught, but her mother refused to budge. She did three years of school in one, and she failed. She inexorably stumbled over maths, geometry and bookkeeping, despite being top of the class in the other subjects. She was plagued by trauma and illness, but she did not give up. In October, she went back to Bianconi College where she covered the entire remaining classical curriculum in a few months, and she passed her exams. In less than ten months, she covered the entire grammar school curriculum. She ended up studying up to twelve hours a day and, thanks to her love for the liberal arts, she succeeded[79].

A ray of light

At Bianconi College, Maria experienced great joy and great sadness. In a page from her *Autobiography*, she summed up her suffering and took inspiration from the seven words uttered by Christ

---

formal school assemblies" (Maria Valtorta, *Autobiografia prima*, op. cit., p. V). We have photocopies of two of these annual essays: *Due cose sono belle nell'universo: il cielo stellato sopra il nostro capo, e il sentimento del dovere nel nostro cuore* [Two things are beautiful in the universe: the starry sky above our head, and the feeling of duty in our hearts], Bianconi College, Monza, 17 February 1912, signed Maria Valtorta; and *Il trionfo della croce e la donna* [The triumph of the cross and the woman], Bianconi College, Monza, 29 January 1913, signed M. Valtorta – Elena Cattaneo.

[77] Twice she had the task of drafting the essay at the end of the school year to be read in front of the whole-school assembly.

[78] "Encephalitis brought on by an excess of mental effort, said the doctors" (Maria Valtorta, *Autobiography,* op. cit., p. 110).

[79] For more detail, cf. ibid., pp. 94-5.

on the Cross. She used the word "suffering"[80] seven times, writing about the suffering caused by her mother's behavior; suffering caused by poverty[81]; suffering for not receiving the nice postcards that the other girls did; suffering for not being able to impose further hardships on herself[82]; suffering because nobody visited her[83]; suffering because she did not have nice underwear like the other girls; and suffering for having been deprived of beautiful liturgies at Holy Communion, unlike others. With this word, 'suffering', Maria Valtorta recalled her spiritual life in that period, when she wrote her *Autobiography* in 1942. We could say that she was just like any other young pupil of the time, and this proves what God can do when He acts in a soul that makes itself available to Him, regardless of its past. This is what happened to Maria in a wondrous way on Good Friday 1943. Despite her young age and her apparently normal life, she was already acting in an unusual way. "And then there was the night... I could not bear to see Jesus up there all alone, while I was warm under the covers and asleep. I would take Him down and place Him over my heart with lots of kisses, little words of love, and fall asleep like that, happy to sleep with Jesus over my heart"[84].

Something wondrous took place during the spiritual exercises in November 1912[85]. Maria feared they would be the last ones, from the rumors she had heard from her mother, and so they were. Those were "spiritually wonderful", said Maria, while having a personal conversation, which became her main goal in life: "You shall not be innocent love. *You will be penitent love.* The uncontaminated virgins (...) the *creatures who knew the sting of evil (...) and then managed to rise*

---

[80] cf. ibid., pp. 107-8.

[81] This poverty, however, was induced by her mother Iside who was harsh and without maternal love.

[82] It was not a form of masochism or of rebellion against her mother, but the response to what happened inside of her that made her spiritually decisive at Marcelline College in Milan.

[83] Again, the lack of affection from her mother, which also forced her father to do the same, seems evident.

[84] ibid., p. 114.

[85] ibid., p. 115. Every year, the nuns started the school year with a few days of spiritual exercises. That year, Fr. Corradi held them, who later "died in the odor of sanctity" (cf. ibid., p. 118).

again and be reborn with a new soul, with a radiance not inferior to that of the pure through the grace of God, and *certainly more meritorious*, for it was painful and laborious beyond every other mode of conquest"[86]. And this became "the program-phase, the guide-phase and the warning-phase for my whole future life"[87]. We can wonder how this personal conversation differed from the one she had on 23 April 1943. Maria never stated the difference, but we can argue that they differed only on the outside. Here she was at 15, she was very young, inexperienced, and lacking the support of a real spiritual guide; she was afraid of her mother's violent reaction; she was afraid that even a single word about her experience would have led to her leaving the school that was a haven of peace for her. That is why this gift ended here and remained locked in her memory. On the afternoon of 23 February 1913, against her and the nuns' will, her mother – with her heart's door "firmly closed, grim, and bristling with iron lances that I couldn't even lean against"[88] – removed her from Bianconi College and brought her back home. We can then say, despite various and false opinions, that Maria Valtorta had completed secondary school, even though this had been done in haste after her failure at the Technical Institute. Therefore, she was not illiterate, and it is not true that she only attended secondary school for two years[89]. She knew Latin and Greek, she was passionate about Italian, and she could produce excellent writing[90]. "She had an exceptional memory

---

[86] ibid., p. 122.

[87] ibid. It should be remembered that this reflection was made in early 1943; that is, thirty-one years later. Indeed, it would be with her until death.

[88] ibid., p. 131.

[89] "In fact, with a great sense of duty and excellent success, she carried out the complementary and technical courses run by the gymnasium and the high school, held at the renowned boarding schools run by the Sisters who were valuable teachers to her. However, because of her ill health and because she failed mathematics, she did not obtain a high school certificate" (Maria Valtorta, *Autobiografia prima,* op. cit., pp. VI-VII). cf. also Jean-François Lavère, *L'enigma Valtorta* [The Valtorta Enigma], Centro Editoriale Valtortiano, Isola del Liri (FR) 2012, p. 37.

[90] Marta Diciotti succinctly lists the books that Maria Valtorta kept, but sums them up: "She had the Catechism of Pius X and the Bible. I think she knew the Gospels by heart. There were no texts of theology or any studies on the Holy Scriptures at home, and there never had been. We preserved

and had effortlessly learnt by heart, the four Gospels and the entire *Divine Comedy*. And she used to say that whatever she read was engraved in her memory like a record in a gramophone"[91]. She also had an exceptional sense of direction. "Even as a child, sometimes people would blindfold her, make her spin around, tell her to stop suddenly and ask her where North was. And the child, still blindfolded, took just a few seconds to indicate it correctly. There's more. Since she was a child, she felt clearly as if she had some wires coming out of her fingers, and these wires went around the world sensing what she wanted and bringing it back to her. She felt like an antenna, capable of searching, receiving and transmitting facts and news"[92]. Wouldn't this alone be enough to describe her as a 'natural psychic'?[93] Probably, yet this does not affect in the slightest, the importance of the gifts that she was later to receive. Saint Pio of Pietrelcina faced the same situation[94].

---

her poor library which was otherwise unusable at the time because of her mother [she died in October 1943], who kept it incomprehensibly closed" (Albo Centoni, *Una vita con Maria Valtorta. Testimonianze di Marta Diciotti*, op. cit., p. 304). Actually Marta Diciotti, in her simplicity, omits some important books of spirituality that Maria had and that she did read, whose authors are for example: St. Teresa of Avila, St. Thérèse of the Child Jesus, St. Francis of Assisi and Blessed John van Ruysbroeck. At a certain point in her mystical life, her Guardian Angel Azariah asked her to make a list of the books she had. Maria obeyed, receiving praise for her precision and for also adding the books she had lent to others. This list probably exists but has never been published.

[91] Maria Valtorta, *Autobiografia prima*, op. cit., p. VI.

[92] ibid., pp. VI-VII.

[93] In the sense that these gifts were not divine gifts due to her correspondence with divine Grace, but natural abilities. cf. AA.VV., *PARA Dizionario Enciclopedico* [PARA Encyclopedic Dictionary], Armenia Editore, Milano 1986, pp. 589-91, Medium and Medium Issues item.

[94] Given that a real detailed biography of St. Pio of Pietrelcina does not exist, just read the chapter: A very special child, Renzo Allegri, *A tu per tu con Padre Pio* [Face to Face with Padre Pio], Arnoldo Mondadori Editore, Milano 2000^{10}, pp. 32-40.

Florence

Her family, especially her mother, decided to move from Voghera to Florence and, on the morning of 1 March 1913[95], she moved into a new flat. It was on the third floor and she had a view of Fiesole; it was nice and comfortable. Maria started a new life there; she had finished school for good. She remained in Florence for twelve years until 1924; that is, from the age of 16 to 27 when, in order to avoid a big rise in rent and unable to move to Reggio, Calabria for lack of houses (due to the devastating earthquake in Messina-Reggio on 28 December 1908), the Valtorta family moved to Viareggio for good, after buying a small house by the pine forest on Via Antonio Fratti.

Her thirst for knowledge never abandoned her, and even if school was over, she never stopped studying. "I would get up early, pray, tidy up my room and the parlor[96] [...], and help in the kitchen. I did not work so much at the time but studied a great deal, played the piano, read a lot, went for walks with Father, sometimes to the movies with him and also with Mother, rarely to the theatre in the cold months and often in the summer. I went to bed rather early at night when we were without conversation because frequently, we went (or others came) to spend the evening in friendly conversations"[97]. This description of daily life in Florence tells us that those twelve years were not pointless. Her classical knowledge increased, although privately. This was nothing in comparison to what she would need from 1943[98] onwards, but she wasn't naive at

---

[95] cf. Maria Valtorta, *Autobiography*, op. cit., p. 136.

[96] Her mother Iside demanded a typically middle-class life that reflected her (small but decent) social life.

[97] ibid., p. 139. A few days after the beginning of the conversations, Maria wrote "I have *read* countless 'Lives' but have myself *bought* the ones with points of contact with my paltry life, and from the effects they have in me – while the others excite my sterile admiration. (Maria Valtorta, *Notebooks 1943*, Centro Editoriale Valtortiano, Isola del Liri (FR) 2001, dated 10 May, p. 24). From this, it is understood that despite theological ignorance, Maria Valtorta was anything but semi-illiterate.

[98] One must always keep this difference in mind when reading her writings. In this way, it will stand out that she could not be the only source of the writings themselves, as Blessed Gabriele Allegra notes: "Digitus Dei est hic" ["The Finger of God is here"] (Emilio Pisani, *Pro e contro Maria*

all. Whoever reads her writings and finds refined - not trivial words, should not be surprised: they were the norm for her. So, she was neither illiterate nor naive nor ignorant despite having had no theological or biblical education[99].

Among the families that she came across in her apartment block was that of a Colonel who had separated from his wife and was living with his son, Mario. He lived in the same building as Maria and she would often go down from the third to the first floor because the Colonel had a nice little garden where she could have a chat with his son who, at the time, was somewhat listless, and she would help him find a purpose in life. On the second floor, there lived an only son, Roberto, from Bari, "handsome, rich and cultured – with a degree in literature. [...] He had come to Florence to do some research work at the city's libraries. [...] He was also very good, serious and calm"[100]. And they fell in love. Summer went by and on 4 January 1914, as soon as he came back from Bari, Roberto went to Maria and declared his love for her. Maria recounted only the first part – that he had come back from Bari – to her father Giuseppe, to the maid and then to her mother, not mentioning the declaration of love. But her mother Iside saw immediately what was going on and she became verbally very abusive. Words became insults[101] and as a direct

---

Valtorta, op. cit., pp. 120, 127). The exact same expression has also been used by the lawyer, Camillo Corsànego (cf. ibid., p. 76).

[99] For example: "I don't know anything about mysticism or asceticism" (Maria Valtorta, *Lettere a Madre Teresa Maria 1* [Letters to Mother Teresa Maria volume 1], Centro Editoriale Valtortiano, Isola del Liri (FR) 2012, p. 315).

[100] Maria Valtorta, *Autobiography*, op. cit., p. 141

[101] "My Mother... brutally tore away the veil of my chaste innocence as a virginal, pure woman. So, I thus found out *that evil can be done between man and woman. Until that evening of 5 January, I had not known.* And this laying bare the shameful parts of life, with no pity for my ignorant age of sixteen, was what struck me and separated me *forever*, definitively, from the woman who produced me. [...] I did not even grasp completely how foul and ugly they were ... There were, of course, those who did take the trouble to do so - and precisely the Colonel's housekeeper who, well informed about everything by way of my mother's tactless enquiry, and endowed as she was with a malign heart, took pleasure in blowing on the fire and instructing me about all the evil I could have done. And yet, believe me, God's goodness

consequence, trust between Maria and her mother ceased. "My mother shut me out and cursed me for a sin I did not commit. I withdrew heartbroken. *But I withdrew forever*"[102]. It's easy to imagine the obscenities that were uttered. It must have been terribly painful for Maria, considering that in 1943, she would still describe the episode in detail: "My youthful flesh died together with Roberto when I was 18"[103]. Later, Maria realized that her mother had acted out of sheer selfishness because she did not want to lose her only daughter's assistance; and whoever had tried to take her away from her would have incurred her terrible wrath[104]. Roberto died in the war in 1915[105] and this put an end to all hope. But there was still Mario, the Colonel's son. Their friendship grew stronger, and her mother Iside welcomed this because his presence would keep other suitors at bay. Meanwhile, Maria gave way to despair[106] which today we would call depression, but the pain is the same. Due to a lack of proper care, impossible back then, the greatest risks were very real. The torment was so dreadful that Maria started thinking of suicide[107].

In the summer of 1916, the night between the 17-18 June, Maria had a prophetic dream. Four characters: the Devil who wanted her for himself; St. Peter who, symbolizing divine justice, said that she did not deserve anything; St. John, who on contrary supported her

---

did not permit me to understand all the vulgarity of certain things. Almost out of mental deficiency, I did not understand. The good Jesus did not want my poor soul to be aware of all the evil of sensuality so soon. And not just evil, but those animal laws which, although are not *evil* because they are necessary for the continuation of the human race, are so disquieting when made known to us all at once. God concealed from me much of the evil that my mother and Mario's housekeeper dissected under my nose - the former out of imprudence, the latter out of wickedness. May God forgive them" (ibid., pp. 144-8).

[102] ibid.

[103] ibid., p. 157.

[104] cf. ibid., p. 155.

[105] cf. ibid., p. 143. She heard the news six months after the start of the Great War (cf. ibidem, p. 155).

[106] cf. ibid., p. 153.

[107] "The temptations to suicide were harder to overcome for I was continually led towards them by the steady, corrosive trickle of all the moments in the day" (ibid., p. 169).

salvation; Jesus, who was cold to start with, but then uttered the words that marked Maria's entire life: *"Maria, know that it is not enough not to do evil; it is also necessary not to wish to do it"*[108]. Maria understood the meaning of the dream. "I understood that I had been forgiven and redeemed"[109], and then: "I awoke with my soul illuminated by something unearthly"[110]. Despite this, her heartbreak persisted, together with her suicidal and sexual thoughts[111], but the gift she had received helped her to overcome all obstacles. In the summer of 1916, as usual, she went on holiday to Viareggio, in Via Umberto I. As well as her family, there were also her cousin of the same age and her mother's dissolute brother. After the dream of 17-18 June, Maria never felt alone. It was just a feeling, but a frequent one. Then during the night between the 17-18 August, she had a paranormal experience[112]: first, a step that had been placed on the windowsill shook, then the dog started to snarl. They woke up but it was not an earthquake because the chandelier was not moving. After half an hour, there were "three very strong blows, as if an open hand had knocked on the door"[113]. She was drenched in a cold sweat out of fear, and she was afraid it might be a dead relative calling her. "Grandma, is it you?"[114], she cried. But there was no answer. Everybody arrived and her mother Iside reprimanded the girls, Maria and her cousin, who in her eyes were responsible for this prank.

Once back in Florence, they had to move because an earthquake had damaged their old house so they went to live in Via Pippo Spano.

---

[108] ibid., p. 163. For the entire incident, cf. also ibid., pp. 160-4.

[109] ibid., p. 163.

[110] ibid.

[111] cf. ibid., pp. 168-9.

[112] cf. Maria Teresa La Vecchia, *Antropologia paranormale. Fenomeni fisici e psichici straordinari* [Paranormal anthropology. Extraordinary physical and psychic phenomena], Pontificia Università Gregoriana, Roma 2002.

[113] ibid., p. 160. Probably, the cause was neither mystical nor preternatural, but it was a paranormal fact that cannot be defined with precision, like the majority of events of this type, which are difficult to categorize. cf. also AA.VV., *PARA Dizionario Enciclopedico*, op. cit.; Jean-Pierre Girard, *Encyclopédie du Paranormal* [Encyclopedia of the Paranormal], Éditions Trajectoire, Paris 2005.

[114] ibid.

The Great War was still on and, in late October 1917, there was the defeat of Kobarid/Caporetto. The Italian government urged young women to help out in hospitals and Maria was able to fulfil three very different wishes: first of all, to help those in need, asking to be sent among the troops and not among the officers; then to get out of the house; and finally, contracting a serious disease with the hope of dying.[115]

Following Roberto's death, Maria Valtorta felt an emptiness in her heart. But the human heart and intelligence hate emptiness, and that is what happened to Maria too. They must somehow be filled and, sure enough, the past came back. Mario had grown up, he was now a midshipman and he had his eyes on Maria. He had even told her mother Iside. It was Maria herself who then, to her mother's surprise, decided to reject his advances, though she kept loving him throughout her life and she kept referring to him as "my Mario"[116]. Even so, with great courage on 3 November 1919, Mario tried to be clear with her mother, asking for Maria's hand. As with Roberto, it was a complete failure: her mother Iside reacted in the same way, and in a fit of anger, she asked Mario never to set foot in her house again. Up until then, Maria had not become aware of a particular call from Heaven. She was not thinking of consecrating herself to a religious life. What had happened years before at Marcelline College and the dream that had made her realize that she had been forgiven and welcomed, did not prevent her from desiring a normal, loving, family life, children included. Her passionate side[117] which she mentions herself, was still quite important. WWI arrived and it was terrible. Maria became a nurse in a Florence hospital. She enrolled, with her mother's permission as a Samaritan Nurse[118]. On 15 November 1917, she entered a hospital for the first time. She had the *mindset* of a very shy schoolgirl and she wrote, smiling: "The first day – rather, the first morning, seeing myself observed by so many eyes, shy as I was, I

---

[115] cf. ibid., *Autobiography*, p. 176.
[116] ibid., pp.182, 210, 235.
[117] ibid., p. 154.
[118] They were the Nurses of the Red Cross at the time, which assisted in the field hospitals both on the front lines and behind the front lines of the war. Maria worked in Florence, obviously behind the front line: her mother, Iside probably would not have agreed to anything else.

stumbled and made a mess... I bumped into a night table and knocked everything to the floor: cups, glasses, bottles etc. Fortunately, the wounded man had just picked up the watch and thermometer... That was my baptism – a bit noisy, if you will, and a bit costly"[119]. But she adapted very quickly and "I soon became skilled and capable, though"[120]. Her pity for those soldiers who were torn apart by grief, must have been great. She loved her job in the ward, among patients of all kinds, including in the infectious-disease ward. She thought that was the best time of the day. She stayed at the hospital for 18 months and everybody loved her: patients, nurses, nuns and doctors[121].

The dreadful Great War, the *useless slaughter* according to Pope Benedict XV, at last ended. "When news reached me, I rushed out of the hospital and ran to the Church of St. Mark to thank the Nazarene... I offered Him myself then, asking Him to take my life, but not to let other wars come"[122]. "Since then, I have always repeated my offer, for this and other motives [...] knowing quite well what I was doing"[123]. This offer was not due to a euphoric moment, so it was not abandoned during her life. Indeed, it was taken very seriously by the Lord, and the event that marked Maria deeply and forever, took place very soon after.

Harmony apparently destroyed

It was 17 March 1920, and this is the almost aseptic account by Maria herself, "Near my house, as I walked giving my arm to Mother, who on account of her notably impaired vision trips over evey little projection and falls, I was struck in the back by a small delinquent, the son of a Communist and our milliner. With an iron bar taken from a bed, he came up from behind while shouting, 'Down with the

---

[119] ibid., p. 179.

[120] ibid.

[121] ibid., p. 128.

[122] ibid., p. 188. Contact with the physical devastation of wounded soldiers must have deeply disturbed her; in the religious climate she already lived in, she still remembered it in 1943.

[123] ibid.

rich and the military', and he gave me a blow with all his might[124]. The noise was so loud that my mother thought he had hurled a stone and that the stone had bounced on the pavement. But it was the noise of the iron on my vertebrae"[125]. The pain was awful, and the consequences were dramatic, both short- and long-term. In fact, her life changed forever. Humanly speaking, she had become like one of the many wounded soldiers from the war who had never completely recovered. She spent three months in bed with a temperature as high as 40°C and underwent three incorrect treatments that nearly killed her. What happened? "An abscess in the kidney, which on breaking, poisoned my blood for which I had attacks of septicemia"[126]. The long-term result was a paralysis of the lower limbs that left her bedridden until her death[127]. Due to what had happened with Mario and this accident, the situation became very serious and Maria was taken to Montecatini (Lucca) to recuperate for 50 days, and then from 20 September to Reggio, Calabria to continue to recover from the huge blow. The main purpose of her stay in Reggio, Calabria was to get well again after the terrible assault, but things did not go so well. Without those medicines that today we take for granted, Maria had to suffer very strong pain, very high fevers, and various crises. Eight months after the assault, her health was still not getting any better[128]. Fortunately – in fact, thanks to God – things started to improve very slowly, and after two years in Reggio, Calabria she was able to move back to Florence[129]. But her depression got worse due

---

[124] In the will signed on 1 November 1952, and confirmed on 18 February 1957, Maria Valtorta writes: "…for the hatred of a spiritual and mental degenerate who at 23-years-old made me physically unhappy for the rest of my life". (From a photocopy of the will). A sign of her forgiveness: she never mentioned it.

[125] Maria Valtorta, *Autobiography*, op. cit., p. 202.

[126] ibid., p. 205. In general cf. ibid., pp. 202-6.

[127] Yet Maria did not spend her days cursing this fanatical and ideological person who was the cause of future pain and tragedies. Maria Valtorta remembered him, but always without rancor: her life had really been changed by divine Grace.

[128] ibid., p. 210.

[129] Marta Diciotti recalled that, years later, a diagnosis was made by Professor Bolaffi of Lucca. In his opinion, there was a spinal injury and

to her mother Iside. Mario, who remained "my Mario" all her life, renewed his advances to Maria Valtorta and, after consulting three different people[130], all of whom told her to accept his proposal, she agreed. Her mother Iside, however, maintained her ban and with measures, which we can guess but we don't know in detail, she ensured that he left for good. Signora Iside prevented everybody from interfering, including her husband, who was so dependent on her that the weak attitude he showed was comparable to cowardice[131]. Maria complained in her letters – her parents had gone back to Florence leaving her in Reggio with her cousins – but all was in vain and, in the end, Maria found herself alone, hopeless, ill and abandoned[132]. Sent on a mission by the Navy, Mario fell in love with a Russian expat, perhaps an aristocrat persecuted by the Bolshevik revolutionaries, and he started seeing her, giving everybody the idea that he had gone mad. Maria found out and her sorrow, if possible, got even worse. They crossed paths on New Year's Eve in 1923, but on that occasion, he pretended he did not see her. Time went by and in 1943, Maria wrote that: "My new sorrow did not detach me from God. Rather, it was an increase of love for Him"[133]. To be closer to God, she thought of joining the Third Order of St Francis, but in the end, she refrained from that as she was ashamed of her sins[134]. On 2 August 1922, she went back to her parents in Florence. After a

---

therefore, the patient could not have had a life expectancy of more than 15 years (cf. Albo Centoni, *Ricordi di donne che conobbero Maria Valtorta*, op. cit., p. 193). In fact, Maria Valtorta lived for another 41 years!

[130] "...all three - the priest, the elderly devout lady, the good–hearted jurist - exhorted me *to accept this love* without fear of mother's 'excommunication'. And they all adduced arguments to whose correctness there was no objection" (Maria Valtorta, *Autobiography*, op. cit., pp. 200-1).

[131] Giuseppe Valtorta's inability to act in this situation undermines his father figure. Perhaps this serious lack could even explain why – according to the visions that Maria had later – he went to heaven after his wife.

[132] cf. Maria Valtorta, *Autobiography*, op. cit., pp. 224-5.

[133] ibid., p. 230.

[134] cf. ibid., p. 231.

temporary respite, her mother's harassment started stronger than ever. But by then, Maria was drawn to other things[135].

The Gospel of Luke

Until then, Maria Valtorta had neither owned nor read the Gospels. At the start of 1924, she found the Gospel of Luke at home[136], which had been brought by her father a couple of years earlier. And it was a real novelty. The following year, in 1925, she bought all four Gospels. From then on, she never walked away from them. "I have never been able to separate myself from the Gospel since then. It is my spirit's daily bread. I do not even need to read it any more because I know it by heart, but I still reread it because I always find a new fascination therein. When I feel very bad, when I am quite afraid of something, I place the little volumes with the Four Gospels bought in the beginning of 1925 over my heart, and I am no longer afraid of anything. From those pages, Jesus seems to be saying to me: 'Fear not', and to things: 'Do no harm to this woman'... But the Gospels! If I experience a doubt, a moment of melancholy, I pray to the Holy Spirit, to whom I am mostly devoted, and then I open the Gospels casually. I always find a word to comfort me, or find an answer to why something is bothering me"[137]. We must note, however, that Maria had by then read a series of important authors including Dante and many other Italian classics. She did not know the entire Bible yet, but in 1942, she wrote a sentence which shed more light on our spiritual knowledge of her. "Ruysbroeck says – [Valtorta is] one of the few people I understand along with St. Paul, St. Catherine of Siena and St. Francis of Assisi among the ancients, and St. Thérèse of the Child Jesus and Sister Benigna (Consolata

---

[135] It is noteworthy that up to this point, there were no priests around her. She had had contact with several priests, but they were always casual, confessional encounters and nothing more.

[136] cf. ibid., p. 240. No wonder this ignorance existed. After the Council of Trent, in order to avoid the errors of the Protestants, the Catholic Church severely limited the Bible to people. It was replaced by devotions, liturgies, the catechism and sacred art.

[137] ibid., p. 241.

Ferrero) among the contemporaries"[138]. And then she cited St. Teresa of Avila and her *Cammino di Perfezione* [The Way of Perfection][139]. So she had read and she knew these authors. Their spiritual thoughts had entered her mind and become part of her education. It is necessary, therefore, to dispel the idea that Maria Valtorta was a semiliterate person and lacking in religious education. In fact, she did not have an excellent religious education, but she nonetheless had some. She did not know the technical terms of theology, but she was aware that religious life had a certain path to follow and it was not based only on the respect of the Ten Commandments but went far beyond. She did not know the Bible[140], but before the Second Vatican Council, very few people, except for a few clergymen, read the Bible daily. The religious tension that Maria Valtorta was experiencing was created also by the non-'devotional' books she had been reading.

Viareggio, her home

The Valtortas had been renting an apartment in Florence, but the owner managed to evict them using an economic ploy. So in September 1924, they decided to move to Viareggio for good. Thanks to their past holidays, they had many friends and

---

[138] ibid.

[139] ibid., p. 245. It is noteworthy that she still had no spiritual guide: up to this point, Maria Valtorta seems a *Sunday Catholic* and nothing more.

[140] In November 1943, she wrote: "I can formally assure you that I was familair with only the four Gospels. I have known them by heart for years. I also once read the Songs of Songs, thirteen or more years ago in a Protestant edition, which I later left with Msgr. Guidi, (who is now dead), the Parish Priest at St. Paolino's at that time. In a book providing general culture, I read the Proverbs of Solomon. And *my knowledge ends there*. To read the Bible is, for me, like walking in an unknown world that would remain impenetrable. I understand only the superficial meaning and what is commented on by the annotations at the foot of the page, which, I remark, are different from the ones given to me by the Master. When I was at school, they had made me study Sacred History from a little textbook adapted to our young age, and you know what those texts are like: reduced to the minimum" (Maria Valtorta, *Notebooks 1943*, op. cit., dated 4 November, p. 449).

acquaintances there and, on 21 September, they bought a small house in via Antonio Fratti and moved in on the 23rd[141].

In December 1924 following an inspiration, Maria Valtorta bought the four Gospels and *The Story of a Soul* by St. Thérèse of Lisieux. These regular readings led her towards God with a mounting impetus. "I immediately read *The Story of a Soul* (…) My soul was melting with love. I had found a harpist capable of making the strings of my spirit resound. […] When I read the act of offering to Merciful Love, I wept with joy… I had found what I was seeking"[142]. And on 28 January 1925 without consulting any priest, she offered herself as victim soul to God, knowing very well how many sorrows she would suffer to save souls despite an enemy voice that told her: 'Be careful about what you are doing! Think it over! And what if you die afterwards?'"[143] She was in fact persecuted; but towards the end of 1942 she wrote: *"I have been renewing it every day since then"*[144].

She decided to consecrate herself to the Church and to join the Pauline nuns[145], but she was too ill by then, and this wish of hers remained just a dream. She then turned to *Catholic Action* (Azione Cattolica)[146], which did not exist under this name in her own parish.

---

[141] cf. Maria Valtorta, *Autobiography*, op. cit., p. 250.

[142] ibid., pp. 253-4.

[143] ibid., p. 254.

[144] ibid.

[145] A Religious congregation recognized by the Church, founded by Blessed Giacomo Alberione (1884-1971) with the aim of spreading the Catholic faith using the tools of social communication.

[146] "These are the 17 associations to which Maria Valtorta belonged in various years of her life: the Daughters of Mary (1910), the Apostolate of Prayer (same year), the Slaves of the Most Holy Mary of St. Grignon de Montfort (1928 and 1936), the Female Youth of *Catholic Action* (1929), the Sisters of the Holy Infant Mary (1938), the Third Franciscan Order (postulated in 1929, vested in 1930, and professed in 1941), the Apostolate of the Infirm of Verona (in 1942), the Third Order of the Servants of Mary (in 1944), the Congregation of the Holy Face of Lucca (in the same year), the Family of Sorrow (in 1949), the Volunteers of the Suffering in Rome (in the same year), the Archbrotherhood of Mercy of Viareggio (in 1950), the Pious Union of the Crucified and Immaculate Mary (in 1951), the Cooperators in the Apostolate of the Editions of the Pious Society of Saint Paul in Rome (in 1952), the Apostolate of the Suffering in Gallione di

But due to her Parish Priest's refusal, this remained just a wish too[147]. The desire to serve, however, continued to be strong, and in 1927, she had the misfortune of helping a young man affected by septicemia for over three months. It was a daily, tiring job, but she reached the goal of seeing the young man recover. She was still young, and many people thought that she saw a husband in him after all that had happened to her, but this was totally false. The story ended with her being slandered but she kept silent to avoid her mother Iside's reproach[148].

In the autumn of 1928, she tried to join the Third Order of the Franciscans. She was accepted, but she had to postpone the clothing ceremony[149] which eventually took place on 23 November 1930, along with the renewal of the vows she had already made in the past[150]. Another act of charity, given her health, was to accompany the son of a disgraced mother to a special boarding school in Cremona in 1929. It was a harrowing journey for a heart that was already suffering from the thin air of the Apuan Alps, but she made it all the same. During an interview with a manager of *Catholic Action*, she found out that this organization existed in her own parish – San Paolino – contrary to what she had been told. So, looking within herself, she had to admit that she really wasn't wanted before[151]. Yet the story had an incredibly happy ending. In December 1929, she joined the spiritual exercises organized for the members of *Catholic Action* of her parish. Again she experienced the happy times she had had at Bianconi College and she was full of joy. Moreover, confiding in Msgr. Sanguinetti – who was the preacher during those spiritual exercises – at last she felt understood and welcomed, and she was appointed as *delegate* for culture. So, from being previously excluded,

---

Caserta (in the same year), the Fellowship of Mary (in the same year), the Militia of Mary Immaculate (in 1953)" (Luciano Raffaele, Preface to Maria Valtorta, *Il Poema dell'Uomo-Dio* [The Poem of the Man-God], op. cit., p. XVII). [Not in the English edition].

[147] cf. Maria Valtorta, *Autobiography*, op. cit., pp. 259, 270.

[148] cf. ibid., op. cit., pp. 261-3.

[149] cf. Maria Valtorta, *Notebooks 1943*, op. cit., dated 16 August, p. 241.

[150] cf. Maria Valtorta, *Notebooks 1945-1950*, op. cit., dated 21 January 1946, p. 178.

[151] cf. Maria Valtorta, *Autobiography*, op. cit., pp. 263-7.

she now made her triumphant entry in Viareggio's *Catholic Action*. It goes without saying that later, using Msgr. Olgiati's *Sillabario del Cristianesimo* [Syllabary of Christianity], she trained the members very well and she made her pupils look very good at the yearly diocesan contest[152].

The spiritual key

With the passing of time, Maria Valtorta's life became more and more spiritual. She still had other problems, but she could now approach them with great devotion and mysticism. At the end of 1942, that is, before the great visions, personal conversations and all the other extraordinary mystical experiences, Maria Valtorta wrote: "Do you, [Father Migliorini] think my suffering suffices? No. It is enormous! To such an extent that without the special grace of God, my being could not stand it and my heart would split in agony"[153].

On Good Friday 1930, her condition got worse. She had an angina attack in the very first hours of Jesus' passion. "I really thought I was dying"[154], she emphatically recalled. She almost had to take her clothes off while in church because she was suffocating and was seized by a cold sweat. To Maria, this was just "...the gift of the dying Jesus to his little victim"[155]. By then, the key for reading her life was entirely spiritual, but that spirituality was not foregone. That very summer, the Valtorta family, cutting back on expenses a little, started putting up holidaymakers in their home. It was a very common way in Viareggio to boost the family's income, and that is why Iside decided to make use of it. The events that followed show that this was a very good choice, not just during WWII, but particularly in the following years. The first lodger was a distinguished professor, accompanied by his secretary. Unfortunately, his arrival was both providential and odd: first, his secretary insisted on the removal of the crucifix from his bedroom, and then they turned out to belong to a congregation of spiritists. Maria sensed this at once during their first summoning of the spirits, as she felt as if she were being pushed

---

[152] cf. ibid., p. 269.
[153] ibid., p. 273.
[154] ibid., p. 274.
[155] ibid.

out of the house. Then as she was taking medicine in her bedroom, the fight was terrible: "Unseen hands seemed to be pressing down upon my chest and blocking my nostrils...*something* was pushing me away from the house"[156]. In the description of this event, it is discovered that her mother Iside as early as 1921, had gone to see an occultist because of Mario. She embraced sorcery and sometimes she met various witch doctors. This occultist had given her a talisman for Maria to wear, but Maria despite never wearing it, felt very unwell all the same[157]. The following day she realized that outside the door, there was an advertising poster showing a hand and the word 'Mustafà – Fortune-teller – Occultist'. At that point, Maria was very determined and forced her mother to choose between her and the necromancer. Her determination made Signora Iside set matters straight with the professor. He had an argument with Maria, and he accused her of going to church, which made it difficult for him to summon the entity, Gabriel. After a last summoning on 17 August 1930, during which Maria felt very unwell, this unwelcomed lodger finally left. "I am convinced that spiritism is satanic": this is what she always thought of this technique for summoning the spirits of the dead. Whether it works or not is another story. However, years later in February and March 1960, Father Berti of the Servite Order, her publisher Dr. Emilio Pisani and Dr. Luciano Raffaele, the secretary of the Italian Parapsychological Society went into Maria's bedroom when she was already absent from this world, to say their goodbyes as they were leaving for Rome. Marta Diciotti recalls: "Suddenly, I hear Maria clearly say, 'Go away! Go away! Go Away!' I ran [...] and saw Maria who, pointing at the door, was telling Dr. Raffaele, 'Go Away! Go Away! Go away!' I tried to intervene in favor of Dr. Raffaele who was the target of that order... but it was all in vain. Firmly and determined, she kept pointing to the door, saying, 'Go Away! Go Away! Go away'. He didn't even try to take her hand and left showing his disappointment"[158]. During that time, Maria was completely absent; she did not respond to any intellectual stimulation. She did not seem to comprehend. But from this episode,

---

[156] ibid., p. 275.
[157] cf. ibid., p. 276.
[158] Albo Centoni, *Ricordi di donne che conobbero Maria Valtorta*, op. cit., p. 278.

we can clearly see that she refused any contact with the spiritist and parapsychologist; she could not even stand his presence there. Maria Valtorta's relationship with spiritism and spiritists were always of this nature.

A complete woman

In 1930, two other important events took place. Her mother Iside who did not want to lose her daughter, would have still liked to see her married to an old, rich man who would agree to let Maria go on looking after her mother. She had a few men in mind, but they were all coldly rejected. What had happened was that her Parish Priest understood Maria, and with his permission, she had made her private vows of chastity, poverty and obedience. She had also moved the ring that she used to wear from her right hand to her left hand, and her mother had to give up, once and for all, despite her various remonstrances[159].

But she had to face struggles in other areas as well. Even though she had been appointed by her superiors as the president of *Catholic Action* in her parish, she was not elected due to a conspiracy by prejudiced and jealous people. However, when the spiritual exercises of the young girls of *Catholic Action* (the Little Circle)[160] began, Msgr. Sanguinetti listened to her and understood her. So he put pressure on Msgr. Giuseppe Guidi, the Parish Priest of San Paolino at that time (who remained the Parish Priest until 1933 when he was replaced with Msgr. Rocchiccioli). Maria Valtorta was promoted and was asked to give lectures in her role as '*delegate* to the Culture of Young Catholics'[161]. In her *Autobiography,* she recalled some of those lectures[162]. Maria was not interested in offices and honors; she just

---

[159] cf. Maria Valtorta, *Autobiography*, op. cit., p. 283.

[160] This was the nickname of the young people who belonged to the *Catholic Action* in Viareggio. cf. ibid., p. 269.

[161] ibid.

[162] cf. ibid., pp. 291-3. In 1969, this is how Father Berti recalled that time: "Therefore in 1931 in Viareggio, having become a delegate of the female youth culture of *Catholic Action*, she distinguished herself by her conferences, which were greatly appreciated, excellently prepared, increasingly attended, profoundly put together and crystal clear, as

wanted to serve the Church and save souls from eternal perdition. In any case, her nature, her dignity and her energy became apparent and renowned when, in 1931, the Italian laws of the time suppressed all youth associations other than the Fascist ones. Maria's standing regarding politics was clear: to defend Catholicism and its vision of the world. She did this when she was very ill after WWII, but she also did it in this instance. Unaware of what was going on outside on the morning of 31 May, Maria saw the chairwoman of *Catholic Action* bursting into her home breathlessly, together with twelve friends. After calming them down, Maria asked what had happened and found out that they had been ordered to hand over the logbooks, the minutes of meetings, and the Association's flag to the police. Filled with fear, and struck down by a myriad of sudden (and made up) illnesses, these women were not up to doing so, and they asked Maria to do everything. And so, she did. That evening, Maria and two friends of hers went to the police headquarters with the logbooks, the minutes and the flag. The police officers were probably thinking that they would get everything without a fuss, but Maria insisted on meeting the delegate and on being given a receipt. The delegate refused to see them but Maria did not give up. The guard called her 'Maria of Lourdes' and in the end, she was introduced to the delegate under this nickname, and she got her receipt. They left triumphantly and Maria smiled at the thought of being called by that name[163]. It was not just an act of personal and social courage; Maria was looking for a sign to do a much braver thing: to offer herself up to Divine Justice as a victim soul for the salvation of sinners. State persecution of the Church through its associations was the sign that Maria was looking for. She had decided to offer herself to God on 8 September, Maria's feast day, but she became impatient and she asked God to suggest the words to her[164], without having to say them or write them herself. On the first Friday of June, during the Mass celebrated for the young girls of *Catholic Action*, she experienced an hour of terrible

---

confirmed by various people who listened to them with keen interest, and who still remember their subject after more than 30 years" (Maria Valtorta, *Autobiografia prima*, op. cit., p. VI).

[163] cf. Maria Valtorta, *Autobiography*, op. cit., pp. 297-9.

[164] At that time, she had no spiritual director or spiritual friendship with whom to consult.

agony and she prophetically foresaw a fragment of what was to happen also in Italy: "wars, famine, deaths, massacres - and endless despair"[165]. On 1 July of the previous year, on the feast day of the Most Precious Blood, she had written her act of offering to Divine Justice, to be a victim soul to Divine Love, and on the same day[166] in 1931 coming out of her heart, she felt that very same offer that she completed with her very own words. And from then on, Maria Valtorta wanted to call herself 'Maria of the Cross'[167] for the act of offering she had made.

A new goal: sacrifice

Her act of offering to God was not made in vain. If and when an offer is accepted by God, there are at least two consequences: on the one hand, a life ever closer to God, meaning an ever greater participation in divine life and a greater enjoyment of the infinite sweetness coming from Him; and on the other hand, this offer, decided upon and lived with equal earnestness and firmness, has its own physical consequences, well exemplified by Jesus Christ's life on earth. A life as 'Maria of the Cross'[168] in various ways.

---

[165] ibid., p. 300. "While I wavered between a yes and a no, the day of the Sacred Heart of Jesus came in June 1931. At the sung Mass with the voices of the young girls of *Catholic Action* ("the Little Circle"), right after the Glory be to the Father, a mental vision and mental knowledge of all the calamities which have tortured us over the past ten years presented themselves to me. An apocalyptic contemplation ... I was seized by such anguish and uncontrollable weeping that I could no longer see anything but the abyss into which the world was plummeting and the need to set victims as props to obstruct, or at least slow down the world's race to the precipice. They had to lead and guide me out of the church at the end of Mass because I was crying so much that I couldn't see ... When I got back home, I wrote my act of offering, which I solemnly pronounced later on the feast of the Most Precious Blood. Here it is" (Maria Valtorta, *Notebooks 1945-1950*, op. cit., dated 10 February 1946, p. 189ff). And it is followed by her rather long-worded script of her act of offering.

[166] Maria Valtorta, *Autobiography*, op. cit., p. 300.

[167] cf. ibid., pp. 299-300.

[168] ibid., p. 300.

And that is what happened in Maria Valtorta's life. Obviously, it all looked inconceivable in the eyes of science. "None of the twenty-nine, that's right, *twenty-nine*... Aesculapius [physicians] who have come over these past twelve years (1931-1943) to tap, press, pierce, poke around, and listen, has ever managed to understand"[169]. This was one of the reasons why many of them became convinced that Maria was not ill but only mad, a hypochondriac, a psychopath or a hysterical person. That is, "a madwoman"[170], as her mother used to say.

And so began ten years of pain, also on a spiritual level. It was not a real hard-heartedness but rather the consequence of contemplating the awful pain that would hit society and therefore human beings that was crushing her. "It was not that I felt abandoned by God. No. His love was always upon me. But if Jesus caressed me, the Father made His hand heavier on my heart. A period of compact penance began. Everything related to the sense of supernatural love, disappeared. I am referring to the sweet dreams which had been my joy for years, and to the trust that God would spare us from all that we are undergoing now. The hour of Gethsemane had come at once - fully and somberly - and may I say that it lasted ten long years, for only since 1941 has its severity relented. Do not think that I experienced aridity in my heart. No, never. Just as I have never been left without the comfort of Christ's love. But I have suffered intensely and morally over an *exact* perception of all that was about to happen in the world... I have shed all my tears for this reason. I wept so much, beseeching the Eternal to avert this tremendous scourge, mortifying myself with harsh penitence to placate, appease and soothe Divine Justice, that when the scourage arrived, and everybody more or less lost their head, I did not have a single tear left. I had already tortured myself in advance, seeing the full unfolding of the tremendous tragedy... I have suffered physically from a break-out of serious maladies, each more frightful than its predecessor, and the series has not yet come to an end... I have experienced all the pain in my body which has become a compendium of infirmities! And what's worse, these maladies have not left the spiritual part immune, but have

---

[169] ibid., p. 305.
[170] ibid.

disturbed it with an unbridling of sensations which in themselves alone are martyrdom"[171]. It was an important turning-point or growth for Maria because love for God and for one's neighbor[172] as taught by Jesus to his disciples and as an essential element of spiritual life, and even more so of a mystical life, was by now knowledge she had acquired[173].

Whenever a soul gets close to God who has summoned it – usually, but not compulsorily, as nothing is 'automatic' regarding spiritual life – things that are difficult to explain or to describe, and unbelievable events, happen. The mystics, as paramysticism teaches, are generally the proof of it[174]. Starting from 1943, many spiritual events happened to Maria Valtorta, events which could be described

---

[171] ibid., p. 301. And it goes into even greater detail: "The matter is as follows. And let us hope that I can succeed in explaining it properly. There were no more dreams, no more caresses, no more soundless words which were nonetheless so perceptible to the soul. No more. As if Jesus had gone very, very far away with his love. *But I felt He was in me like never before.* He was simply silent. He loved me as before and even more, but He did not make himself felt in any way. The hour of darkness had come for me; I had wanted it – no one had forced me to undergo it; I alone had imposed it upon myself by asking the Father for it. Now I had to suffer with whatever most painful aspects might be joined to it. When *His time* came, Jesus remained alone, separated from the Father. It was the Man, the Man alone, who was undergoing his punishment […] Pain shared by the heart of a compassionate Cyrenian, loses its crushing weight. But when *we alone* are the ones who have to bear it, it compresses us to the point of suffocation … If this happens with human pain, it takes place much more when this pain rises to spheres that are more select than human ones" (ibid., pp. 302-3).

[172] cf. *Il Castello Interiore* [The Interior Castle], Teresa d'Avila, *Tutte le opere* [Teresa of Avila: The Collected Works], Bompiani Il pensiero occidentale, Milano 2011, p. 1282ff. The beginning of the sixth mansion.

[173] cf. *Rubén Pineda Esteban, La Immolación como la clave de appreión y el nesxo de unión entre teología y vida mística en las obras de María Valtorta* [The Immolation as the key of apprehension and the link between theology and mystical life in the works of María Valtorta], Facultad de Teología del Norte de España headquarters in Burgos, Burgos 2010. This is a PhD thesis. At the moment, it is the most elaborate theological thesis.

[174] Saint Pio of Pietrelcina is far from being the only proof of this. cf. Renzo Allegri, *A tu per tu con Padre Pio*, op. cit.

as extraordinary had they not been so many and so frequent. But some of them had already occurred before: on 4 January 1932, Maria Valtorta saw for the first time her Guardian Angel – who later revealed its name, Azariah[175], to her – beautiful and smiling. In January it is cold, sometimes very cold, even in Viareggio, a town on the Tyrrhenian Sea about twenty kilometres north of Pisa. On that 4 January, a Sunday, Maria had returned home after Mass and several meetings with *Catholic Action*. Inside, the air was made impossible to breathe by four coal foot-warmers that polluted the whole house. Maria complained but after her mother's reproaches, she kept quiet to keep the peace. A couple of guests arrived, and Maria had to wait on them, running to and fro. Suddenly she was overwhelmed and she fainted. She stopped in a dressing room where she fell to the floor with a thud, and she also broke some glass, injuring herself. She was unconscious for half an hour without anyone noticing or anyone asking where she had gone. But as she fell, a beautiful, angelic creature appeared: "What splendor in his face and clothing, which seemed to be made of lily petals strewn with silver dust and diamonds! What a smile! I would be willing to suffer everyday like that day to see him again!"[176]

She could therefore bear the pain, the family troubles, the lack of understanding that she would experience and accept; it was far from easy, though. She wrote this thought, for instance, about the young girls of *Catholic Action*: "Sometimes, I confess, I could tell them to go jump in the lake. I am so tired, run down and aching!"[177] It was the beginning of 1932, and *the best had yet to come…* Meanwhile, Maria continued to identify with the cross of Christ. The events took place again and her acceptance of pain increased. From 1932 onwards, she rarely went out because her heart was weak and she had to lean on her mother, who was herself in pain. So the two of them, dressed as ageless, elderly, stumbling ladies, must have been a pitiful sight. Nonetheless, she kept holding lectures at the parish church, but her heart was getting weaker and weaker. She had had to stop several times and be rescued, despite her mother Iside, who stubbornly

---

[175] Maria Valtorta, *Lettere a Madre Teresa Maria 1*, op. cit., p. 46.

[176] Maria Valtorta, *Autobiography*, op. cit., p. 307. For the whole story, cf. ibid., pp. 307-8.

[177] ibid., p. 311.

refused to accept her daughter's illnesses and insisted that her own were more serious. More than once, the doctors got the treatment wrong and more than once, Maria was close to death. It was on these occasions, despite her past experience as a nurse, that she started to understand the tragedy of the sick and of sickness[178]. On 18 December 1932, after three years of doubts and fears about what would happen to her – almost a premonition – she held a conference on Joan of Arc. She started talking while standing, but despite her ferocious efforts, at some point she had to sit down and then she had a heart crisis. They rescued her and she took two hours to recover. The premonition was correct! It was to be the signal of a new spiritual growth characterized by suffering.

Her last Holy Mass in a church

Maria Valtorta had always wanted to attend the Holy Mass and on Christmas Eve in 1932, she went out accompanied by six women and some cognac in her pocket. But it was cold and the heart pain came back, violent and sudden. She managed to hold on until Communion, but when she received the Eucharist, her heart went crazy. Maria took a pill and some cognac, then when she had made it back to her seat, she asked to return home where she arrived exhausted. It was her last Holy Mass in public on 24 December 1932, which she attended while being still able to walk. In the meantime, something that even she thought was unthinkable happened: "[A] series of strangers came looking for me[179] in search of advice and prayers in ever-growing numbers. They were simple people who wanted to meet her. It was as if a sixth sense made people, open to the supernatural, discover the inner qualities of sickly Maria Valtorta. This was troubling to her though because she would have needed

---

[178] "I have had persecutions because the world always persecutes when encountering us, even if misfortune leaves us among the dead; and our own relatives are in the world, to whom we are a burden, and they tell us so. And the friends who deride us as crazy people; and the doctors who torment us in a *thousand* ways; and the strangers who, knowing nothing, want to blather about us with unmerciful criticisms…" (ibid., p. 335).

[179] ibid., p. 336.

silence and rest; but it also boosted her because she felt useful to those who needed solace.

In 1934 on Good Friday, she said that on that day she was "pierced by love on contemplating my Jesus on the Cross"[180]. "Two days after that moment of ecstasy and that cry of desire which rent my chest, I was nailed onto the Cross"[181]. We can clearly see here the rule of the call-answer-gift, typical of mystical self-immolation. The experience was without a doubt a mystical one, and the rule was therefore followed. And the consequences were extremely important for her life. Maria's real transformation or metamorphosis occurred a few years later. From then on, she referred to herself as 'Christ's violet'[182], and from then onwards, she was bedridden except for some brief and secret exceptions. As, for example, during the 1934-35 winter when her mother was ill due to a serious carelessness, and Maria got up at night to tidy up and then she went back to bed; but that was an exception[183].

The Doctors

Her history with doctors continued which was made up of a lack of understanding, serious mistakes, and a lack of attention. And we must understand that, despite being ill, Maria was not like any other person. It is typical of mystics to suffer from mysterious illnesses - just think of the illness of St. Pio da Pietrelcina during WWI[184]. If a doctor does not understand this, he ends up making serious mistakes in both tests and treatments and with Maria, this was always the case. Her descriptions sometimes even sound humorous[185]: "After another

---

[180] ibid., p. 342.

[181] ibid., p. 343.

[182] ibid., p. 350.

[183] ibid., p. 365.

[184] Renzo Allegri, *Padre Pio un santo tra noi* [Padre Pio a saint among us], Mondadori, Milano 1988, p. 145ff.

[185] "On 5 May, after a careful medical examination during the usual weekly visit, he changed my medication ... He had already changed it a dozen times before. Away with the trinitrine, viretone and the cardiotonic. He wanted to give me calcium injections because pulmonary tuberculosis was present ... Tuberculosis? Since when? It had not shown up in any tests,

consultation with a surgeon, 'it's appendicitis! You need to undergo surgery at once!' (Boom!) They had also diagnosed that in 1920 and 14 years later, appendicitis has not shown up yet. I am still waiting for it. And I survive on salad, peas and such delicacies with a bowel which, according to the surgeon, is almost perforated! Another consultation and 'it's a genital insufficiency'. (Three times: Boom!) I have never had that kind of ailment! This is more than incompetency! On the contrary, there was a tendency towards super-incompetency! But it must be a breeding ground. It's easy for male doctors to treat women! What they cannot classify something with a proper name, they call it hysteria, and we are stuck! After a treatment of ovarian hormones, the result: the heart had not improved and an ovary inflammation led to a tumor that is causing me great pain and troubles, *not purely physical* [186]. Then, since they had failed to hit the

---

and there was nothing in me that made anyone assume I had it. I repeat: maybe it is present now, but nine years ago, there was really nothing. Enough. I refused the calcium injections. *I did not want injections* ... And now I have had over 13,000 – that's right: thirteen thousand ... Then I had to swallow calcium, cod-liver oil, cholesterol taken orally, phosphates and vitamins ... My stomach turned into a sink ... There were so many things to take, and all of them at least an hour apart and separate from meal times. So I asked the doctor with a Brother Juniper reaction (a character in a novel), 'Will you tell me, then, at what time I can eat?'. For he entreated me to nourish myself to excess and to rest. The only thing he added was that for half an hour each day, I *had* to stay in the sun. The result was a ruined stomach which was an obstacle to nutrition, not superabundant, but rather less than usual because I always had indigestion from all those concoctions that I gulped down. I had heart crises which were more violent than ever, an increase in fevers, and finally, I had first-rate congestion due to the sun and to the hardening of my arteries, to the point of having juvenile sclerosis with the formation of an aneurysm. But before stating the rest, I shall make a remark. If another person had to savor that diagnosis, it would have scared them. I took it in joyfully. [I had] tuberculous to the point where I was going to die soon, according to the doctor. And what did I want? To consummate my sacrifice Oh, human foolishness! That hurry of mine was cowardice and egotism" (ibid., pp. 353-4).

[186] Despite all her serious illnesses, her sexual urges did not leave her alone. On 6 July 1944 she wrote something that would be unbelievable if it were not written in her own handwriting: "During the night, an orgasm

bull's-eye, ladies and gentlemen, it was time for a change of treatment. The phthisiologist (who specializes in tuberculosis) came back once again. Oh, what *human* inconsistency! Properly instructed by the doctor in charge, he took back his *entire* previous diagnosis from a short time before, and whereas he had previously put me on fresh tap water and fruit juices for my blood pressure, he now ordered high-nutrition. Whereas he had previously ordered complete immobility under the pain of death, he now ordered me to get up and go to the pine wood. Whereas he had previously decalcified my arteries with all the nitrates possible, he now ordered calcium again without interruption because there was bilateral tuberculosis (boom!) which if not checked by high-nutrition, air, movement and calcium, it would take me to the cemetery within three months (boom, boom!) amidst tremendous haemoptysis (boom, boom, boom!). It was 4 September 1934. Today is 8 April 1943. I have been eating less and less and I have not taken in any fresh air except for what comes in from the window. I have not moved about, I have not ingested calcium, and here I am... waiting... I had to engage in movement, but *none* of the three physicians commited himself to taking me by ambulance to have an x-ray done... They knew that moving me risked death. In short, one gave me alcohol, another prohibited even watered-down white wine; one administered heavy doses of caffeine, and another prohibited coffee; one overfed me provoking crisis after crisis, and put me on water and fruit juice... It was enough to drive you crazy!"[187]. To conclude, the doctors made Maria Valtorta's life very hard, taking her several times near death's door. Then the Devil himself started to torment her: first, with an inexplicable, painful,

---

(incorrectly translated as 'anxiety' in English) brought me out of sopor at 3 am. It had been a long time since it had happened to me. I went on crying desolately. I think my heart was dislocated even more. I then prayed. Afterwards, I made my usual offerings. And when I came to the one for Nennolina [Antonietta Meo, who died at six and a half years of age] [...], Nennolina appeared to me. Dressed in white, almost as tall as Marta, with her thoughtful, shining eyes, smiling and luminous [...]. Then Jesus came [...]. And even in human terms, I am content... because I am *still* a woman" (Maria Valtorta, *Notebboks 1944,* op. cit., 6 July, p. 422). This episode was caused by an ovarian tumor.

[187] Maria Valtorta, *Autobiography*, op. cit., pp. 358-9.

piercing melancholy; and the awful, yet typical, suggestions: "Do you see how your Jesus listens to you? He has taken everything away from you and now He is taking away your doctor too. And He's taking him away right now when you, poor fool, were deceiving yourself about being more secure [...]. The war is going from bad to worse; peace is a myth, isolation is growing around you, you are losing your doctor... You imbecile, you have deluded yourself!"[188].

Physical and spiritual storms, the usual signs that the Lord is purifying you[189].

Meanwhile, life went on among the appalling, sudden and useless outbursts of her mother Iside, among a physical crisis and premonitory dreams. Maria's equated that the suffering that she had accepted – whatever type of suffering – meant the salvation of souls[190]. In 1935, between the arrival in the Valtorta household of Marta Diciotti and her father's death, Maria also joined the Prayer Apostolate with the permission of her Parish Priest, but for reasons unknown, for a long time she did not receive a membership card from this Association[191]. So, she compiled a 'calendar of suffering', and every day she offered her sorrows for someone's good[192].

---

[188] ibid., p. 349.

[189] cf. 1 Cor 2:14-5.

[190] "Immolation constitutes the substance of Christian spirituality, as also demonstrated by the lives of mystics from all periods of time. Many of them experienced mystical-oblation; they found its root, model and fulfillment in the oblation of the divine Trinitarian love which was revealed and shared with humanity by Jesus Christ, the High Priest, with his birth, life, death and eternal gift to the Father in the Holy Spirit" (Luigi Borriello – Edmondo Caruana – Maria Rosaria Del Genio – Raffaele Di Muro (editor), *Nuovo dizionario di mistica* [The new dictionary of mystics], Libreria Editrice Vaticana, Città del Vaticano 2016, entry *Immolazione* [Immolation]).

[191] Maria Valtorta, *Autobiography*, op. cit., p. 367.

[192] "On Mondays, I made reparation for violations against the law of God and the Church, for justice, and to obtain a holy death for those in agony. On Tuesdays, for the abuses and contempt of the word of God, for resistance to grace, and for the souls in Purgatory. And so on. On Saturdays, when I offered and suffered for sacrilegious confessions and for the sins of the senses, I added the intention of expiating to redeem women who were lost" (ibid., p. 368).

The arrival of Marta Diciotti

The arrival of Marta Diciotti marked a big change. This young lady was very important for Maria Valtorta: she became much more than just a cleaning lady – she was a *family member*[193] to her. Even though she could never compete in culture and holiness, nonetheless she was totally loyal and discreet until Maria's death, and her service was likewise complete. Marta Diciotti was born in 1910 and she came to Viareggio with her mother in 1923. With her mother Isolina's death, she found herself alone, working as a legal secretary and learning to use the typewriter[194]. She knew Maria because they lived in the same street (via Antonio Fratti) and she often went to keep her company. Then one afternoon, Maria had seen the late Signora Isolina in a dream, asking her to take Marta on to save her from the evils of the world. After all, Maria's mother needed help in the management of the house and she had been looking for someone, so Marta Diciotti was just what she needed. So on 24 May 1935, she joined the Valtorta household[195] and she never left, although she was tempted on various occasions to do just that by Signora Iside's bad temper[196].

The death of her father Giuseppe

After unimaginable suffering, Maria's father died as well. Giuseppe Valtorta left this world during the night of 30 June 1935. Many years later, his daughter wrote[197] to Father Migliorini: "Bladder

---

[193] A term that is not used often, but which is perfectly adequate to describe the relationship between Marta Diciotti and Maria Valtorta. A person who was practically, even if not legally, "adopted" by her, lived in the house, shared her worries, pains and joys as is normally done in a family.

[194] This ability was of great use to her after 1946, when she helped Maria Valtorta transfer the manuscripts onto typed sheets.

[195] cf. ibid., p. 347; Albo Centoni, *Una vita con Maria Valtorta. Testimonianze di Marta Diciotti*, op. cit., pp. 34-5.

[196] In a letter to Father Migliorini, Maria Valtorta praised Marta for her low expectations and for being indispensable. Without her, Maria would have been brought to a hospital for long-term care and her mother to a hospice (cf. Maria Valtorta, *Lettere a Padre Migliorini* [Letters to Father Migliorini], Centro Editoriale Valtortiano, Isola del Liri (FR) 2011, p. 10).

[197] ibid., p. 140; letter dated 3 May 1946.

stones with consequences to the prostate. (...) My poor father, a giant who was struck dead in great agony"[198]. It was a huge blow for Maria. "I was alone, by then, alone, do you understand (Father Migliorini)? Alone. There was nobody left on this earth. God and father were in Heaven. But Heaven seemed to be so deaf and far away!"[199] Maria did not see her father's body after he died and this made her sorrow even more acute.

As her mother Iside did not have a husband to harass any more, she targeted Maria and Marta even more, causing painful situations, at times even farcical, as she could not even stop herself from eating[200]. "And mother hurled herself without restraint, at Marta, at me, at everybody... A real lunatic! She has performed more cruel and foolish acts herself over the past eight years than a whole psychiatric hospital"[201]. She often burst out in a paroxysm. To calm her down the doctor also gave her some bromide, but this did not prevent her from doing awful things to the family.

Signora Iside obviously felt the need to strengthen family ties: with the excuse of her husband's death, she rekindled her relationship with her disorderly and reckless brother, who in the past she had categorically refused to either help or be near to. Then she accused her late husband of forcing her to keep away from him. The reckless man all but changed his way of living and took advantage of the situation, throwing away the money that should have been used for the family's bare necessities, to the extent that they had to do without woolen vests. It may sound a trifle, but let us not forget that the room in which Maria lay in bed was not heated, so they needed anything that could keep them warm[202].

After this dangerous behavior, there also came the unbelievable allegation that Maria was "a debauchee with the worst, most degrading vices"[203]. The rumor was started, rather absurdly, by two

---

[198] ibid.

[199] Albo Centoni, *Una vita con Maria Valtorta. Testimonianze di Marta Diciotti*, op. cit., p. 357. On this page, the events of her father's death are also written.

[200] cf. Maria Valtorta, *Autobiography*, op. cit., p. 390.

[201] ibid., p. 385.

[202] cf. ibid.

[203] ibid., p. 389.

single ladies who were staying with the Valtortas as lodgers. Maria's physician who, for obvious reasons, examined her quite often, was explicitly regarded by these two as a very handsome man. Maria noticed that they were trying some risqué approaches and, in the end, she had to complain. She did not do it out of jealousy, but that is what they thought, and she ended up being accused of jealousy. The two women then, once they knew a little more about her past, and as the Alto Tirreno Navy Squadron had dropped anchor at Viareggio, they started to presume that her beloved Mario was also there – Maria's earthly love[204] – so on their own initiative, they started to make untoward enquiries about him. Marta was the first to find out: she warned them, but it was useless; she told Maria, but as she could not act directly, she warned her mother. But the mother got it all wrong and at first, she attacked Maria with every possible insult and allegation. Then she turned to the two ladies in the same way and in the end, she threw them out. Their reaction was suitably proud and violent, slandering Maria within earshot of the Barbantine nuns who were looking after her, to the point that these were immediately withdrawn from service. From that point on, the allegations got worse and worse, and all types of dirt was told about Maria Valtorta. There is no need to think about demonic possession and obsession to understand their cruelty. Events like these real absurdities of human behavior prove it beyond words.

The persecution by Iside and a thirst for writing

However, the persecution by her mother did not stop. On the contrary, it went on until her death. The Valtorta household was at the mercy of her touchiness. "One day we would have lunch at ten and another at three; one morning we would get up at four and another at eight. One day we would eat three times and another just once, perhaps without soup, only bread and a little cheese... a real

---

[204] As is often the case with people with certain gifts – one can take Saint Pio of Pietrelcina again as an example – normal, paranormal and mystical facts are intertwined. Mario was considered dead by Maria Valtorta since 1932 because she believed she had seen him and talked to him in her dreams over and over again, and several times he asked her to go with him to the afterlife, [although he did receive] a clear refusal from her. cf. ibid., pp. 387-8.

madhouse!"[205] Signora Iside was also very stingy with the money that her husband had left her. It was not a lot, but enough to cause all sorts of tension. He would have left everything to his daughter, leaving only what was due to his wife, but the latter never acknowledged her husband's wish, and she destroyed his will, living in fear that Maria might want to uphold her own rights. But by then, Maria had embarked on a different course, "What concerns would she show me regarding the possession or lack of money? I have never had whims and I have always been able to repress my desires, therefore… […] in these conditions […] mother should give me only what is necessary to live; I ask for nothing else"[206]. But Signora Iside could not put up with anybody and anything any longer.

Indeed, there is an obscure episode that casts some serious doubts upon her actions against Maria. On the advice of a few acquaintances, Maria had tried to write a book to strengthen the faith of good Christians and to make some money too. Maria had already chosen the title – The Heart of a Woman [207] – but her mother was violently against it and in the end, to keep the peace, the project was set aside. Curiously enough, probably blinded by envy from that very moment on, her mother started to add a finely chopped up concoction to the soup which she served to Maria. And then Maria would feel sick. One day she let Marta taste it and she felt sick too. Then Maria told her physician and her Parish Priest about it and both told her not to eat it anymore, on the contrary, to give it to Signora Iside instead. Maria followed their advice and this time it was her mother who felt very sick; therefore, Maria demanded to eat what everybody else ate and she was fine.

Signora Iside's eccentricities didn't prevent the Lord from operating wonders through Maria. At the beginning of 1939, Annamaria, a 14-month-old girl, was on her deathbed. After one month of contracting a very serious and contagious lung disease which was treated as best as they could back then, her father, who had been praying and had been asking for prayers, turned up by chance at the Valtortas' door in need of some cotton wool. He spoke

---

[205] ibid., p. 390.
[206] ibid., p. 391.
[207] The manuscript was destroyed years later by Marta Diciotti and Dr. Emilio Pisani, following the wishes of Maria Valtorta.

to Maria about the child who lay dying, and about his own doubts regarding God's providence. Maria prayed to God, offering to take upon herself the disease to get the child well again, and to dispel the father's doubts. The child suddenly got better with no relapse whatsoever. Her father developed a trust in God once again, but Maria Valtorta was struck by pleurisy that would still greatly affect her at the end of 1942. The swap was therefore accepted by God, and Maria remarked: "I am dying. I am dying of this too. But what does it matter? I am full of defects. But what does it matter? At one time, I was even worse. But what does it matter? Charity covers a multitude of sins"[208]. As a matter of fact, she was wrong - she did not die at once, but 19 years later, after many other humanly unbelievable events.

A humorous strictness

One of Maria Valtorta's lesser-known traits which shows her absolute normality, was her ability to joke. Marta Diciotti said that she was "a skillful impressionist: she could imitate gestures, voices, and expressions in a surprising way, and when she pulled out all the stops, she made us all roar with laughter [...]. She could also imitate her mother very well. [...] When someone talked to her, or to us, in a rather pompous, self-important way, she would look at you with a wicked spark in her eyes and you knew that if she could have, she would have said, in the same tone as the speaker, 'Ah yes! Here we need an extra-exclamation mark!'... [...] She immediately sensed exaggeration, ridicule and falsehood..."[209]. She always maintained this style, even when she was totally enveloped in pain and in para-mystical experiences. Marta Diciotti also recounted this episode: a Servite Friar who knew of Maria and of her charism, one day went to see her because he wanted her supernatural opinion regarding a very important matter. Clearly, this Servite Friar hadn't had much experience with mystics, but perhaps he had heard of fortune-tellers or similar people. "I remember that he urged her by repeating 'Concentrate! Concentrate!'. She looked at him puzzled. And he repeated, 'Concentrate! Concentrate!'. 'To do what?' Maria asked.

---

[208] ibid., p. 398.
[209] Albo Centoni, *Ricordi di donne che conobbero Maria Valtorta*, op. cit., p. 256.

'Because the Lord must give me an answer' he repiled. To which Maria responded, 'He must? Are you saying that He must? But the Lord is not at our beck and call! He's not our valet! If He wants to give me an answer, He decides when and how. He wakes me up during the night if He wants. At all hours. There is no need for me to concentrate. Do not fear. If I get an answer, I will let you know'. And with these words she sent him away. And he... well, he never showed up again"[210]. This and other similar episodes which were even decades apart, tell us how stable Maria was and the way she behaved. To do things this way, one has to be able to joke, one has to have a holistic vision of what happens, and one has to have inner calm and impartial judgement. That is, one must be psychologically normal, and able to fully and humbly make use of the intelligence that the Lord has given us.

Just before Heaven opened up

Maria Valtorta had had several premonitions about the war, but when she saw what she had foreseen and experienced it firsthand, this affected her enormously. She had prayed, made sacrifices, fasted, and cried to prevent war, but the terrible devastation had come at last. On 12 August 1939, the feast day of St. Clare, a new premonition warned her that the 'fierce hour'[211] had come. At that time, one of her *daughters* of *Catholic Action* had gone to Poland. Maria had always followed her with prayers and sacrifices to ensure she would not stray from the righteous path. On that very day, the premonition was followed by a voice that spoke about that girl: "Tell her to come back at once"[212]. Maria immediately wrote a letter to that former pupil of hers, which was placed in the last post-bag in time, allowing her to get out before the closure of the borders. And the girl was able to leave on the last train out of Poland. This was not the only

---

[210] ibid., p. 236.

[211] Maria Valtorta, *Autobiography*, op. cit., p. 408. The German invasion of Poland began on the morning of 2 September 1939.

[212] ibid.

premonition: while she was writing her *Autobiography*, she had already "foreseen precisely what would happen later"[213].

The year 1940 arrived: "Many deceived themselves about our 'non-belligerence'. I did not. I redoubled prayers and sacrifices, but I now did so to obtain mercy for us in the terrible contingencies of the war"[214]. Meanwhile, her illnesses worsened and ravaged her. In the spring of 1940, her mother fell ill with a strange ailment, which Maria attributed to the wrong and bizarre way she ate. In any case, the situation within the Valtorta household was getting worse. As she wrote in her *Autobiography*: "I have gotten worse since then as never before in nearly ten years. To the already existing illnesses, others were added: neuritis with a spasmodic aching so intense that I begged the doctor to let me die. I went as far as brushing a very strong tincture of iodine over my whole face to numb the trigeminal nerve which gave me maddening pain – pain that I could not alleviate with any analgesics because of the state of my heart. In addition to neuritis, there was pachymeningitis which left me numb as if I had been mummified. The smallest movement caused me to howl. My kidneys failed and the chronic cystitis was complicated by pyelocystitis, culminating in renal and vesical hemorrhages. My peritonitis increased producing intestinal occlusion. The pleurisy worsened on the right side where some painful adhesions formed. In the very cold December of 1940, Marta was away for a few days and I was left without hot-water bottles[215] and heating. I suffered from pulmonary congestion that came upon me which got worse and worse in the numberless relapses I have had since then"[216]. Maria Valtorta had also to go through these serious contingencies, but it was exactly this

---

[213] ibid., pp. 322-4. A whole series of premonitions and how they presented themselves to her are described in detail here.

[214] ibid., p. 409. Blessed Elena Aiello, a contemporary mystic of Maria Valtorta, also felt the same danger. In addition, she managed to send Benito Mussolini three letters, mandated by Jesus himself, in which He invited him not to go to war (cf. Vincenzo Speziale, *Le profezie della Beata Madre Elena Aiello* [The prophecies of Blessed Mother Elena Aiello], Edizioni Segno, Tavagnacco (UD) 2014, pp. 53-67).

[215] The only winter heating for Maria as there was no heater in the room.

[216] ibid., p. 411.

difficult situation that urged her to look for a priest who could help and advise her.

Father Romualdo Migliorini, spiritual director

At the time, Father Romualdo Migliorini[217] was the Superior of the community of the Friar Servants of Mary in Viareggio. Two of Maria's girlfriends from Castelnuovo Garfagnana asked Father Pennoni, a Servite Friar himself, to pay a visit to the Valtortas. He obediently asked his Superior for permission but as Fr. Pennoni was very ill, Father Migliorini took it upon himself to pay Maria a visit. He went to see the ill woman, and after a rather cold start, there started a friendship as the visits became more and more frequent. With time, this became spiritual direction and help in all contingencies. He became the first, the only and the real spiritual director of her life. Maria could write well and fast, and this struck Father Migliorini enormously. After Maria wrote a few letters to him, he had the idea to get her to write something about herself. Hence the *Autobiography* which she wrote between February and April 1943[218]. It is a fundamental work if one wants an insider's understanding of the life of Maria Valtorta up to that date because she set out her own truth about her life, told before God, without omitting anything important and without belittling anything. The necessity to 'tell everything' before God forced her to also expose uncomfortable truths about herself and about her family. But this

---

[217] Father Romualdo Maria Migliorini was born in Volegno di Stazzema (LU) on 21 June 1884, and died in Carsòli (AQ) on 10 July 1953 from miliary tuberculosis. He entered the Order of the Servants of Mary in 1900 and was ordained a priest in 1908. For three years, he remained in Italy, then (in 1911) he was transferred to Canada where he exercised the ministry of Parish Priest. He was later sent to South Africa where he became a regular superior and the Apostolic Prefect. He was ordered to return to Italy in 1939 where he became the Prior of Sant'Andrea in Viareggio (LU) until 1946. After the vicissitudes with Maria Valtorta, he was transferred to Rome in 1946 with the command not to return to Viareggio. He died in Carsòli (L'Aquila) on 10 July 1953, in the holiday home of the students of the Order (cf. "Bollettino Valtortiano", op. cit., n. 18 – September 1978, p. 70).

[218] Marta Diciotti recounts the events (cf. Albo Centoni, *Una vita con Maria Valtorta. Testimonianze di Marta Diciotti*, op. cit., pp. 31-4).

allows us, after Father Migliorini, to better understand the story and the personality of Maria Valtorta – at least until the fateful day on 23 April 1943 when, although apparently everything stayed the same, everything changed.

PART TWO

And Heaven entered her room

The second part of Maria Valtorta's life ends on the day of her death, 12 October 1961. During these years she never physically left her bed, nor did she leave her bedroom[219]. That was her enclosure until her death, during which she led a mystical life full of gifts, both on a personal level and on a social level. Illnesses continued to affect her cruelly, endlessly and without interruption. Doctors came and went to her deathbed without realizing what was really going on and they looked for remedies which always proved to be either ineffective or, even worse, harmful. Her mother Iside lived on until October 1943[220], then Maria was left alone with Marta Diciotti. While the loss of her mother was very painful, on the other hand, it meant the end of her cruel harassment and of the incessant reproaches. Marta Diciotti acted as her support and as her family every day until her death. Marta was a simple woman, but she was exemplary in her service and devotion to the woman whose many, beautiful secrets she knew, as she knew of the many humiliations she had had to endure. She never did shy away from her, and their friendship allowed Maria Valtorta to write and do everything that she did. Without the humble and continuous service of Marta Diciotti, Maria would not have been able to write practically anything[221].

---

[219] As already mentioned, only once did she get out of bed and take a few steps. This occurred when she tried to give first-aid assistance to her mother, but it was an unsuccessful attempt because her back did not support her and she immediately fell to the ground.

[220] According to Marta Diciotti, the only doctor who understood the origin of Maria's illnesses, although it is not known to what extent, was Dr. Lamberto Lapi who died on 26 October 1943 in an ambush during the war. Maria had also had a premonition about his death. (cf. Albo Centoni, *Una vita con Maria Valtorta. Testimonianze di Marta Diciotti*, op. cit., pp. 126-7).

[221] Maria Valtorta's esteem for Marta was very great. On 29 October 1942, before she began her literary production and her adventure as a seer, she wrote favourably of Marta to Father Migliorini: "I who remember the very large number of infinite servants who passed through our house [...] and I who see what Marta does: grocery shopping, housework and tasks in

In 1943, there began the 13,193 notebook pages with no corrections or amendments, and the hundreds and hundreds of letters sent to many people, who made Maria Valtorta known not only throughout Italy, but also around the world as her writings have been translated in over 30 languages. Her writings have been both criticized and celebrated; they are a source of passionate praise and insults, of huge misunderstandings and misrepresentation. Maria Valtorta has been, and is, a powerful provoker: her writings, if they are read, urge one to take sides; they question one's conscience, and require an examination of one's life that not everybody can bear.

In this second part of her life, we shall explore the path which her writings caused her to follow. It was not Maria who went into the world, it was the world which went to her, in the shape of many lay people and clergy who – in various ways and for different reasons – wanted to meet, question and talk to her. Hence the many events and the need to clarify a few things. We must understand and 'prove' that Maria Valtorta was a very normal woman, suffering from many serious illnesses, and with great superhuman gifts. However, she was not mentally ill, or addicted to any altered state of consciousness, or vain to the point of becoming famous by making up stories, and least of all, she was not schizophrenic and suffering from a multiple personality disorder. She suffered from physical illnesses, not mental illness and above all, her soul was not affected. To sum up, she was mentally sound, spiritually exceptional, and she dedicated herself to chronicle the life of Jesus or, to be more precise, to illustrate the life of Jesus by writing down his dictations/personal conversations.

The second part of her life started at a precise date and time: after an initial comforting experience on 2 March 1943[222], Maria Valtorta

---

all areas, with seriousness, honesty and ability, and at the more than modest salary of L. 50 per month, I repeat fifty, but I who see and reflect on all of this believe that if Marta were to become tired of all this, I would be taken to the hospital and mother to a nursing home because we wouldn't be able to find anyone with so few expectations and with all those qualities that we need and that Marta possesses" (Maria Valtorta, *Lettere a Padre Migliorini*, op. cit., p. 10).

[222] The "little bird" she kept in a cage and named Giacomino had died. Sensitive as she was, she complained in prayer but ended up also offering up this pain. At a certain point, she perceived that she was wrapped in an

had her first true and detailed personal conversation at about 11.45am on Good Friday, 23 April 1943.

God's pen

Doctors had told her that she had two or three years to live[223] because her many illnesses, especially her heart disease, would get the better of her. It was not to be. She was often on her deathbed[224] and yet she recovered every time, and she was able to do a job that not even someone young and in good health could have done. It must be added that Maria Valtorta's psychological and spiritual situation was excellent: she was physically ill, but she was intellectually and psychologically very bright. She wrote simply to Father Migliorini, mentioning the *Nozze spirituali* [Spiritual Weddings][225] by John van Ruysbroeck, which she had given to him, stating: "You have asked me if I understand Ruysbroeck and I have answered honestly that I do. Do not think that I am proud or deluded. I would not understand him by myself. What is Maria Valtorta? Nothing. [...] She is the divine eagle; it is Jesus who takes me up there where my human eyes do not reach. [...] God opens up streams of light, yes, He is a real sparkling stream, and I am flooded with light, and I am guided and comforted"[226]. And in the same letter she went on: "And here goes Ruysbroeck again: 'To swallow and to be swallowed'. How right that is! We consume God and we are consumed by Him. [...] There is a generosity contest between God and me. He gives to me; I give to Him. He adapts His Immensity to my nothingness; I adapt my

---

invisible human body, and a clear inner voice tried to console her (cf. Maria Valtorta, *Notebooks 1943*, op. cit., dated 13 May, p. 33).

[223] cf. Albo Centoni, *Ricordi di donne che conobbero Maria Valtorta*, op. cit., p. 193.

[224] It has been pointed out to me by a friend who is a doctor and a continuous reader of her writings, Dr. Ezio Bocedi of Carrara (MS) that the physical state of Maria Valtorta, certainly from 23 April 1943 onwards, was equivalent to a person in perpetual agony.

[225] Maria Valtorta probably knew the text in the version that Domenico Giuliotti translated from a partial French version by Ernest Hello: John van Ruysbroeck, *Nozze Spirituali* [Spiritual Weddings], G. Carabba, Lanciano 1923.

[226] Maria Valtorta, *Lettere a Padre Migliorini*, op. cit., pp. 15-6.

nothingness to His Everything, and I do all my *poor nothing* to honor him"[227]. That's how Maria Valtorta was on the eve of the big event: clear-headed, calm, and aware of what she knew in relation to spirituality, including Ruysbroeck, a master in contemplative life: a prominent figure of Rhineland mysticism, who expressed very well in his books, the prelude to all that Maria Valtorta would later write herself.

So, on that day, at that time, what had happened sporadically in Maria Valtorta's life became at first a daily occurrence and then it happened several times a day. We can say that for Maria Valtorta, that was the start of her paramystic period. The personal conversations began, which became proper dictations; then there were the extraordinary visions. At 11.45 on 23 April 1943, Maria suddenly called for Marta and asked her to run to Father Migliorini and tell him to come at once because something extraordinary had happened[228]. Father Migliorini listened to what Maria had heard and written[229] and he gave her the advice that would change her life: "She

---

[227] ibid., pp. 17-9.

[228] The description of the event made years later by Marta Diciotti is however important: "Certainly she found herself [...] I don't know [...] surprised, perhaps alarmed, probably afraid of being deceived by demonic seduction [...] it is certain that she immediately wanted to be able to speak with Father Migliorini. [...] I don't know what excuse I made [with Signora Iside, since it was almost noon, an unusual time] [...] So I went to Sant'Andrea quickly, I looked for Father and asked him to come to Maria, and informed him of what had happened" (Albo Centoni, *Una vita con Maria Valtorta. Tesrimonianze di Marta Diciotti*], op. cit., pp. 66-7).

[229] cf. Maria Valtorta, *Notebooks 1943*, op. cit. All the dictated works of 1943 are now printed in chronological order in this book. And there is further precision to be made. It is she herself who writes: "Since childhood, I have always had a great fear of apparitions. Even in boarding school, when the nuns said: 'Think if Jesus appeared! What a joy', I said: 'No, please! If I couldn't get out through the door, I'd jump out the window.' I remember the terror I had one evening when I accidentally closed myself in the college chapel. It was June. The Sacred Heart was on the main altar. I had asked to be able to go and say hello to Him while the recreation period was ending. And it was granted to me... I don't know how it happened; I didn't hear the the doors closing. I must have been praying intensely... When I returned to myself and went to the exits (three doors) I found them all

was advised by Father to write down everything that she was told; and she was also specifically asked to report everything to him"[230]. And that is what she did, systematically obeying, at least until Father Migliorini was tragically transferred to Rome. But that's another story, as we shall see. The first conversation and the many others that followed had some peculiarities which must be noted. (1) It was sudden[231]: having finished writing and having delivered her autobiography, Maria Valtorta's duty was to pray, to repent and to bear the suffering which Divine Providence had given her; nothing suggested this divine irruption. The conversation was instant. (2) It was also unexpected. Maria Valtorta, who considered herself a great sinner, would never have thought that she could deserve such divine care. (3) The conversation was not sought out: the humility that she derived from the crucifix and from the religious readings on which she had fed, stopped her from making any demands. (4) She never wanted it; on the contrary, she was frightened. That is, quite rightly, Maria feared the devil's deception and that is why she immediately turned to her spiritual director. (5) It was not evoked. That is, it was not a séance: Maria Valtorta recoiled from spiritism although she had to talk about it time and time again with her cousin Giuseppe Belfanti, who was a spiritist and a follower of Pietro Ubaldi. (6) It was not fabricated: it was not the product of deceit to trick her spiritual director in a surge of vain pride. It cannot be considered a

---

closed. I went back to the altar and started to go to the sacristy... But unfortunately, I looked up at the simulacrum... and, due to the shine of the moonlight; it seemed to me that it was moving, bending towards me. I became mad with terror. I screamed so much, I kicked so much that, although the chapel was isolated, they heard me and came to help me... If they hadn't heard me, they would have found me dead with fear in the morning. Suffice to say, I am afraid of what comes out of the supernatural" (Maria Valtorta, *Notebooks 1945-1950*, op. cit., dated 9 October 1947, p. 426).

[230] Albo Centoni, *Una vita con Maria Valtorta. Testimonianze di Marta Diciotti*, op. cit., pp. 66-7.

[231] Both Saint Ignatius of Loyola and Saint Teresa of Avila are in accord in specifying this fact as a sign of the presence of the divine (cf. Ignazio di Loyola, *Esercizi Spirituali* [Spiritual Exercises], Edizioni San Paolo, Cinisello Balsamo (MI) 1995, n.330; Teresa d'Avila, *Il Castello Interiore* [The Interior Castle], Figlie di San Paolo, Milano 2005, chap. 6.2 p. 143ff).

fabrication due to its very own dimension, and temporal and spatial characteristics. (7) On the contrary, it was certainly endured, it forced itself and she could not stop it, prepare it, or define it with her own strength or by her own merits. (8) This literary style and lifestyle remained unchanged till the end. All her personal conversations and then her visions had all these characteristics. (9) We must also add that Maria "was very careful and fearful of the private revelations and prophecies related to specific people and things [...] and she was terrified of the generic ones [...]. She was afraid of having misheard, she was always afraid of making mistakes: she would shut herself off and she would keep obstinately silent despite the repeated calls by Our Lord to spread the message [...]. And this happened [...] not because she was an indecisive, irresolute and a fearful woman. She was quite the opposite: uninhibited, very resolute and very brave. It was because she had a deep respect for the famous 'secrets of the King'"[232]. We can infer, from all this, that her conversations were generally founded on real compassion and on a deeply mature spirituality. But there is a problem: the term 'personal conversation' can also be used to describe what had happened to her during the spiritual experience at Bianconi College just before leaving it in 1912. She was 15-years-old, but this event did not upset her much. The same thing happened two years earlier in 1941: she heard a soundless voice which replied to her questions[233]. It must be noted, however, that at both those times, she did not have a spiritual director, whereas now, the experience seems fundamentally new. It does not mean that only this is true, for there were clear words even in the first two. How can we explain the difference, then? If we just look at the facts, it was probably the same thing. But the difference lies in the presence of a spiritual director. This time, and afterwards, she had someone to speak to who knew theology, who believed her and who looked after her. Maria was able to trust him and really embark on a new journey.

From this day on (23 April 1943), Maria's life changed as she adjusted to her new mission. Maria, who called herself 'Violet'[234] from

---

[232] Albo Centoni, *Una vita con Maria Valtorta*, op. cit., p. 251.

[233] cf. Maria Valtorta, *Notebooks 1943*, op. cit., dated 13 May, p. 28.

[234] cf. Maria Valtorta, *Autobiography*, op. cit., p. 59. She used the name "Violet" to refer to herself several times, for example in Maria Valtorta, *Notebooks 1945-1950*, op. cit., pp. 124, 206, 227, 248, 273, 507, 538, 590.

the very beginning of her autobiography, and then 'Violet of the Cross', was later repeatedly called 'Little John' by the inner voice to indicate three things: the love she possessed set on the example of the apostle John; the suffering in her union with Jesus, who was suffering for redemption; and her role in transmitting the conversations and the visions that she was increasingly receiving[235]. It was not a name that substituted her own name, only a nickname describing her new role.

On 23 April 1943, besides being the date of her first conversation, it was also the day when she started to be filled with a stream of mystic and paramystic gifts, all linked to her personal conversations and visions.

After a few scattered conversations until 13 May 1943, the daily occurrence became the rule and sometimes these gifts occurred several times a day[236].

The stream from then on was daily and, as it happened every day although with very few differences, it caused her to gain more and more experience until it peaked in 1946 when it resulted in a library made up of 13,193 handwritten notebook pages. The first period until the end of December 1942 was mainly characterised by personal conversations or dictations. The use of the word 'dictation' is important because it means that Maria Valtorta was not writing of her own initiative; she was writing down only what she heard; she was neither using 'automatic writing' nor was she seeking or was subjected to 'states of altered conscience' to write. In other words, she just wrote what she heard and in fact, she always said or made it clear when the words were her own. A second period had a prelude in December 1943 and lasted for the whole 1944. During this period, the conversations and visions were continuous. We can add a third stage with the end of the visions which completes *The Gospel as Revealed to Me;* that is, until 24 April 1947. In the last period, her

---

[235] For example: "My little John, I entrust you with my Word. Send it to the masters, who use it for the good of creatures. It comes from the One Shepherd, from the Good Shepherd, who has written the truth of His Word with His Blood" (Maria Valtorta, *Notebooks 1943*, op. cit., dated 10 September, pp. 296-7).

[236] For example, the conversations of 1 June 1943 (cf. Maria Valtorta, *Notebooks 1943*, op. cit., pp. 46-8).

charism was fading and Maria herself was not mentally present, for she was spiritually absorbed in God. This lasts until her death on 12 October 1961.

1943: Her yes to open Heaven

The death of her mother Iside was of paramount importance this year. Her health, afflicted by various illnesses not always well-treated by her account too, deteriorated quickly; and in September, the situation got even worse. Signora Iside had a prophetic dream herself, three days before her death – that is, on 1 October 1943. She saw the Lord Jesus who hit her three times on the shoulder with a stick "speaking words of severe disapproval of her behavior"[237]. The woman was very frightened and Maria tried to comfort her while saying to Marta: "Here we go, let us prepare ourselves because in three days' time, mother will not be around anymore"[238]. In any event, three days later – as in the prophetic dream on 4 October 1943 around midday – she died: the tyrannical and horrible mother of Maria Valtorta thus ended her days on earth. From then on, Maria's family and daily life was with Marta Diciotti, alone with her every day until her death. Her relatives in Reggio, Calabria and her cousin Giuseppe Belfanti remained far away and practically unable to live with her and help her, except for the time in 1944 when they were evacuated to Sant'Andrea di Còmpito – a village located between Pisa and Lucca near Altopascio.

Along with her autobiography, all her dictations and her visions were passed on to her spiritual director, written down in strict confidentiality and an open heart, in an honest, objective, fearless way. However, in her various writings, Maria Valtorta also warned him against what, in her opinion, could be possible mistakes and misunderstandings. Father Migliorini decided intuitively to make

---

[237] "O sister, what fear! The Lord appeared to me! How severe it was! He was holding a rod, and with that he beat me three times on the shoulder, saying: 'Enough, do you understand? Stop tormenting and being domineering. I do not want it any more.' And then he left" (Albo Centoni, *Una vita con Maria Valtorta,* op. cit., p. 484).

[238] ibid., p. 482. The full story as recounted by Marta Diciotti can be found on the same page and on the following two pages.

Maria write everything down[239], and she always did that from the autobiography until the day he was transferred by the authorities to Rome in March 1946. Everything went through his hands. Furthermore, when Father Migliorini realized that the dictations were happening continuously, and acknowledged the value of their contents, he had the idea of copying them using a typewriter. Maria would write in a notebook using a fountain pen which she regularly refilled[240]. Unfortunately, the way this was done caused a few problems with printing. Maria would write in a notebook; Father Migliorini would come by, take the notebook and copy it out. Meanwhile, Maria would go on writing in a new notebook or in one that she had already started. At the next visit, Father Migliorini would bring back the notebook he had copied out and would take another one for the same process[241]. Then the printed pages would go back to Maria to be corrected[242] without making any changes to the content. The typing errors were inevitable, and this was the only kind of corrections she would make. At first this turn-round of notebooks and printed pages seemed to work, but then a few anomalies were discovered. Luckily, Maria, no doubt on the suggestion of Father Migliorini, dated and sometimes even timed every dictation and vision. That way, it was possible to piece together the exact sequence of the many locutions because the same notebook could contain dictations and visions even with dates very far apart[243]. The first

---

[239] For example, cf. Maria Valtorta, *Notebooks 1943*, op. cit., dated 13 May, p.25. Furthermore, Father Migliorini asked her to write down her "past impressions" (ibid., p. 26).

[240] In the house-museum in Viareggio, the various fountain pens that Maria used throughout the years are beautifully on display in a glass cabinet. When she realized that sometimes the dictations (and then the visions) could be long, she prepared several pens already loaded with ink, ready to be used as soon as the one in use ran out of ink.

[241] cf. Maria Valtorta, *Notebooks 1943*, op. cit., dated 22 August, p. 265.

[242] cf. ibid., dated 12 September, p. 304. While she corrected the type-wriitten pages, she also had particular spiritual highlights. (cf. ibid., dated 15 November, p. 479).

[243] Cf. Emilio Pisani, *Catalogo dei quaderni autografi di Maria Valtorta* [The Catalogue of autographed notebooks by Maria Valtorta], Centro Editoriale Valtortiano, Isola del Liri (FR) 2010.

edition of *Notebooks 1943*[244] was editorially published following the notebooks. However, the result was obviously rather shambolic: it happened that a dictation should have been followed by the immediate continuation of the next one, but the notebooks did not follow this order, thus causing confusion. The editorial mistake was put right in the following editions. From then on, they were published in chronological order and the chaos stopped[245].

Father Migliorini was fundamentally important for Maria Valtorta. She was very obedient, but not subservient; she remained fully in control of her actions, and she knew, as always, how to be firm even with him. She wanted to remain hidden because she wanted this herself, but also because she was explicitly told by the inner voice. So she warned Father Migliorini: "I urge you to keep everything I say and write to yourself. Believe me, I find it hard having to say and make certain things public. It seems impossible that this may happen to me! And to think that such an overpowering Will is not going to leave us in peace until we listen"[246].

In the following days, good and bad visions were intercalated between dictations. The vision of 20 July 1943 was particularly

---

[244] The titles of the dictations and of some visions have been grouped into four volumes: *Notebooks 1943*, *Notebooks 1944*, *Notebooks 1945-1950*, and *The Little Notebooks*. Frankly, the title and the editorial method – not coming from the writer herself – raises many valid doubts. Those years were of war, civil war, massacres, and various bombings. In addition, the city of Viareggio was right on the Gothic Line. It is very easy to regard the [Notebooks] as memoirs, diaries (very widespread at that time) or stories of war since battles were fought there for months and months, and the massacres were numerous. Perhaps a more significant and spiritual title would have been more appropriate. A similar thing can be said of her main work, *The Gospel as Revealed to Me*, especially after discoveries by various scholars: Lavère, Aulignier, De Caro, Matricciani, and La Greca. Two hurdles need to be avoided: letting her main Work be perceived as a novel, perhaps a historical or imaginative one; and letting it be perceived as the fifth Gospel, or a completion of the four Gospels. Even with simple book titles, one should always be careful to avoid these possible erroneous interpretations which the Church obviously cannot accept.

[245] It is enough to compare the two editions of *Notebooks 1943*, the 1976 and 2006 editions, to see the difference.

[246] Maria Valtorta, *Notebooks 1943*, op. cit., dated 1 June, p. 46.

significant which Maria Valtorta described as follows: "Since the night of the 18th, Jesus has been showing me a horrendous beast - so horrendous that it fills me with disgust and makes me feel like shrieking. Its name is well-known [...]. No human reality can depict supreme Beauty and supreme Ugliness with precision [...]. If this is a pale representation of Satan, what must he be really like? It is enough to make you die twice over"[247]. And she gave an accurate enough description of it, with the same gloomy tone. Maria added this reflection to the description of this vision which had been going on for two days. There were often even longer episodes in the following years: "If the beast was in a corner, my white, handsome, blond Jesus was very close by [...] The Light in the light!"[248] We should understand that Maria did not like to speak about the 'beast': in fact she did that very rarely and only when pressed; her preferred choice was always the Lord Jesus[249].

The war in Viareggio

The war had been raging for several months. The front line was gradually moving up towards Northern Italy. The *Wermacht* (the German defense power) having left Rome, built a defense line that went from Viareggio across the whole peninsula as far as the Adriatic Sea. They called it the Gothic Line and it lasted until the end of the war[250]. So, Maria found herself on the front line for many months, with no other defense than her prayers and her continuous sacrifices. Then 1 November 1943 came with the first British bombing: bomb after bomb and shelling from British warships. Obviously, even the few links that had been previously in place were interrupted, and this caused all sorts of problems, on top of the number of dead, the

---

[247] ibid., pp. 181-2.
[248] ibid., p. 182.
[249] The whole *of The Gospel as Revealed to Me* is made up of approximately 1,797,000 words. The terms "Jesus", "Jesus Christ" and "Christ" are used about 11,000 times; "Satan", "Lucifer" and "Demon" are used just over 1000 times.
[250] cf. Federico Bertozzi, *Attaccarono i fogli: si doveva sfollà!* [They put up the notices: it was time to evacuate], Pezzini Editore, Viareggio (LU) 2014. pp. 80-5.

injured and the destruction caused to houses and buildings. The bombing began on the evening of 1 November[251], and the whole neighborhood fled to Valtorta's house, not because the house was particularly solid or had a basement strong enough to withstand the bombing, but because that small crowd was hoping to escape the bombs thanks to Maria's prayers. The next day, 2 November, she wrote: "Yesterday, among those who came… and the visit from the not very pleasant English, I was not able to write any more […]. In my state, which is very serious, it would be a lie to say my heart did not suffer. If a loud noise, a cry, a collision between two cars, seeing a person fall, a dispute, a piece of news and other such things made an impression on me, what my physical heart must have suffered as a result of that devastation is really understandable"[252]. And she added words full of fear: "Has everything happened now? May God so will, for I confess to you that the idea of dying buried alive or in agony in a hospital doesn't appeal to me. I accept my five illnesses and agree to accept another five, another ten, with all its torments, but I only ask to be left in my house where Jesus has done so many

---

[251] "The population, deprived as it was of bomb shelters, sought refuge in the pine forests, on the beach and in the surrounding countryside. But unfortunately, the enemy bombs that fell there in only a few moments time, reaped their innocent victims especially women, old people, children and the sick that had not been able to escape quickly enough. As usual, the enemy aircraft, with the possibility of hitting objects of military importance that do not exist here and have never existed, sowed destruction and death among the civilian population especially in the humblest neighborhoods of old Viareggio. The bombs, thrown haphazardly and exploding with a terrifying crash, completely demolished many houses while many others were seriously damaged by them. So the families that remained deprived of their small, but characteristic and neat one- or two-storey houses, numbered more than a hundred […] The effects of the air raid on the population were three dead and 17 injured" ("The Telegraph", 2 November 1943, cited in *http://ilforum.forumcommunity.net/?t=21289139*, consulted 5 January 2019). These serious facts are often underestimated by both critics and non-critics of Valtorta.

[252] Maria Valtorta, *Notebooks 1943*, op. cit., dated 2 November, p. 444.

things for me, and which is sacred to me for His sake, for it was given to me by Him and because my parents have died in here"[253].

The war did not end then, but it forced her to evacuate and leave her house for eight months, with all the discomfort and pain that all this implied. But we can still admire the realism and the faith that guided Maria even at that time.

Marta Diciotti was also a good witness during wartime. So we learn that Maria, despite being bedridden at home, kept herself up to date on what was happening "We would read the newspaper. Yes, we had to have the newspaper hot off the press. We would buy both *Il Corriere della Sera* [The Evening Courier] and *La Tribuna* [The Tibune], and then a few illustrated weeklies, particularly *La Domenica del Corriere* [The Sunday Courier]. With all these, she was able to, as they say, read between the lines, make her own assessments, and express some extraordinarily enlightening judgments"[254]. Maria kept herself up to date by also listening to the radio. So she was not detached from the world: she knew what was going on thanks to the newspapers that she read; she could judge people and the facts; she knew, she anticipated, and she was careful all the time. She was not an ascetic closed in a high-walled convent; she lived in a bedroom, but her ears were wide open to what was going on in the world. Realism, information, caution, openness and prayer; no exaltation, no personalism and not even any intimacy.

Dictations and visions

The literary output of Maria Valtorta was very large, and reading *Notebooks 1943,* one has the clear sense of a varied and academic

---

[253] ibid., pp. 444-5. Maria showed love for her home at other times too. In her will she wrote: "I love my house where so much Heaven lived and from where I brought souls to Heaven, from those of my Belfanti cousins to innumerable others" (Albo Centoni, *Una vita con Maria Valtorta*, op. cit., p. 233). Maria Valtorta's scholars are divided among those who brought her remains to the chapel in the garden of the church – the Basilica of the Most Holy Annunciation in Florence – managed by the Servants of Mary and those who claim that Maria Valtorta should return and stay in her beloved home in Viareggio.

[254] Albo Centoni, *Una vita con Maria Valtorta*, op. cit., pp. 90-1.

education. Actually, we can say that year was also a period of training: an exercise in listening to the inner voice which later became visible too; an exercise and a habit in writing fast with a fountain pen, getting used to having more than one always filled with ink and ready for use (Maria Valtorta never used ballpoint pens[255] or pencils, only fountain pens); an exercise in not being distracted by what was going on around her, including her mother's cries; and an exercise in observing what she saw in order to describe it in detail in her writings. The gifts of Maria Valtorta, the writer, were pushed to the limit during this year of training. In comparison with the following years, the visions of 1943 were very few. Then she had the first, very detailed visions. On 28 June, she saw a terribly sad Jesus with blood on every single hair. On 1 July, she tried to explain the Trinity symbol that she saw, and the resulting spiritual effects it had on her – but "the reality I saw cannot be described"[256]. On 20 July, she was very scared by a vision of Satan. On 13 August, she saw Jesus again carrying the Cross with no one around. On 19 September between 8 - 9 pm, she saw the Holy Virgin and she described Her in detail in two pages: She was the glorified Virgin who shone everywhere and in every detail. In the end, a little later: "Mary tells me wordlessly that She is teaching me something else: to see Her children even in one's enemies. For them too, She has given her Son and accepted them as children as She accepted us"[257]. On 25 December she saw the Virgin Mother: "at the end of my bed on the right-hand side and coming close to my bed, holding the Child in her arms [...]. When she was close me, I saw the Divine Baby sleeping, placid and beautiful, resting on Mary's right arm and breast"[258]. And as early as 20 November, the Holy Virgin had already given her perceivable caresses: "I received Our Lady's caresses on my head and cheeks"[259].

On 4 November, Maria Valtorta replied to a question that Father Migliorini asked: "In regard to your desire that I tell you what knowledge I had of the Sacred Scripture, I can formally assure you

---

[255] Also because ballpoint pens were patented in 1941 and arrived in Italy only in the late 1940s.

[256] Maria Valtorta, *Notebooks 1943*, op. cit., dated 1 July, p. 130.

[257] ibid., dated 19 September, p. 323.

[258] ibid., dated 25 December, p. 603.

[259] ibid., dated 20 November, p. 496.

that I was familar with only the four Gospels. I have known them by heart for years. I have also once read the Song of Songs, thirteen years ago or more, in a Protestant edition [...]. I have read the Proverbs of Solomon. *And my knowledge ends there*"[260]. This piece of news that Maria Valtorta conveyed so truthfully to Father Migliorini, her spiritual director, is very important in relation to what would happen in the following years. Before her evangelical visions began, Maria Valtorta only knew six out of the seventy-three books of the Bible. We could call it absolute ignorance and this very ignorance cannot explain what she would write in the following years. The precision of the minute historical details that she wrote about exhaustively could not have come from the little knowledge of the Bible that she had.

The 'dictations', that is, the personal conversations, were not made of a vague and watered-down spirituality and they were not photocopies repeated a thousand times. On the contrary, they were made of a strong and almost stern spirituality. The moral truths were remembered almost daily, and the Jeremiah-style was always present, although it was not the only one. Social themes were also discussed, for instance. Here is one of these pages: "You thought that I was giving evangelical counsel on poverty. I was, but not poverty as you understand it - not only that. Money, land, buildings and jewels are things you love, and it requires sacrifice for you to give up possessing them or else it causes pain for you to lose them. But for the sake of a vocation to love, you are even able to strip yourselves of them. How many women have sold everything to keep a husband or lover – which is worse – and continue a vocation to human love? Others throw away their lives for the sake of an idea. Soldiers, scientists, politicians and heralds of new social doctrines, immolate themselves every day to their ideal, selling their lives, giving their lives for the beauty – or what they deem to be the beauty – of an idea[261]. They become poor *of the riches of life* for their idea". Even on its own, this passage shows that Maria Valtorta was never abstract, mawkish, or raving: her clear-headed materiality was ever present in all her writings.

---

[260] ibid., dated 4 November, p. 449.
[261] ibid., dated 29 June, p. 122.

Ecstasy

For Maria Valtorta, 28 November marked a new beginning. She wrote: "For three days, the rivers of ecstasy have been opened for my soul, and I rejoice at the vision in addition to the words. My soul has become whiteness and light, for the whiteness of the Virgin Mother and the Light are in me. Glory be to God for His goodness"[262]. However, she had already had this experience. On 22 May of the same year, in reply to a question by Father Migliorini, she had tried to distinguish between 'sense of ecstasy' and 'ecstasy', saying that she had experienced the former several times but never the latter. But in fact, what she writes about the 'sense of ecstasy' is just another way of referring to 'ecstasy'[263]. "All vitality is concentrated on a point, focussed in such a way that *everything* else loses its value [...] creating a kind of veil around us [...]. I believe that if this continued, it would kill us in a short time [...]. It is like an increase in our spiritual vitality, a passage given from a younger to an older age, whereby, after each immersion [...] we find we have grown in grace and in supernatural wisdom. [...] This 'joy' which takes us away from what is humanly perceptible to immerse us in a realm of the divinely suprasensible, is given to us by God"[264].

Around Christmas 1943, she had new personal conversations. It was not only Jesus who dictated, but the Holy Virgin also gave her a spiritual commentary both on 8 December, the Feast of the

---

[262] ibid., dated 28 November, p. 519.

[263] "If, instead, you are speaking of that sense of ecstasy wherein human vitality is not suppressed but all vitality is concentrated in one point, focused in such a way that everything else loses value and we live only amidst the things of each hour, as if surrounded by a robe isolating and protecting us from them, creating a kind of veil of fire around us within which we move and act, gazing solely at the hub attracting us, then I have definitely experienced it many times" (ibid., dated 22 May, pp. 38-9).

[264] ibid., "In the context of Christian mysticism, ecstasy understood in a spiritual sense, in which man transfers all his intellectual, sensitive and volitional faculties to God, in Jesus Christ, has value without any doubt [...] The phenomenology of this ecstasy can have different effects, such as the total forgetting and almost annihilation of the 'I'" (L. Borriello – E. Caruana – MR Del Genio – R. Di Muro (editor), *New Dictionary of Mysticism,* op. cit., entry *Ecstasy,* p. 753).

Immaculate Conception, and on Christmas Day. They were an in-depth analysis which added to the two conversations – or dictations – of God the Father. These gifts did not only bring joy: on the contrary, the stress was such that she wrote: "I felt a crazy urge not to write anything else by resisting [...] the dear Voice, if [It] did not want to content me by keeping silent so as not to give me the occasion to serve the curiosity of others"[265]. Then a desire to escape, but also serious pain of various types: "Believe me, Father (Migliorini), I am suffering a lot [...]. I am amidst thorns of every kind because the good Jesus reveals horizons of blood and fire to me, and Lucifer tries to upset me by pointing out that I shall soon be left alone (without the Master) and that He is already tired of me"[266].

Both for her and for Italy and the world, 31 December of this dramatic year came at last. Now apparently alone among intense and sometimes unbearable pains, with the help of Marta alone, among the bombings from the sea and from the air, the supernatural presence was more and more intense and lively, and therefore, she was not forsaken. If the cornerstone of Maria Valtorta's life was self-immolation for the love of Jesus and for the Church, then the perspective was broadened by a series of conversations which blossomed into a series of almost countless, material – not symbolic – visions.

1944: Her "fullness of time"

The New Year began with a lovely event for Maria Valtorta: she contemplated the Holy Face of Jesus![267] From then on, this was not an extraordinary episode, but something that she took for granted. For Maria Valtorta, 1944 was a very important year for many reasons, both material and spiritual. The conversations continued; then came the 'Ignatian' visions; she experienced the evacuation and the dark night of the soul; she fought the war for her cousin Giuseppe Belfanti and in the end, she savored the return to her home in via Fratti, which had miraculously survived the war, in a badly damaged Viareggio.

---

[265] ibid., Maria Valtorta, *Notebooks 1943*, op. cit., dated 1 October, p. 345.
[266] ibid., dated 11 August, pp. 230-1.
[267] Maria Valtorta, *Notebooks 1944*, op. cit., dated 1 January, p. 19.

The personal conversations from the beginning, took a new direction: not only Jesus, but other characters joined in, one after the other. The merciful and eternal Father[268], Jesus right from the beginning, the Holy Spirit[269], the Blessed Virgin[270], St. John[271], St. Paul[272] and St. Francis of Assisi[273]. This chain of personal conversations at the beginning of the year ended (in a manner of speaking), with the sudden, neither rehearsed nor sought, vision of the martyrdom of St. Agnes[274], followed after a few days, by the vision of her entombment[275]. This vision was the starting point for a new line of spiritual experiences for Maria Valtorta, which can be described as 'Ignatian visions', because as this saint teaches in his *Spiritual Exercises[276]*, Maria Valtorta could see the people and the places; she could observe what the various people did; she could hear the words and the dialogue besides the noises, sounds and music; and she could also – and this was specific to Maria Valtorta – perceive the smells and the environmental conditions. She was really inside the scene. We must specify that in the *Exercises* of St. Ignatius, we find the so-called 'application of the senses', in which the retreatant is guided to experience with their own five physical senses whatever happens during the contemplation itself. We can therefore say, that what St. Ignatius asks a retreatant to achieve on their own, Maria Valtorta received as a gift without any effort in recreating environments, places, people and gestures. She just had to accept it; all the rest came from God. It was as though Maria Valtorta lived continuously in the *Exercises* of St. Ignatius of Loyola.

Despite all this, she could not read hearts or minds so she did not know why those characters acted the way that they did; it was always

---

[268] ibid., dated 6 January, p. 26.
[269] ibid., dated 10 January, p. 45f.
[270] ibid., p. 48f.
[271] ibid., dated 11 January, p. 55f.
[272] ibid., p. 61f.
[273] ibid., dated 1 May, pp. 272-3.
[274] cf. ibid., dated 20 January, pp. 103-4.
[275] ibid., p. 76f. This is the episode that happened on 20 January 1944 at 4 pm.
[276] cf. Ignatius of Loyola, *Esercizi Spirituali* [Spiritual Exercises], op. cit., pp. 190-5.

and only an external observation[277]. Another factor was that Maria Valtorta was present and acted in the situations in which she was placed, but without ever deciding herself where to go. And yet she moved! The scene in which she was placed had 360-degree views, but all this was not caused or prepared by anything human: there was no conjuring technique – typical, for instance, of the spiritist or esoteric world – to create what Maria Valtorta saw; not even a specific prayer. It was always a sudden storming in of the supernatural, ordered by an external agent (God, obviously) that imposed complex visions, neither sought or demanded, and completely precise from a scientific point of view. This was the typical type of vision that Maria Valtorta had. This is the practice of all 657 chapters of *The Gospel as Revealed to Me*. The personal conversations, on the contrary, were very different, and she went on having those, uninterruptedly, in the form of dictations.

---

[277] Maria Valtorta only described what she observed from the outside. By contrast, here is an example of a narrative technique in which the author recounts and explains even the internal thoughts of the various characters, which instead does not exist in the entire Valtortian work: "Mother and son, having dinner, exchanged a few words among themselves. She asked him for some news from school; how he had spent the day; she often reproached him for the way that he lived his life. He was so young and she wanted to motivate him; she encouraged him to move around a bit during the day, out in the open air; to be more lively, more manly, to go! Studying was important, yes, but also some entertainment was needed. She suffered so much to see him so bored, pale and groggy. He gave her short answers: yes, no; he promised coldly and waited impatiently for the end of dinner to go to bed, early early, because he used to get up early in the morning. He was always alone growing up, and he had no familiarity with his mother. He saw her, felt her very different from himself, so brisk, energetic and casual. Maybe he took after his father. And the void left by his father for a long time was between him and his mother, and had grown larger and larger over the years. His mother, also present there, always seemed to him as distant" (Luigi Pirandello, *The Rest is Silence,* Mondadori Modern Library, Milan 1960).

Father Migliorini was not able to follow her in flight

Meanwhile, something that should not have happened and which would cause great suffering in the future, took place. Father Migliorini – who remains a very important and, in many senses, a very positive figure for Maria Valtorta – had been warned to keep the contents of the personal conversations relatively secret, but the secret was to be comprehensive regarding Maria Valtorta, her name and her gifts. His job should have only consisted in assisting the infirm woman and in preparing the manuscripts. The publication and the diffusion of the texts could even take place, but the disclosure of the 'medium' was to be made only after the death of Maria Valtorta. Some of the personal conversations had been clear: "You can use my words for yourself, for your soul, for your preaching, to guide and comfort other souls, of clergymen or not. *But [Father Migliorini] must not reveal their source*, for the time being"[278]. Another warning followed dated 23 August[279]: "Go and spread the Word. Go with discernment and care. Do not apply it to all in the same way. [...] Not an open resounding dissemination, but a slow, ever broader outpouring – and it should remain nameless. [...] When your hand is still in peace during the wait to rise in *glory*, then – *only* then – will your name be mentioned"[280].

But Father Migliorini's heart had been deeply shaken by various events: the defeat of the Italian army in Russia, and the consequent retreat with the victory of the enemies of God and of the Church; the bombings of Viareggio and the frontline getting closer and closer which frightened him and made many people despair; and his hypersensitivity to psychics which attracted him in an almost irresistible way. All this sparked a desire in him to comfort those who seemed to be suffering more, giving them hope through words from Heaven. Signora Antonia Dal Bo Terruzzi had recently died on 4 January. Assisted till the end by Father Migliorini, she had offered herself to God for the soldiers and the salvation of Italy, and in her last months of sickness, she had also been known to Maria Valtorta. For her funeral, a small remembrance card was printed with an

---

[278] Maria Valtorta, *Notebooks 1943*, op. cit., dated 8 July, p. 165.
[279] ibid., pp. 259-60.
[280] ibid., dated 23 August, pp. 267, 268-9.

extract of a dictation and the footnote: "Dictated by a Heavenly Voice to its 'Spokesperson' in Viareggio on 12 January 1944"[281]. When Maria Valtorta got a hold of it, she added in writing: "One could not be more reckless then this!" Then she accompanied it with a small note on which she wrote: "Clear evidence that Fr Migliorini is reckless, is here, in the misguided footnote to the epigraph that Jesus had dictated for this host and for the peace of her relatives who had witnessed her awful agony and thought she was damned... but instead it was Satan's hate for the blessed victim"[282]. This simple event, together with the following similarly serious acts of recklessness, led to Father Migliorini being transferred to Rome with no possibility of him returning to Viareggio.

The evacuation

The war was raging and what Maria Valtorta had feared and known from Heaven was taking place punctually. The German Gothic Line was eventually drawn between Viareggio and Pesaro. The small town in Versilia was one of the epicentres of the fighting, and the much-feared evacuation order arrived. The pictures of that historical moment are horrifying. But compared to the risk of losing the house with all its furniture and contents, the main problem was Maria Valtorta's serious physical condition because the probability

---

[281] Albo Centoni, *Una vita con Maria Valtorta. Testimonianze di Marta Diciotti*], op. cit., p. 142.

[282] Maria Valtorta, *Notebooks 1944*, op. cit., dated 14 January, pp. 57-8, [Footnote not included in English edition]. Marta Diciotti also explained: "It was precisely with that remembrance card that the real troubles began for the person of the 'spokesperson'. In fact, until then Father Migliorini, with his generous heart full of charity towards souls, had yes, imprudently, and untimely copied and disseminated typed copies of the Writings, but he had also carefully kept the person of the spokesperson concealed, even leaving others to believe that it was a man. But here, precisely with this remembrance card, he committed his first serious imprudence" (Albo Centoni, *Una vita con Maria Valtorta. Testimonianze di Marta Diciotti*, op. cit., p. 140). For Marta, this "[was] unfortunately the primary cause of the difficulties encountered with the Writings, and of the anxieties that ensued. [...] [There was, in fact, a] triple (it seems to me) warning from the Lord who disapproved of such behavior" (ibid., p. 107).

that she might die because of the journey or even during the journey, was very high. Three things accumulated during those horrible three days. First Maria Valtorta's health, which got suddenly worse. From 9 April 1944, it caused a cardiac crisis which wore her out with a painful drowsiness that could last for 11 continuous hours of haze and agony, during which she was powerless. At the same time – but this was typical of these things – the dark night of the soul began with an apparent lack of complete spiritual help from Heaven[283]. In such circumstances, the other members of the Valtorta household (her cousin Giuseppe Belfanti, his daughter Paola and his second wife Anna) received the news on 10 April of an evacuation order and began to prepare with difficult decisions to be made: what to bring and what to leave behind, with the danger that they might not find it on their return; where to go in order to be safe from air raids and how to get there. After a long debate, they excluded the possibility of using an ambulance for fear of the Nazi eugenics policies – and of a few eager, Fascist collaborators – that did not care much for certain sick people, of whom Maria Valtorta knew and was afraid. She would have liked to go to the Carmelite convent in Camaiore, but in the end, they decided to go to Sant'Andrea di Còmpito[284] in the hills of Lucchesia (nowadays a 45-minute drive) because it was safer from the dangers coming from both ground and air attacks. It turned out to be a wise decision because Camaiore was seriously damaged whereas Sant'Andrea di Còmpito was left untouched. The order to leave came on Monday 24 April[285] which she did at 3.30pm, sitting in the back of a Balilla model car beside Paola, Father Migliorini (who was carrying the holy oil!) and a nurse. Besides the chauffeur, there

---

[283] The evocative image of what was happening to her is that of the crucified Lord Jesus as he pronounces the words: "My God, my God, why have you forsaken me?" (Mt 27:46).

[284] cf. Maria Valtorta, *The Little Notebooks*, op. cit., pp. 15-20. This entry dated 28 June 1944 is a good example of the character of Maria Valtorta. She never gave up easily, she was always ready to assert her reasons, and she was always determined in her words. Grace entered her character's roots and acted, to make her love towards Jesus and all people explode in abundance.

[285] cf. Maria Valtorta, *Notebooks 1944*, op. cit., dated 9 April, pp. 268-70 footnotes.

was also the dog Toi and a birdcage. So the car was quite full. It must have been rather uncomfortable and expensive but anyway, they arrived in the evening, safe and sound, although exhausted. The new house was on two levels – the ground floor and a first-floor attic – on the village outskirts at the bend by the entrance to the village, so from her window, Maria Valtorta was able to see the comings and goings of soldiers, evacuees, and residents. She also acted as a sentinel, as requested: she would ring a bell whenever she spotted the arrival of soldiers. Maria Valtorta lived on the first floor, which was very close to the roof tiles and this caused many problems: extreme cold in the winter and scorching temperatures in the summer, besides the problems of being bedridden and the sight of unwelcomed visits from rats[286] which were scuttling around on the rafters and sometimes pooped even on the bed of the invalid![287] She remained there, evacuated and in poverty, for eight months until 23 December[288] of the same year.

---

[286] Marta Diciotti remembered: "Far from her room in Viareggio, a testimony of her great love, Maria Valtorta spent eight months of real exile in a little room on the first floor of our refuge for refugees in Sant'Andrea di Còmpito. In this new environment, nothing suited her, starting with the air and atmospheric pressure. When it rained, an umbrella was needed because the ceiling in the the room was poorly made and the roof was damaged by time and bullets. There was extreme heat in the summer, and a very brutal cold during the cold seasons: and the poor woman experienced both because she spent the spring, summer, autumn and the first few days of 'winter' there" (Albo Centoni, *Una vita con Maria Valtorta. Testimonianze di Marta Diciotti*, op. cit., p. 89).

[287] "In that primitive environment (the horrendous prison, as she called it), where moles ran around on the roof and where, when it rained, we had to shelter with an umbrella, and in many places, in the bedroom", ibid., p. 198). To Father Migliorini she wrote in a colorful way: "At night over our heads, the … Cossacks in the form of squadrons of mice that for 12 hours, from 6 to 6, hold a market on the roof, and wake Giuseppe [her cousin] who is deaf. During the day, alarms with relative confetti ring very close. This morning was terrible" (Maria Valtorta, *Lettere a Padre Migliorini*, op. cit., p. 63).

[288] cf. Maria Valtorta, *Notebooks 1944*, op. cit., dated 13 December, p. 637.

The dark night of the soul

Besides the external discomforts – living outside one's home without one's own little comforts and habits – she was also affected by the internal ones, much worse than the former[289]: a hard, dark night of the soul which lasted from 9 April to 12 May, with only a short break on 20 April thanks to the visit of the Blessed Virgin. She hit rock bottom on 25 April: "Awful night. Awful day. At midday, another break away from Father Migliorini which makes everything worse again. I call the Blessed Virgin Mary, but even She seems to be far away. There is no more Heaven for me"[290]. On 26 April, she saw the emblem of the cross; on 1 May she talked with a visible St. Francis of Assisi; on the same day she saw St. Anthony of Padua, but there was no conversation. Then she wrote: "I pray. Then what? Nothing! I take Communion. Well? Nothing! Nothing at all. *Total* void. *Total* darkness. *Total* silence"[291]. On 2 May, she received a letter from Father Migliorini which made her even more depressed because he assessed her state in terms of doctrine, without realizing that the pain she suffered went beyond every theory. On the 4th, the Blessed Virgin Mary came back, but the devil kept on tormenting her. On the 13th, Jesus corrected an oversight in chapter 613 of her *Gospel*: she had only omitted one word, without noticing, but the whole meaning had changed, and it all made no sense. This event is important because, besides describing Maria's state of mind, it also explains the precision that the personal conversations and the visions expected of her. We shall see the importance of details and how, what looks like a pointless or verbose description, was in fact essential to the truth of her writings[292]. In the evening after 6pm, the enemy arrived: "My God, what a fight! I am dumbstruck! – I am overwhelmed again by

---

[289] This is Marta Diciotti's memory of those days, of which she had been an eyewitness: "The period began with those forty terrible days of agony, during which she suffered the terrible abandonment that made the horrors of hell known to her. It seems that those were days of frightening spiritual aridity, in which she believed she had lost His Goodness, for her demerit" (ibid., p. 89).

[290] Maria Valtorta, *Notebooks 1944*, op. cit., dated 9 April, p. 268.

[291] Maria Valtorta, *Lettere a Padre Migliorini*, op. cit., p.64.

[292] cf. Jean-François Lavère, *The Valtorta Enigma*, op. cit.

that wave of despair which gives me sparks of madness. I try to recite the Rosary but I can hear the devil laughing scornfully and making fun of me. [...] These are the times when Satan tries to convince me that I am a liar, a madwoman, someone who fools all the people. He tries to convince me that it is all a lie, that I am damned... If I were alone, I would scream, but I am in someone else's home, and who can understand me?"[293] On the 13th, the devil, was still there: "I am deep in sorrow [...]. I find him there, ready to give me his nightmare: 'God does not love you. You are damned. You are a liar. A madwoman. A heretic'. [...] a real nightmare. He takes every comfort away. He even overshadows the sunlight and the sight of natural beauty that in a different state of mind would have cheered me up. He makes me unable to do anything. He spoils the peace that I used to get from praying and the joy of praying. I talk and I can hear that thought. I write and he upsets my mind. I read and he drowns the words. He is there, always there... As soon as I come to my senses, the first sensation is about this thought. Even before I open my eyes, my mouth, or move my hands, he is already at work, drilling my heart and my mind. As soon as the Master or the Mother finish talking, he resumes his work like a woodworm eating tirelessly away wherever it dwells. One only has to try it to understand what he really is like..."[294]. On 15 May, despite the continuous assaults and a cardiac crisis, she started to see the end of the tunnel. When she regained her strength, Maria herself lucidly explained: "I want to explain something, not to be misunderstood. I did not rebel at the lack of extraordinary manifestations. I have *never* wanted them; I have *never* demanded them since I had been granted them. God grants them for free, and none of his children can force Him to grant them. But what made me suffer was the feeling of neglect because I had been separated from God"[295]. On the 16th, Jesus could tell her, among

---

[293] Maria Valtorta, *Notebooks 1944*, op. cit., dated 13 May, p. 290.

[294] ibid., p. 290. Marta Diciotti recounted that "The demon stopped at the door of her room where he was never able to enter. Once I brought her a cup of tea, and he was standing there in the doorway. She feared that it would make me fall to the ground which, of course, did not happen, fortunately" (Albo Centoni, *Ricordi di donne che conobbero Maria Valtorta*, op. cit., p. 239).

[295] ibid., p. 291

other thoughts: "Now you are cured. You have defeated Satan. But because I have given you enough time to do that, it's time to get back on to your feet after the Enemy's sudden and horrible assault to your soul, sudden and scornful. He has assaulted you like the lion mentioned by Peter and he has beaten you up. He has run away because you, with that little strength left – just an ounce – and with that little voice left – just a whisper – have lifted the cross and said my Name"[296]. And slowly, the dark night made way for the sunrise, which came out shining but not before the 18th. The drafting of the future *Gospel as Revealed to Me* was also interrupted between 8 April and 16 May: no vision of the Gospel during those days. In a month, that was a unicum until April 1947. As you can see, Maria Valtorta never became verbally delirious, blasphemous, rebellious or fanciful; on the contrary, she transferred her suffering to her prayers, and she endured it through her prayers. Only her writings have revealed what really happened, even though Marta Diciotti had a glimpse of it[297]. The question is, was it really a dark night of the soul?[298] It is not a silly question because from the answer depends on the truthfulness

---

[296] ibid., p. 294.

[297] "She experienced the privation of God which was her hell suffered on this earth […]. For me, basically, it remained a mystery and it more or less remained so even for many subsequent years" (Albo Centoni, *Una vita con Maria Valtorta. Testimonianze di Marta*, op. cit., p. 385).

[298] I want to point out that it is not about discernment in general, but only about discerning whether it is about the night of the spirit or not. The theme, in both areas, would lead to an endless bibliography because it is the central theme of Christian life and of living. First, I would like to point out the Spiritual Exercises of Saint Ignatius of Loyola: a way to discern. It is "all the ways of preparing and disposing the soul to free itself from all disordered affections. Then followed (316-27) the rules for proper discernment. However, St. Ignatius stops at the difference between consolation and desolation. Our theme will be treated only starting from Saint John of the Cross, with the text *The Dark Night: a true summation of what happens in these cases*. In fact, he describes what the symptoms are and how to behave if God privileges a person by making them go through this beautiful and, at the same time, tremendous moment of Christian life (cf. *Esercizi Spirituali. Ricerca sulle fonti* [Spiritual Exercises. Research on sources], Edizioni San Paolo, Milano 2014; cf. also John of the Cross, *Tutte le opere* [The Collected works], Bompiani, Milano 2010).

of her faith, her actions and writings, and her state of mind. Indeed, we have the proof that her offer to give up her life to Divine Justice was real and was kept. Was it a real dark night of the soul, or just a – albeit painful – temporary depression, maybe caused by the evacuation, and all that this meant for her? A necessary precondition is that the subject always follows the Catholic orthodoxy, and that this remains the doctrinal environment he/she lives in. As for Maria Valtorta, this was so obvious that no-one has ever questioned it[299]. The necessary discernment urges us to verify at least three elements that are typical of the dark night of the soul: "(1) there is no satisfaction or consolation from the things of God or from any creatures either; (2) one cannot meditate or discuss with the same zest and benefits as before; (3) the memory turns to God solicitously and with painful care, and the soul thinks it is not serving God"[300]. There are also three other signs, not essential, but it is better if they are there as they improve discernment: (4) the presence of material difficulties consisting in illnesses, social malaise or persecutions of various nature; (5) the judgment of those who could observe directly what was happening, expressed with behaviour, words and actions; (6) the spiritual state of the subject; that is, their state at the end of

---

[299] Even her most absolute critic, Father Pier Angelo Gramaglia, has not pointed out anything on this level, even though in his text on Maria Valtorta – according to what is also his typical style – he uses hostile language: cf. Pier Angelo Gramaglia, *Maria Valtorta. Una moderna manipolazione dei Vangeli* [Maria Valtorta. A modern manipulation of the Gospels], Edizioni Piemme, Casale Monferrato (AL) 1985. cf. also Pier Angelo Gramaglia, *Confronto con i mormoni* [A comparison with Mormons], Edizioni Piemme, Casale Monferrato (AL) 1985; Pier Angelo Gramaglia, *Esoterismo, magia e cristianesimo* [Esotericism, magic and christianity], Piemme Editions, Casale Monferrato (AL) 1991; Pier Angelo Gramaglia, *Lo spiritismo* [Spiritism], Edizioni Piemme, Casale Monferrato (AL) 1986; Pier Angelo Gramaglia, *Perché non sono d'accordo con i Testimoni di Geova* [Why I disagree with Jehovah's Witnesses], Edizioni Piemme, Casale Monferrato (AL) 1984. It should be noted that when this author studied Maria Valtorta, he had no Valtortian epistolary available.

[300] Borriello Luigi – Caruana Edmondo – Del Genio Maria Rosaria – Suffi Nicolò (editor), *Dizionario di mistica* [Dictionary of Mysticism], Libreria Editrice Vaticana, Città del Vaticano 1998, entry *Notte Oscura* [Dark Night], p. 914.

the dark night. The first four signs are evident in Maria Valtorta with the lack of the gifts that she had been receiving for at least 12 months and a day[301], and with the difficulties due to the evacuation, during which she had risked her life on her journey to Sant'Andrea di Còmpito. God's silence and the lack of His gifts, together with the enemy's horrible assaults, who had been trying to convince her that she was deluded and damned, are evidence of this. The terrible journey and the evacuation to the attic room in Sant'Andrea di Còmpito are the negative physical aspects that overwhelmed her during April and May1944[302]. The statements of those present have confirmed the rest. Marta Diciotti recalled: "In the following months, Father Migliorini made an important observation: he noticed that she had made spiritual progress, and she had also improved the way she expressed herself: 'She is much, much better' he said"[303]. This is another testimonial that shows that it was not depression and, as a matter-of-fact, Maria Valtorta remained clear-headed in every circumstance, she never lost her temper, she was not prone to hysteria, and she kept praying as always.

Giuseppe Belfanti

After being artfully struck in the back with an iron bar, Maria Valtorta was assisted by several relatives who housed her for two years in their hotel in Reggio, Calabria. Among these relatives was Giuseppe[304], one of her mother Iside's cousins, and therefore, Maria

---

[301] Albo Centoni, *Una vita con Maria Valtorta. Testimonianze di Marta Diciotti*, op. cit., p. 384.

[302] Again, Marta Diciotti testified: "I found her there, desperate, inconsolable, in her closed silence. She made every human effort not to disturb and not to weigh on others, but I, who was always at her side, realized her silent desolation. Tears, despite herself, often flooded her face..." (ibid., p. 384).

[303] ibid., p. 385.

[304] Now an inexplicable piece of the story is this phrase of Jesus: "The other" knows and speaks as long as he can. Do you remember Punturieri? Well then? Of what use was he? To bring Giuseppe here and to give him to Me" (Maria Valtorta, *Notebooks 1945-1950*, op. cit., dated 19 December 1945, p. 128). Who he was and what type of relationship Punturieri had with Belfanti and Maria Valtorta is not known to us. In another passage he

Valtorta's cousin once removed. After that, when war broke out, those relatives from Reggio moved to Viareggio to Valtorta's home to escape the bombings. They also remained close during the evacuation, when Giuseppe rented a small house next to the one occupied by Maria Valtorta; and he and his wife also spent nights with Maria, so that she would not be alone. The two cousins, Giuseppe and Maria Valtorta, loved each other, but Giuseppe had a thing for spiritism: he accepted and followed the ideas of Pietro Ubaldi[305] (Foligno 18 August 1886 – São Vicente, Brazil 29 February 1972), who is still known today as the theorist of 'The Great Synthesis'[306]. Until 1944, the two cousins had exchanged letters in which Giuseppe – a follower of Pietro Ubaldi and convinced of being a spiritist himself – promoted spiritism[307] while Maria Valtorta tried

---

is connected to Pietro Ubaldi, but without specifying anything else (cf. Maria Valtorta, *Notebooks 1944*, op. cit., dated 14 November, p. 617.)

[305] AA.VV., *PARA Dizionario Enciclopedico*, op. cit., p. 1015. To understand his attractiveness, it is necessary to know that "he was nominated for the Nobel Prize [1964] (he was preferred over [Jean Paul] Sartre) and he corresponded with Albert Einstein" (Paola Giovetti, *I grandi iniziati del nostro tempo* [The great initiates of our time], Edizioni Mediterranee, Roma 2006, p. 125).

[306] Pietro Ubaldi, *La grande sintesi* [The great synthesis], Ulrico Hoepli Editore, Milano 1939 (currently published by Edizioni Macro, Cesena). Even priests did not notice his mistake: "His friend Don Brizio Casciola, a priest in Montefalco, near Foligno, [...] [described him] perfectly as organic and coherent, who faces, we can say, all the most delicate problems pertinent to science and life. He presents himself as informed by extraordinary means, of the latest results. He finds new connections and anticipates theoretical discoveries. All in an irreproachable, lucid, and elegant literary form; with a very high tone, a warm and pure spirituality, a throbbing humanity" (cited in Paola Giovetti, *I grandi iniziati del nostro tempo*, op. cit., p. 124).

[307] In the preface of this text, he says: "In this case, however, an unknown medium (Pietro Ubaldi) is unprepared, doubtful for a long time on the opportunity to make his making known, without means and without support, modest, and shunning any notoriety, without any interested purpose. But rather, [he is] forced into a life of martyrdom to express his rare mediumistic gifts. He saw his product, timidly offered, briefly go around the world, spreading quickly, 'automatically', as if by his 'own

to talk him out of it, and bring him back to the Catholic Church. What were the main ideas of Pietro Ubaldi? The disciples of this English teacher from Gubbio divide his life into four stages: 1891-1911; 1911-1931; 1931-1951; 1951-1971. These are 20-year periods with different characteristics. The first one is the period of academic studies: he earned a degree, learning English, French, and German. At the beginning of the second period, he got married and had two children; then he managed his and his wife's properties; he travelled extensively to the United States, but in the end, tired of all this, he delegated the administrative tasks to others while keeping usufructuary rights. The third period starts with the alleged apparition of Jesus (1927). As he could not be idle, he started giving English lessons in the state schools of Gubbio; and he started (and continued) to receive messages in his heart from God Himself – or at least that is what he said. Be careful: he was not a spiritist *strictu sensu* [in the strictest sense], dedicated to séances. He was certainly a *medium*, but he had no need of special techniques to receive messages; he just had to listen to his own heart. "With my sensitivity, the mind becomes as powerful as lightning and the spiritual currents of the world are tangible. These subtle forces are real, and I move forward among them, steering my ship. At first, I feel lost […]. I asked a chain of human kindred spirits to start and act as a psychic circle […]. As I reach the state of nervous tension which is necessary to jump into the current, this drags me […], one must merely dive into the noùri (spiritual currents) to be able to tap into all energetic elements"[308]. Out of this 'current of telepathic communication'[309], Ubaldi derived all his knowledge to the point of creating – as it sadly usually happens in these instances – a brand new vision of the world. His most important work, *La grande sintesi* [The great synthesis], describes his thoughts in about 1,000 pages; but it is not exhaustive because

---

prodigious strength'" (Marc Antonio Bragadin, preface to Pietro Ubaldi, *La grande sintesi,* op. cit., p. XII). In the eyes of Giuseppe Belfanti, this martyrdom equated Pietro Ubaldi with a very different martyrdom to that of Maria Valtorta and her writings. Here you can see divine mercy towards this man.

[308] Pietro Ubaldi, *Le Noúri* [The Noúri], Ulrico Hoepli Editore, Milano 1937, pp. 28-9.

[309] ibid., p. 28.

Ubaldi, before declaring his job done – or, as he preferred to say, his communications – wrote a total of about 10,000 pages. The theological themes are obviously very present, but as he tried to speak of the Trinity, his vision was essentially a monistic one[310]: one God, the only Substance, which manifests itself in trinity mode as static matter, dynamic energy and spirit or life. In saying this, he denied the Trinity, and he stopped at one single reality which manifests itself in three different ways. Of his fundamental and main work, his followers state that: "It is described by Ubaldi as a 'hymn to the glory of God' with the goal to outline the new 'cosmic awareness'. The aim is to shape the universal awareness that all humanity must be able to achieve during the third millennium. What he outlines is a 'real revolution', a new science configured for the paths of love and of spiritual growth. (In this book), his theory of knowledge is introduced, outlined in a unitary vision described as Monism"[311]. In another text – *Dio e universo* [God and Universe][312] – he explained that: "(his) system is based on the 'reincarnationist column', without which all his vision would collapse. So, he describes a biological catharsis which will produce a process of spiritualization capable of getting hold of the Law of the Spirit to conquer and fulfil the divine Self"[313].

---

[310] cf. Pietro Ubaldi, *La grande sintesi*, op. cit., p. 15ff. "From polytheism to monotheism to monism, your conception of Divinity expands. This discussion is, therefore, the hymn of his glory" (ibid., p. 16). In order to understand the serious temptation that Maria Valtorta suffered: "The highest nouric source is what man has called God, and the Bible is the largest document of world nouric reception, drawn from the highest sources. The Jewish people give us the example of a gigantic inspirational phenomenon that has continued for centuries and centuries, placed in preparation for the event from which the civilization that was to rule the world was to be born. And Christianity has been awaited and prepared by this very high inspirational mediumship" (Paola Giovetti, *I grandi iniziati del nostro tempo*, op. cit., p. 125).

[311] http://www.pietroubaldi.com/?page_id=54, consulted 18 December 2015. This web page, which is part of the website that officially represents the ideals of "The Pietro Ubaldi Cultural Center", summarizes the content of the books he published.

[312] ibid.

[313] ibid.

In *Ascensioni umane* [Human Ascension][314] he explains: "the inevitability of human evolution through a gradual process of extending the self in everyone. A vision of humankind is outlined which moves beyond violence and indifference towards harmony and unification of the conscience"[315] following an evolutionary path. But a big battle is raging now: "the difference between the evolved and the un-evolved man is outlined and clarified, as well as the difference between his idea of a super-human – as inspired by the Gospel – and Nietzsche's idea of a Übermensch. [...] that is, between the two principles of animalism (strength) and spirituality (intelligence), in such a way as to generate public usefulness by considering everything as part of an organic system, the universe system, which contains within itself the law of the future"[316]. In the works of Ubaldi, Christ has His relevance, too: "Christ is presented as the reference point of all his vision, the essence of the evolutionary, redemptive and salvific process"[317], but not as God in the flesh, thus denying the Incarnation. The sociologists of religion[318] consider the cult of Pietro Ubaldi a post-spiritist, because despite the many affinities with Christianity, it is the spiritist aspect which prevails and dominates[319].

---

[314] ibid.
[315] ibid.
[316] ibid.
[317] ibid.
[318] Massimo Introvigne – PierLuigi Zoccatelli (under the direction of), *Enciclopedia delle religioni in Italia*, Elledici, Torino 2013, pp. 1055-6.
[319] Despite everything, a year later Maria Valtorta wrote: "Do you remember when I read those books by Ubaldi and, since God so willed, I drew deeply into Christian thoughts from them? You smiled at this ... property of mine for seeing, feeling, savouring, and understanding God alone, even in the works of a devil. But I can account for it quite well. It is because God has given me ... special, miraculous lenses, which cancel out the evil words and turn them into good ones. I think of the Gospel: 'You will step on snakes and scorpions, *and they will not harm you*' [Lk 10:19]. God is good!" (Maria Valtorta, *Notebooks 1945-1950*, op. cit., dated 8 September 1945, p. 108). Up until 1944, Pietro Ubaldi had written six books – to which 18 others were added until 1971, for a total of about 10,000 pages – namely: *I grandi messaggi* [The great messages], *La grade sintesi* [The great synthesis], *Le Noúri* [The Noúri], *L'ascesi mistica* [Mystical asceticism], *Storia di un uomo*

The debate between Giuseppe Belfanti and Maria Valtorta was not a literary or philosophical discussion without consequences[320]: he had stopped going to Church and receiving the sacraments and this deeply upset Maria, who feared eternal damnation for her cousin[321]. Maria prayed and did penance for him; and Heaven worked wonders, without taking Giuseppe's responsibility away. Maria's wish was amazingly fulfilled. The visions she had from mid-January to mid-October 1944 – when her cousin was preparing to leave Sant'Andrea di Còmpito to return to Reggio, Calabria – were not in an orderly succession; they did not follow one after another in a continuous and orderly way: 1, 2, 3, 4, etc., but they were written with large gaps between them: 52, 322, 327, 435, 236, 36, 41, etc.[322] In the end, the

---

[The history of a man] and *Frammenti di pensiero e di passioni* [Fragments of thought and passions]. He died in Brazil on 29 February 1972.

[320] cf. Maria Valtorta, *The Little Notebooks*, op. cit., pp. 42-6. This dictation of 17 October 1944, answered several questions posed by Giuseppe Belfanti and some of his ideas, claiming that Pietro Ubaldi's theories were the result of a "lying and cunning spirit". The fundamental concept was that Ubaldi's theories were "nebulous", against the simplicity and clarity of the Church's doctrine that Maria Valtorta expounded. Dr Luciano Raffaele specified from a text written by Giuseppe Belfanti, unpublished elsewhere, his various spiritual experiences with a friend, and the clear repulsion of Maria Valtorta: "For heaven's sake: Maria did not want to know about it and she ridiculed and condemned me and my manifestations, of which she had a sacred terror" (Luciano Raffaele, preface to Maria Valtorta, *Il Poema dell'Uomo-Dio* [The Poem of the Man-God], Tipografia Editrice M. Pisani, Isola del Liri (FR) 1961², p. XXIX). [Not in the English edition].

[321] After all, on the one hand, there is a miracle; that is, her life combined with the simple precision of what she saw and described. On the other, a cloudy kaleidoscope which was only lucid in appearance of Ubaldi. Today we could also say: the Christian fact is opposed to the New Age cloud, or even her factual and real rationality is against his irrational of phantasmagorical images.

[322] Data was collected from the texts and presented in the original Notebooks. Some examples to help understand the chapter jumps and the big differences between them: 28 February 1944: chapter 44, Adoration of the Magi; 4 March: chapter 274, Jesus walks on water; 5 March 1944: chapter 17, Eve's disobedience and Mary's obedience. To be even clearer in seeing the jumps: chapter 45 was already written on 3 February 1944, and

Voice itself told her how to precisely organize her writings, and then everything fit into place, matching the previous and the following chapters. This bizarre, yet extremely precise method[323] produced various results, such as her cousin's conversion: after much hesitation, as soon as he was back in Reggio, Calabria in November 1944. Giuseppe was convinced of Maria Valtorta's truthfulness and of Pietro Ubaldi's arbitrary invention, and rejoined the Church and the sacraments. On top of this result, there came the demonstration of the precision adopted by Maria in her writings: in the end, all the chapters come one after the other in a harmonious narrative, fitting one into the other perfectly: no mistakes and no oversights; one single, regular text, even though adjoining episodes were written one or two years apart. The critical analysis of Maria's texts demonstrates this precision and becomes even more convincing for the acknowledgement of the supernatural nature of her writings. The method and the episode itself prove once again that God makes miracles and despite this, He leaves mankind free to accept it or refuse it.

---

chapter 43 would be written on 10 June 1944. Chapter 273 would be written on 7 September 1945 and chapter 275 on 8 September 1945; Chapter 273 fits perfectly between these two, despite the temporal distance. Compared to chapter 17, 16 was written on 8 March 1944, and chapter 18 on 25 March 1944. Dr. Luciano Raffaele who wrote: "Despite so much and such scrupulous precision, and indeed, in contrast with similar meticulous care, a surprising peculiarity emerges: especially with regard to the Pre-gospel and the Passion, the events, and therefore the chapters or paragraphs that contain them, they are not progressive. That is, they do not appear in the manuscripts, in the chronological order of the facts and in the logical development of the events, but in a non-continuous manner. Therefore, the progression of the individual parts, and the harmonious merging of the same, are not seen until the work is completed" (Luciano Raffaele, preface to Maria Valtorta, *Il Poema dell'Uomo-Dio*, op. cit., p. XXII). [Not in the English edition].

[323] It is not visible, at first glance, when a continuous lectio of the Gospel is made, unless the date of the inscription is checked chapter by chapter.

Everybody back at home

At 11.30am on 23 December 1944, Father Fantoni, a Servite like Father Migliorini, arrived at Sant'Andrea di Còmpito, and to Maria's great joy – who said she almost 'choked' with excitement – took her back to the house in Viareggio, running again a big health risk. In fact, she had been warned the previous night so she could not wait: "My temperature was higher than usual. I packed my suitcases with more energy than a healthy person. I spoke and wrote until midnight and my soul sang: "Thank you, Jesus" [...], a thanksgiving which I still repeat unceasingly – even while I sleep, I think – for I wake up saying, 'Thank you, my Lord'"[324]. We can understand her joy in finding her house virtually intact despite the bombings or the usual looters. She was at home at last: "There now remains the great peace of being here. It is as if the house were embracing me... and, along with the house, my dead loved ones and I with them, rediscover 'my' little Paradise which I lost in April, and all of them return as they were then. And all of them for me. I call this the house of my love, and it is"[325]. And she added a foresight that she received: "What adds a special flavor to this is your goodness, you who ten days ago told me, 'In ten days' time you will be...' I would be blessed, thanks to your goodness and that of my much-desired Lord"[326].

Up to her neck in writing

The war was about to end; the frontline shifted northwards, towards Massa and Carrara; there were no more bombings. The last German guns were around La Spezia and struck as far as Carrara and Massa, leaving Viareggio free from bullets because it was too far away. By now, the Axis powers had collapsed; the war ended in late April. However, the post-war years began, which were awful because of the consequences of what had happened, and because of the attempt of the communists to obtain power in Italy too, although in a different way compared to elsewhere in the world; that is, in a democratic way through free elections. The devaluation of the lira

---

[324] Maria Valtorta, *Notebooks 1944*, op. cit., dated 30 December, p. 647.
[325] ibid.
[326] ibid.

(Italian currency before the euro) caused the collapse of Maria Valtorta's already dwindling finances. Until then, what had been an economically lower middle-class, was plunged to the poverty threshold; she was basically left with only the property of the house, and so she faced destitution with all its miseries. Luckily, Marta Diciotti – a real friend in times of need when economic hardship was hitting hard – remained always loyal to Maria Valtorta, whose health was getting worse and in need of continuous treatments. Life was getting harder and harder.

The Devil's countenance

For Maria Valtorta, 1945 started with the devil's countenance. The words that she wrote in her dictations were filled with particular visions. There were also personal messages for Father Migliorini and other clergy, and men and women, but after the vision of St. Valente the martyr, followed by the priestly ordination of Valentine[327] (16 January), on 26 January, the Devil himself appeared to her. "I was so terrified by the apparition of the devil that if the curfew had not been imposed, I would have had you called. A real devil with no camouflage whatsoever – that is, a tall, tenuous, smoky personage with a low, narrow brow, a pointed face, deep eyes and such a wicked, sarcastic and false gaze that I was on the verge of crying out for help. I was praying in the darkness of my room while Marta was in the kitchen. I was praying to the Immaculate Heart of Mary when he appeared to me next to the closed door. Dark in the darkness, yet I could see all the details of his body, naked and ugly, not because of a deformity, but because of a kind of fierceness and serpentine trait gleaming from each of his members. I did not see any horns or a tail, or a forked foot or wings, as he is generally depicted. But his entire monstrosity was in his expression. To say what he was, I would have to say: "Falsehood", "sarcasm", "Ferocity", "Hatred" and "Lurking". This is what his deceitful, wicked expression conveyed. He was mocking and insulting me. But he did not dare to come closer. He was there, nailed in place next to the door. He stayed there for a good ten minutes and then he went away. But I was ... in a hot and cold

---

[327] Maria Valtorta, *Notebooks 1945-1950*, op. cit., dated 16 January 1945, p. 24ff.

sweat"[328]. It is worth noticing how Maria's realism was very strong here, too: rather than leaving her imagination run free in fantastical settings, this looks like a charcoal sketch with no unnecessary words. The comments added by the inner voice are as concise, flawless, and with a humility that is getting more and more refined: "In a state of dismay, as I wondered what the reason was for that visit, Jesus said, '[It is] because you had rejected him so harshly in his main element'. (While I prayed to Mary, there had insistently come back to me the... I do not know what to call it since it is not a voice or an idea or a mind, and yet it is something saying, 'If you had not been there, something would have happened. By your merit, it did not happen because you are loved so much by God'. I do not know if I am behaving rightly or wrongly, but I think I am actiing properly because when I hear this, I say, 'Depart, Satan. Do not tempt me. For if it is Jesus who is saying this, then I will accept it. But nobody else should say so to provoke self-satisfaction in me'). Jesus then said: "...you had rejected him so harshly in his main element: pride"[329]. The battle went on. And after a few days, on 19 March, Maria wrote a sort of summary of the temptations she had had to endure: "This is not the first time, you know, that Satan has bothered me, tempting me to do this or that. And now that he is not tempting my flesh anymore, he is tempting my spirit. He has been bothering me now for a year, on and off. The first time was during those terrible days in April 1944 when he promised to help me if I adored him. The second time he assaulted me with that intense, violent and long enticement on 4 July 1944, he tempted me to ape the Master's language to humiliate those who had offended me. The third time was when he suggested that I should claim that the dictations were my own words and that I should publish them, taking the credit and the money. The fourth time was when he appeared to me in February this year, (I believe it was already February the first time that I saw him because the other times I only heard him), he terrorized me with his looks and his hatred. The fifth time was last night. These were the *great* apparitions of Satan"[330].

---

[328] ibid., p. 27.
[329] ibid., pp. 27-8.
[330] ibid., p. 42.

And 1945 ended on the same wavelength: on 29 December, Maria Valtorta had a vision of how Lucifer's fall from Heaven had happened. It was revealed to her as a real fact which happened in time and space, and this is totally understandable if one wants to be understood by someone who is always immersed in these two elements. The day after, the voice (Jesus), commented on the vision, and ended up shouting at Satan in such a way that Maria herself was scared and wrote: "'Stay back, O Satan! I rise up in defense between her and you. Roam over the Earth! Corrupt, bite, and rot! But not here on my prey. My Cross is upon her. Go, accursed one! I am who I am, and you are the one defeated! Go away! Go away! Go somewhere else! Go away in the Holy Name known to Me alone! In the Name of the One who is and who struck you with His lightning! Go away, in the Name of God the King, of Jesus the Saviour and the Crucified One, and of Eternal Love!' [...] And I am telling the truth: when I heard Him cry out like that, with all His might and so angrily, though I saw nothing and did not notice any disturbances from an evil spirit, I was nonetheless afraid. The wrath of God is terrible! I have perceived it like this only on one other occasion - in that far-off dictation against Mussolini and Hitler back in January 1944,[331] if I am not mistaken. I will look up the date: 17-18 January 1944[332]. But today it was even more forceful. At the end, His command was such as to burn someone to ashes. All the sounds in Heaven seemed to have joined together in His voice. But they were no longer the sweet songs of indescribable beauty. They were the din of lightning bolts"[333].

How can we not consider these words by Maria Valtorta as a prophecy[334] that before long would have become apparent all over

---

[331] On 25 January 1944, Maria wrote a long dictation describing the precursors and the advent of the antichrist. This essay is a small treatise on the history of theology. cf. Maria Valtorta, *Notebooks 1944*, op. cit., dated 25 January, pp. 107-11. (*Notebooks 1945-50*, op.cit., 30 December 1945, pp. 152-3).

[332] Today it is found in (*Notebooks 1944*, op.cit., dated 17 January, pp. 84-90).

[333] Maria Valtorta, *Notebooks 1945-1950*, op. cit., dated 30 December 1945, p. 153.

[334] To the strong criticisms of Pope Pius XII against any form of communism, Stalin replied, deriding him, asking how many armored

the world? "The other sad affair: my short dream at dawn […]. It was fearful. It took me back to those predictions that deeply disturbed me in 1915 before the wars and revolutions […] and which have continued up to this war and its aftermath. Today I semed to be living in expectation of a fearsome event, together with the whole city, for something awful. And indeed, people had to take cover because the sky was packed with small (since they were very high up) airplanes, all of them black, whose purpose was unknown. Gas? Grapeshot (weaponry)? Bombs? Everyone was fleeing. The streets emptied. I tried to look upwards, but I was told: 'Quick, quick, take cover!' And they all screamed: 'The punishment is starting'. The planes seemed to be Russian. I said: 'But we have only just come out of a storm! Is that still not enough?' And many answered: 'This is sweeping everyone away. Even the Monarchy has come. (This is not a prophecy since even dunces understand it, but there will plenty for everyone'. I woke up terrified"[335].

Her clear thinking in describing what everybody seemed to predict both about the Italian monarchy, and about this new war, was extraordinary. It must be said, that the theme of a possible Third World War, complete with the routes of attack of the various armies, was very common among many circles dedicated to prophecies[336]. Only the collapse of the Soviet Union in 1989 which had not been predicted by any political study, erased this tonne of data. The only

---

divisions the Pope had. The secularist and communist culture, starting from 1963 with the theatrical piece – and then film – *The Vicar* [*Der Stellvertreter. Ein christliches Trauerspiel*] by the German playwright Rolf Hochhuth, a communist sympathizer, ferociously attacked Pius XII with the slander of being anti-Jewish and for not having openly condemned National Socialism.

[335] Maria Valtorta, *Notebooks 1945-1950*, op. cit., dated 3 June 1945, p. 75.

[336] There were about 43 different people, dating from the mid-1600s until the 1980s. cf. *http://profezierivelazione.blogspot.it/2015/09/visioni-sulla-terza-guerra-m Mondiale.html*, [visions of the third World war] consulted 14 October 2018. cf. *Gli enigmatici messaggi della mistica Marie Julie Jahenny (1850-1941)* [The enigmatic messages of the mystic Marie Julie Jahenny (1850-1941)], in: "Il Segno del soprannaturale" [The Sign of the supernatural], Year XXIX n. 366 – December 2018, pp. 11-5. To this are added also the visions of Alois Irlmaier (Cf. *http://profezierivelazione.blogspot.it/2011/11/le-profezie-di-alois-irlmaier-prima.html* [the prophecies of Alois Irlmaier], consulted 14 October 2018).

prophecy that has come true remains the one made by Our Lady of Fatima[337] who had promised the end of all dangers with the consecration of Russia to Her Immaculate Heart, as it did happen.

Heaven in the blood of Jesus

On 29 May 1944, Maria Valtorta was granted the great mystical gift of drinking from His side by Jesus: "First of all, come and drink. You are more fortunate than John. He rested his head on My chest when not yet wounded. As for you, cling to my lacerated chest and drink the love flowing from my wounded heart"[338]. And on 29-30 March 1945, this was replicated even more intensely: 'Listen, little John. Father Migliorini cannot bring you Communion and you are suffering. I am your Priest. I have kept you bent over my tortures, my agony. It is right for Me to give you a reward. Look: many years ago, I was heading to the Cenacle at this hour to consummate the Passover and distribute the first Eucharist. Come and take this, little John'. And letting His mantle fall open, He shows me the ciborium He was holding in His hand. He became solemn and said: 'I am the living Bread descending from Heaven. Whoever eats this Bread will no longer be hungry and will live eternally. This is my Body which I give you in memory of Me. Take it and eat'. And He gave me a large host. I say 'large' because it was as big as an ancient coin (a scudo). Its (material and spiritual) flavour was such that it filled me with delight. He caressed me and then said: 'Now that you are nourished, write. I shall come back tomorrow'. And this evening, at the same hour, He appeared to me again. I had been feeling ill since you were here (Father Migliorini) and I was unable to get over the crisis. I was in a cold sweat, very pale and gasping, with constant dizziness and a darkening of my sight. And yet, I was writing because I *had* to write... Our Lady of Sorrows was moaning from her agony. Jesus removed me for a while from so much shared moral and physical pain, and holding the chalice fully exposed, filled with red, vigorous blood - I would say ' thick', nearly boiling, for it foamed with strange bubbles

---

[337] cf. Saverio Gaeta, *Fatima. Tutta la verità, la storia, i segreti, la consacrazione* [Fatima. The whole truth, the history, the secrets, the consecration], San Paolo Edizioni, Milano 2017.

[338] Maria Valtorta, *Notebooks 1944*, op. cit., dated 29 May, p. 323.

as if it had just come out of an artery - He said: "This is my Blood which I have shed out of love for you. Take it and drink it'. And He brought the chalice up to my lips while drawing me towards it with His other hand. I perceived the coldness of the metal against my lips and the smell of the blood in my nose. But I felt no repugnance. I pressed my lips against the smooth brim of the silver chalice and I drank a sip of this divine Blood which had all the characteristics of our own in terms of fluidity, viscosity and taste. But it flows down into me, bringing me a delight which lifts me high up into joy. I would like to drink and drink... For the more you drink, the more you want it. But reverence restrains me. And I contemplate that beloved Blood, smell its living scent, admire its perfect bright redness. But Jesus has me drink twice more... And then He departs... And the taste and the fragrance of that Blood of my Jesus remains in me. I almost did not want to write this here but in a letter which I was unsure whether to give it to you immediately or let you have it at my death. For certain sublime moments are poorly and unwillingly ariculated"[339]. This is a gift that also other mystics were granted. So, from a certain point of view, there is nothing new. But it demonstrates the usual simplicity that Maria would use – which features also in the descriptions of *The Gospel* – and which is used again here with no exaggerations, with clarity, flawlessly and effortlessly. We should add another extraordinary mystical gift: on 13 October 1945, Maria Valtorta had a vision – not a dictation – in which Jesus, dressed in white wool, made this gesture, real and symbolic at the same time: "He placed His left hand on my left shoulder and drew me to Himself, while with His right hand, He brought the chalice up to my lips, saying, 'Drink.' The chalice was full of a liquid looking like pure water. I glimpsed it in the instant Jesus offered it to me, forcing me to drink. I drank. What bitterness! Oh, it is certainly not the inebriating chalice of Holy Thursday, filled with the living Blood of my Lord! Sweet, mellow Blood from which I would never have withdrawn my lips! This is water of such a nauseating bitterness that no medicine possesses it. It bites the throat and the stomach, making it turn over with revulsion. It brings tears to your eyes and lasts like a parching thirst

---

[339] Maria Valtorta, *Notebooks 1945-1950*, op. cit., dated 29-30 March 1945, pp. 52-3.

from burning acid. Jesus has me drink just one sip ... and then withdraws the chalice and explains: 'This is the chalice I drank in Gethsemane. I drank it all, to the dregs, and the dregs are more bitter. And this is the chalice which men's sins fill up each day, and these then head towards Heaven to have Me go on drinking thereof. But I can no longer drink anything but Infinite Love. And then, you see, I offer it to the generous, to the beloved ones. Thank you for this sip! I will now go to other dear souls. I bless you for the sake of the Father, Myself and Eternal Love.' And He goes off leaving my mouth and stomach searing with poison and my soul filled with peace."[340]. Apart from the gift, which was both painful and peaceful – as is everything that comes from Heaven – we can notice in Maria Valtorta, the lack of centralization and absolutization of her case: Jesus said that He was also going 'to other beloved souls'; that is, to other martyrs of love for the salvation of mankind. This is not a devotional and self-exalting image, on the contrary, it is shared with simplicity and as a matter of course.

The enemy shall not pass!

As we have already seen, Maria could not stand spiritists, especially in action: she thought that their séances were satanic and promoted all sorts of evil, and that if they took place near her (house or flat) she would feel ill. In June, she had refused to host two of these for a fee who declared themselves 'palm readers and fortune-tellers'. But her neighbor decided, around mid-July, to accommodate them. Maria Valtorta could 'perceive' their presence and she was spiritually upset by it. On the evening of 18 July, she could not bear it any longer. During the night and for the following three nights, she recited Leo XIII's exorcism prayer[341], kneeling with great difficulty on her bed. The outcome was not long in coming: the two left in a hurry. This is how the neighbor described the outcome: "He also said that he is not staying on because he is too ruffled. Not by noise or by

---

[340] ibid., dated 13 October, p. 116.
[341] For example, cf. *https://www.papaboys.org/25-10-il-potente-esorcismo-di-leone-xiii-contro-il-demonio-lo-pecono-anche-i-laici* [the powerful exorcism of Leo XIII against the devil, the laypeople also offend him], consulted 1 May 2019.

us at home, since we don't even say a word while the professor [?!] is at work, but by other things which he did not want to explain. And afterwards he wanted to know who you are and what you do. A lot of things. And when we told him, 'She's a sick woman who reads, writes and does embroidery...,' he replied, 'No, I know: she's a saint' (forgive me if I have to write this word in order to be precise). Those good people did not understand what connection I had with the work of the professor (?!) or how he could know about me, to the point where they asked, 'But do you know him?' 'No, by God's grace,' I replied. But I understood all the connections. Well! It's a repetition of 1930. The fact is that the medium took to his heels, and I trust the other will soon follow him ... and the air will be cleansed of the smell of sulphur, which my spiritual lungs cannot bear. And now let us see what annoyance Satan will cause me to take revenge... I certainly won't get off lightly. In 1930, through the mouth of the medium I had driven away, as you know, he said, "You are throwing me out. But you're making a mistake because whoever drives me out meets with pains and troubles. In fact, I was no longer well but they had to go elsewhere."[342]. This event was neither fortuitous nor occasional but it was the constant anti-spiritism of Maria Valtorta: not just a dislike, rather a real repulsion, even at the cost of personal sacrifice. In all her life, she never weakened!

Spokesperson and word for everyone

Maria Valtorta fought as long as she could to remain hidden and unknown. Her existence should have remained anonymous until her death. Only then would the world have known. But it did not happen. Usually very careful about what was going on, Father Migliorini could not keep silent. What he had in his hands was too beautiful; too many tragedies of war; too many appeals for comfort. And because of this, he ended up saying too much[343]. Anyway, irrespective of the spiritual director, something leaked out and Maria Valtorta became the medium of communication between some (very few, actually) people and her inner voice, and even Jesus who appeared to her. After a few

---

[342] Maria Valtorta, *Notebooks 1945-1950*, op. cit., dated 28 July 1945, p. 88.
[343] The matter would be dealt with when he would be definitively transferred to Rome in 1946.

messages and remarks for Father Romualdo Migliorini, the teaching in the visions for her cousin Giuseppe Belfanti, and a few dictations dedicated to him, other people appeared to her in 1944 directed by various people Maria Valtorta was acquainted with or by people who, having 'understood' something, were asking for her intercession. Among the first ones was Dora Barsottelli[344] who had spiritual gifts and was directed by Father Migliorini himself; Sister Maria Gabriella[345]; then Mother Teresa Maria, the Mother Superior of the Carmel of San Colombano near Lucca[346], Sister Teresa Cherubina of the Holy Face[347], Mother Luigia Giacinta[348]; and finally, even some laypersons were addressed in these messages, for instance Maria Raffaelli, to console her for her son Antonio[349]. The contents of these messages were the most varied: clarifications, explanations, consolation and even reproach. The general tone was, however, always merciful, and it invited people to do better.

The pagan sky and Christian Heaven

If it is true that philosophy was not one of Maria Valtorta's strengths, she knew, however, how to make sense of it when she needed to. What she wrote on 8 September 1945 is for various reasons, a wonderful page. She had been contacted by a student – ready to enroll in the Faculty of Philosophy, although upset by the ambiguous behavior of the Christian clergy and laity, and already determined to join the Communist party – who asked her to read *Phaedo* by Plato. By the way, this gives me the opportunity to say that she had read both *The Apology of Socrates* and *Euthyphro*, so Maria Valtorta cannot be said to be illiterate or lacking an intellectual education. The uniqueness of this episode lies in the fact that Jesus

---

[344] cf. ibid., dated 18 April 1946, pp. 249-51.

[345] Maria Valtorta, *Notebooks 1944,* op. cit., dated 9 April, pp. 270-1.

[346] cf. Maria Valtorta, *Notebooks 1945-1950,* op. cit., dated 15 March 1946, p. 226. A very remarkable and essential correspondence between Mother Teresa Maria and Maria Valtorta followed, starting from March 1946.

[347] cf. ibid., dated 24 December 1945, pp. 134-6.

[348] cf. ibid., dated 25 December 1945, pp. 140-2.

[349] cf. ibid., dated 26 December 1945, p. 138.

appeared clearly at her right side, and embracing her, He explained how souls were created, saying beautiful words about Socrates: "The Greek philosopher...is the possessor of just a semi revelation, a barely glimpsed religion, and thus cannot have the whole Truth - but as I say. The soul does not remember because it lives again. [...] I know He said Socrates had followed this thought in a straight line as far as he could, and then, since he lacked knowledge of Divine Truth, he drifted off the straight line and doubled back downwards instead of continuing the ascent. He said, "A second life is lived, indeed, but no longer on the earth. With the spirit in other realms." But I lose track of the rest."[350]. We do not know what happened to that Catholic youth who was tempted to leave the Church, but on this page we have a reading of those 'rays of light' that are present in ancient pagan texts[351], the forerunners of the famous words of the Second Vatican Council: Christians "should be familiar with their (non-Christians) national and religious traditions; they should gladly and reverently lay bare the seeds of the Word which lie hidden among their fellows"[352] followed by the words of St. John Paul II: "The Fathers of the Church rightly saw in the various religions as it were, so many reflections of one truth - 'seeds of the Word'"[353].

The Archangels in her room

While *the Gospel* tells of the life on earth of the Son of God made flesh to the ultimate consequence, *The Notebooks* and *The Little Notebooks* recount the dictations and other visions, including the life of the early Church and the death of several martyrs. Along with this, occasionally, there are visions of paradise or of celestial beings, but

---

[350] ibid., dated 8 September 1945, pp. 108-9 Also in other texts, authors of antiquity are cited, both philosophers and doctors, such as Galen.

[351] Known as *"logoi spermatikoi or sperm sowers"* (cf. Igino Giordani (Introduction and translation of), *San Giustino. Le apologie* [Saint Giustino. Apologies], Città Nuova, Roma 1962, II Apology, X. 1-6).

[352] Concilio Ecumenico Vaticano II [Ecumenical Vatican Council II], *Decreto sull'attività missionaria della chiesa Ad Gentes* [Decree on the missionary activity of the church of the nations], n. 11.

[353] Pope Saint John Paul II, Enciclica *Redemptoris Hominis* [Encyciclical: the Redeemer of Man], n. 11.

realism that dominates even here: they are symbols, yet they are wonderful, without being senseless fantasies. On 21 December 1945 near the end of the year after receiving Holy Communion and for an unspecified period: "trembling with joy, waves of more vast joy, the heavenly domain became progressively illuminated for me and I saw the most radiant azures of the meadows of Paradise... This is a vision of the heavenly regions which no comparison can convey"[354]. Then came the vision of the three singing Archangels, and the description of their faces and their robes. Finally: "I descended from the spheres where I had been and came back to myself, to my agonies, to my bed. But the joy remained..."[355]. And in fact, despite all the ecstasies, we must always remember that physical pain remained Maria Valtorta's constant companion.

1946 and the post-war period

For Maria Valtorta, 1946 was another terrible year. Her writings increased, but her heart was pierced by the tragic and disastrous exit of Father Migliorini. And immediately on 4 January, St. Peter appeared to her and asked her to write to Father Migliorini to keep an eye on his flock[356]". It was just the prelude to the tsunami: the events became more and more pressing and calmed down, so to speak, only on 24 April 1947 when the drafting of the main Work

---

[354] Maria Valtorta, *Notebooks 1945-1950*, op. cit., dated 21 December, 1945 p. 129.

[355] ibid., pp. 130-3. The archangel Gabriel has been described as "Blond – a pure gold blond – with wavy hair barely touching his shoulders [...]. He was looking at me with his sapphire eyes" (ibid., p. 131); Michael is "*terrible in his austere handsomeness*. With brown hair shorter than his companion's and curlier [...] He touches the jewel on his chest. He took it between the fingers of his right hand and lifted it up to show it to me, and in a voice resounding like bronze, he says: Whoever is with God can do everything. And Satan can do nothing against whoever is with God. For *who is like God?*" (ibid., pp. 130-1); Raffaele is "tall, long dark long hair [...] looks the youngest of all [...] has the eyes of a very sweet brown color, a placid, patient look, which is a caress. [...] They greet me. Gabriele sang with his voice like a very spiritual harp (and every note takes you into ecstasy): "Hail Mary" (ibid., pp. 131-2).

[356] cf. ibid., dated 4 January 1946, p. 157.

was finished. On 11 January 1946, Maria Valtorta wrote about the incredible link between a letter from Giuseppe Belfanti and what the visions and the voices had told her regarding Dora Barsottelli of Camaiore: "He uses almost the same words to exhort us not to abandon ourselves quite blindly to Dora's case which is very 'mixed'. And so from 5 December until today, there have been *many* spiritual or human voices saying the same thing. (...) A continuous whizzing of voices saying: 'Be careful! For your own sake and for Father's. Be careful!'"[357]. Taking very seriously what she had been told, almost feeling the imminent earthquake, Maria was extremely insistent in telling Father Migliorini that he should stop taking his other spiritual disciple too seriously: "Do you know that on certain nights I have had to win real battles so as not to scream and have to tell you: 'Leave everything! Leave everything! Don't destroy yourself!'? [...] I don't know if you have noticed this. I don't know if you have failed to note that on certain occasions on hearing you so "sure". The most recent was that morning when you came back from Camaiore for the last time – I had tears in my eyes. Do they speak positively about me? If it is a voice from God, I thank Him for illuminating you in this regard. But I attach *such minimal* certainty to it that I receive *no* joy. [...] I also say to you, as does Giuseppe who perceives things the same way I do from so far away. I questioned the other soul: "Be careful! Be careful! Put yourself in a waiting position, a position of vigilance. Observe from a distance. Time will provide the light [...] – Dora [...] is in a very unstable position. [...] when the 'other' wants to use her to harm us. But don't you understand that even if he does not possess her forever, it suffices for *him* to *have her just enough to make you appear to be 'unable to distinguish between Truth and Lies'* so that they will laugh at you in *the Curias* and so on? But don't you understand that, as a result, this would bring harm to my case? Oh, if I could have you feel for an hour what I experience! But you won't pay attention to me.... And may Infinite Goodness work the miracle of not punishing you and not saying, 'Enough!' to punish you"[358]. Unfortunately, the situation quickly took a tragic and fatal turn for Father Migliorini.

---

[357] cf. ibid., dated 11 January 1946, p. 167.
[358] ibid., dated 11 January 1946, pp. 167-8.

Azariah, the guardian angel

Still more events affected the life of Maria Valtorta during 1946. On 15 January very early in the morning at 5:30am, her Guardian Angel revealed himself in a vision. She had heard his voice many times and she had called him 'the inner advisor'[359]. But this time as she was praying, she saw him and her curiosity was aroused.

She stopped and began a short dialogue: "What is your name? You must have a name! I call you 'inner advisor' but I would like to address you with a name. He appeared to me alongside my bed, on the right towards the foot, and he immediately said with a big smile: 'Azariah'. 'Azariah? Really?'"[360] Azariah would assume an important role later. In this case, rather than observing him, she contemplated him, and with her usual meticulousness she described him in the materialised vision: "I observed him: tall, handsome, with dark brown hair, a rounded face perfect in its lines and color, and large, gentle, very beautiful dark brown eyes. I observed his loose robe: a straight tunic, very chaste and attractive, lacking a belt or mantle, with long sleeves and a square-shaped opening at the neck. The robe was white and silver. The background was a very slightly burnished silver. This robe's embroidery, which seemed to be precious brocade, was a luminous white - whiter than any snow or petal ever formed. And the embroidery was a whole stream of lily stems with an open calyx. They followed in one direction like this: in such a way that the angel seemed to be wrapped in an enveloping sheaf of lilies in bloom. At the neck, on the sleeves and at the bottom were silver stripes. I said, "The same clothing as on 4 January 1932, and the same appearance!" "Yes, it is I. And if on other occasions I appeared to you with the three holy colors, it was to remind you that the Guardian watches, above all, over the life of the three theological virtues in the spirit of the one he protects." I contemplated and contemplated him, pronouncing and savoring his name throughout the night of bitter sufferings and without any shadow of sleep. From now on, the inner

---

[359] cf. Maria Valtorta, *Notebooks 1944*, op. cit., pp. 299, 612; cf. also Maria Valtorta, *Notebooks 1945-1950*, op. cit., pp. 133, 162, 164, 169, 170, 172, 220.

[360] Maria Valtorta, *Notebooks 1945-1950*, op. cit., dated 15 January 1946, p. 170.

advisor will be indicated by the name of Azariah"³⁶¹. And Azariah ended on a theological note: "...every guardian angel is an Azariah: a help from the Lord who in special cases becomes more manifest by his order and for his glory"³⁶².

Between the end of 1945 and the beginning of 1946, the first doubts about Father Migliorini started to emerge. In retrospect, we understand the need for the dictation of 20 January 1946, which consisted of a theological dissertation on the fall of Lucifer, the most handsome among the Angels, with passages of real depth, far from banal³⁶³: it was simply a warning that a similar thing would not happen to him as well. Therefore, Azariah intervened directly from 26 February. Heaven already knew the awful result of Father Migliorini's 'distraction', and providentially sent Azariah to spiritually guide Maria Valtorta and compensate for her imminent spiritual loneliness. The Guardian Angel Azariah commented on the epistle of the 52 Holy Masses of the Roman Missal in use at the time³⁶⁴, which became a

---

³⁶¹ ibid., pp. 171-2.

³⁶² ibid., p. 172.

³⁶³ This is how it begins: "The angels are superior to men. When I say 'men', it refers to all beings designated in this way, composed of matter and spirit. We are then superior, entirely spirit. But remember that when Grace lives in man, and the Blood of the Mystical Body circulates, whose head is Christ, while the seven Sacraments confirm him from birth to death, in every state and every stage of life, we then see the Lord in you, 'living temples of the Lord', and worship Him in you, and you are then superior to us. You are 'other Christs' and have what is called the 'Bread of angels'; but Bread is for men alone. A mystical, insatiable hunger for the Eucharist which is in you, makes us cling to you when you feed on It, to perceive the divine fragrance of this perfect Food!". Ibid., dated 20 January 1946, p. 174.

³⁶⁴ On 16 July 1947, Azariah explained to Mary who Guardian Angels are and their purpose: "People think the mission of the Guardian Angel ceases with the death of the one being protected. It is not always that way. It ceases, as is logical, at the death of impenitent sinners, and with supreme pain on the part of the guardian angel of whoever did not repent. It is transfigured into festive, eternal glory at the death of a saint who goes from earth to Paradise with no stopover for purgation. But he continues as before, as a protection that intercedes and loves the one entrusted to it, in the case of those going from earth to Purgatory to expiate and purify themselves. Then we, the guardian angels, pray for you with charity before

volume published under the title: *The Book of Azariah*. As a matter of fact, Maria Valtorta had given it two other titles: *Angelical Masses* and *Directions*[365] - terms which were probably more suitable for the contents and the needs of the time, and which began with the comment to the second reading – as we would call it today – and went on with advice, explanations[366], spiritual examples for her and for other victim souls, providing a truly spiritual guide in times of solitude and sorrow. It should be stressed that these dictations have been contemporaneous with the visions and the dictations of other figures: these visions/dictations did not interrupt the others, so Maria Valtorta spent more time writing every day, to a level that would be hardly bearable even for a strong, young person[367].

---

the throne of God and, along with our loving prayers, present the entreaties offered for you on earth by relatives and friends." (Maria Valtorta, *Notebooks 1945-1950*, op. cit., dated 16 July 1947, p. 403).

[365] Maria Valtorta, *The Book of Azariah*, Centro Editoriale Valtortiano, Isola del Liri (FR) 1993, p. 10.

[366] Here is an example of an explanation: "My Guardian Angel explained to me the difference between the separation of the soul from the body at death, and the momentary separation of the spirit from the body and soul in ecstasy or rapture. He told me that, whereas the soul's separation from the body provokes death, ecstatic contemplation – that is, the temporary prayer of the spirit outside of the barriers of the senses and matter – does not provoke death. And this is because the soul is not separated, but with its better part becomes immersed in the fires of contemplation. To get me to understand this better, he had me consider that all men, as long as they are in life, have their soul in themselves (be it dead or alive because of sin or justice), but only the great lovers of God reach true contemplation. This serves to demonstrate that the soul preserving existence, as long as it is united to the body – and in this respect, it is the same in all men – has a select part in itself – the soul of the soul, shall we say – which, with a lack of love for God and his Law or even with lukewarmness and venial sins, loses the grace to be able to contemplate and know God and the eternal truths, insofar as a creature can, according to the perfection attained"(Maria Valtorta, *Notebooks 1945-1950*, op. cit., dated 1 May 1948, pp. 479-80).

[367] Few people have had such resistance. John Dee (1527-1608) is one such example: An English mathematician-astrologer-alchemist-angelologist, he was made famous as the protagonist in several comic books and esoteric novels. "In a diary, he wrote that he kept his head buried in a book for 18 hours a day.

Unlimited immolation

A few days later on 10 February, the Voice asked Maria Valtorta to write down her act of offering herself as a victim for the salvation of sinners. She obeyed, writing everything down and adding what she called 'My mystical calendar'[368], detailed and concise at the same time, as if she were telling Father Migliorini of the ugly situation he was in and, on the contrary, what a long spiritual journey she had been on, inviting him therefore to avoid the mistake of comparing her to Dora Barsottelli. Regarding Maria Valtorta's life, this mystical calendar – written also for her spiritual Father and therefore without qualms or ulterior motives – recounts the stages of her spiritual life and the height she had reached. The reader will not find, even here, any emphasis, any improper glorification, or any superfluous detail. This was a constant feature in her, and the apparent expository pompousness of *The Gospel*, therefore has a precise meaning (which we shall see in due course). Among this list of the most significant spiritual events of her life, are those coming up to the difficult days of 1946-7. Then other events took place which made her union with Him even stronger: the martyr accepts and endures an instantaneous immolation, or at least a short, or very short one; Maria Valtorta, like Marthe Robin, Luisa Piccarreta, Josefa Menendez, Alexandrina Da Costa – to name the most famous, but by no means the only ones of the 20th century – accepted a martyrdom which renewed itself day by day until the complete immolation: this is the concept of coredemption; a co-redemption always subject to Christ, yet very real. Obvious, yet not defined, according to the Church; it was rejected, in principle, by the entire protestant world.

The books in the Valtorta household

On another occasion, since she had to write down a list of her books as ordered by the visions, she also wrote down the books she had

---

(Cf. *ttps://www.letturefantastica.com/cacciatori_di_fantasmi_1.html*, consulted 20 October 2018).

[368] Maria Valtorta, *Notebooks 1945-1950*, op. cit., dated 10 February 1946, pp. 194-8., of which she also wrote an abridged version in: Maria Valtorta, *Lettere a Madre Teresa Maria 1*, op. cit., pp. 49-50.

lent out and which had not yet been returned. This can seem a trivial and secondary fact, and it may well have been so in a situation of normal spirituality. However, at the mystical level of Maria Valtorta, and because of what she had to write and describe, it was not so at all. As a matter of fact, Azariah, her Guardian Angel, noticed it and said: "With deceitful reflections, he wanted to make you disobey the order received to list the books you have *with sincerity*. There is nothing to be criticized in your books *or of such a nature as might give rise to talk among those not believing in the supernatural that you are aided culturally in your work*. (This, however, is what is really meant... 12 September 47). But he wanted to frighten you, saying this and that, to lead you ... to leave out *intentionally* some book or other. "To forget is not a sin when it is a *real lapse* of the mind. But *to will to forget*, to carry out obedience as one believes it is humanly useful to do so, is *a sin* [...]. Observe, soul of mine, if you had accepted a mental restriction, one of those Satan proposed to you, and if you had omitted this book of your grandfather's because it might give offense to priests, this other one of your mother's because it was on the Index, that other one of yours because it speaks of God to such a minimal extent that *it certainly cannot explain what you set down on paper*, and all of this to appear holy even in the books you keep as mementoes as you keep the family portraits which you cannot contemplate, sick as you are, but which it would cause you sorrow to destroy because they are the face of your father, of your mother, of your grandparents.... you would have lied, and now *you would not merit* this peace you enjoy and would not see the glorious Gabriel. *You have merited more by this perfect obedience*, which to the superficial may seem to be something ridiculous, *than if you had said a thousand vocal prayers*. This is to tell you the value of the obedience which does not degrade itself with compromises. Always be heroic like this, and peace and light will ever increase in you"[369]. The loyal reply of Maria Valtorta went as far as this. But this event has yet another meaning when we look at it in the long term. Why a detailed list of all her books, even of the ones she had lent to others? The writing of 24

---

[369] Maria Valtorta, *The Book of Azariah*, op. cit., pp. 35-6. Unfortunately, this list has not yet been published. Therefore, we cannot know in detail the books that Maria Valtorta owned and not even if and to what extent they influenced her writings.

March 1946 explains this: Father Migliorini was in Rome for good; and a little over a year remained before she would finish writing *The Gospel*. By now, it was clear to all those who had read the typed pages that the depth of the data was so strong and the claim was so big, that it was necessary to clarify which books of any kind, had Maria been able to consult. It was therefore of paramount importance to know the few books she had at her disposal. The comparison between her library and that of her personal knowledge and the data in her notebooks was, and is, shocking: literally, an abyss! This is the main reason for requesting a book list. The fact that she diligently and accurately wrote everything down was the icing on the cake[370]; but the cake was the book list itself.

The request for Maria's book list is also important for two types of objections: one which was put down in writing and the other which was implicit. The first one implies that everything that Maria Valtorta has ever written was of her own making. This objection was formulated – together with her alleged mental, psychoanalytical and psychic illnesses – by Father Gramaglia in his text[371] which is based however, on a huge lack of data at his disposal[372]. The second

---

[370] A very important icing on the cake for her spiritual life! "God grants these souls a very great desire not to dissatisfy him in anything, however small it may be, or by not being able to make imperfections" (Teresa of Avila, *Il Castello Interiore* [The Interior Castle], 6,3,3, in: *Tutte le opere* [The collected works], op. cit.).

[371] cf. Pier Angelo Gramaglia, *Maria Valtorta. Una moderna manipolazione dei Vangeli*, op. cit.

[372] The non-publication of the library has finally been resolved. Sixty years after her death, the list of Valtorta's books has been published: Maria Valtorta, *I miei libri, le mie letture* [My books, my letters], Centro Editoriale valtortiano, Isola del Liri (FR), 2021. To be as objective as possible, they have published the photos of the sheets of paper on which our writer wrote the list of her books. Excellent, but with the limitation that the list, duly signed by her, dates to 4 October 1943. From page 78, the other books found in the Valtorta house, but not on the list, are also listed. Unfortunately, the complete number cannot be reached accurately. However, the total is this: 277 + 50 (?) + 133 = 460 (?). In fact, there is a collection of books but it not clear if they are counted as 1 or as 50. In any case, 410 or 460 remain insignificant compared to what Maria Valtorta wrote herself. The introduction states: "This publication may

objection claims that the writings were composed by at least three people: Father Migliorini, Father Berti and Father Roschini; the three of them who were all Servants of Mary (and two of them were also theologians and, moreover, founders of the Pontifical University Marianum). That they would have planned the drafting of *The Gospel* with the secret help of a few brothers and talented seminarians, passing them off as the writings of Maria, eternally in agony, in order to make money for the Order. This theory, not serious and far from reality, only needs some terrorist and/or extra-terrestrial plot to be totally humorous. So, the book list does exist, even though it has mysteriously not been made public yet; however, some books have been mentioned. The school books must be eliminated, obviously, despite the influence they had on shaping the environment in which Maria Valtorta lived, but they are not relevant with regard to the data she would need to write *The Gospel* or with regard to her spiritual choices. We must also ignore the books of her mother Iside, a French teacher. So very few are left. In this context, we must take into account another unpleasant event, told by Marta Diciotti: "When Maria became bedridden, or to be more precise, became infirm, the books were locked away by her mother, who jealously kept the keys to herself, together with all the other keys to wardrobes and drawers, which she had in a bunch that she carried around in one of those large pockets that 19th-century old ladies used to have under their skirt. And there was no access to the library. [...] She had various books by D'Annunzio: the *Laudi,* I think, *The Flame of Life, Notturno*... maybe, or am I mistaken in naming these titles? I think that she liked that author. [...] I know that she also had some Japanese books, translated ones, of course. And I know that she admired them, and that she attributed great virtues to them, which she may have learnt

---

have integrated and updated re-editions if other information on books and readings emerges from the existing documentation in the Valtortian archive". It should be emphasized that there are no texts on theology, or on exegesis, or even on scientific religious archeology. She writes: "The existing books in my library belong to three generations: my grandfather, my parents, and my own, which consist of in part, some pleasant literature, all the lives of the Saints or other books of piety and religious formation" (p. 39). The obvious conclusion is that between the texts written by Maria Valtorta and those in her family library, there is no "apparent" relationship.

about or imagined, by means of these books. [...] I gave her two or three books about these people of the Rising Sun myself. When it came to gifts for her, I also thought of a book, from time to time, because I knew that if she liked it, it would have been the most appreciated gift. Those small volumes that had come into the house from 1935 onwards, that is, since my arrival here, we tried not to put on that famous shelf from which they would have never come out, thanks to the strict surveillance of Signora Iside. If we remembered, we tried to keep them to one side and away from her, who would have buried them on those shelves, making them, as inaccessible as the others. This was another of her fixations, of her manias: keeping everything under lock and key, keeping everything under control"[373].

Maria Valtorta would read all sorts of things and had her own tastes. We can smile at the idea of her reading about the valor and toughness of Japanese samurai, yet they may also have been a source of inspiration for a heroically religious life. A very interesting thing is the keys that her mother Iside carried always with her, and that small shelf which was always locked.

Here are references to some sources in which Maria Valtorta talks about the books she had read: "When you gave me that book on the Holy Shroud, Father..."[374]; "My Master gave me a powerful push through a book. Do not be scandalised, Father. It was a book on the Index of Forbidden Books: *The Saint* by Fogazzaro"[375]; "I once read in a book by a jurist stating that criminals always repeat their crimes using the same method..."[376]; "On 28 January 1925, a big package arrived with the books requested and a volume added to it by my dear former school friend, which was a collection of Gospel commentaries intended for young people. I think it was by a priest, Father Baudernom, if I remember correctly"[377]; "And here I was more successful than subdeacon Girard! After two years of shots,

---

[373] Albo Centoni, *Una vita con Maria Valtorta. Testimonianze di Marta Diciotti*, op. cit., pp. 138-9.

[374] Maria Valtorta, *Autobiography*, op. cit., p. 163.

[375] ibid., p. 216

[376] ibid., p. 224.

[377] ibid., p. 253. Perhaps it is Léopold Beaudenom, *Meditazioni sul Vangelo* [Meditations on the Gospel], four volumes, Libreria Editrice Fiorentina, Firenze 1943.

including double ones of morphine, I prohibited them for myself and I felt *no craving.*"³⁷⁸; "I had to prepare the lessons on the booklets by A.C. and on the *Primer on Christianity and Christian Moral* by Olgiati"³⁷⁹; "I repeat: *never sermons* of any kind. *Never religion classes* of any kind. *Catholic Action*, one course attended at irregular intervals, the Leaders' School by Fr. Cresi in 1931 at the Mantellate Sisters Convent of Viareggio. But his mode of expression was so difficult that I understand nothing and told him so frankly as well. None of us understood and no one wanted to confess it to him. I, who have always loved sincerity, did say so. I have no books on religion, except for the two *Primers* by Olgiati and the *Catechism* (by St. Pius X). The works on the history of churches and religions were stolen by someone. I have *The Soul of the Apostolate* by Father Chautard, which the Diocesan Leaders had us acquire and which I have never been able to read because it makes me fall asleep. Religious books: the Gospels and *The Imitation of Christ*. I have read the former for decades. The latter is conserved as a memento of my Mother Superior. Gospel commentaries: a few pages by Giulio Salvadori, and that's all. No revelations. No meditations. Before Jesus made me His instrumentl, I carried out my meditations on my own, as my heart suggested them to me. Without texts or outlines on the Gospels or on the life of St. Thérèse of Lisieux, (*Story of a Soul*) or Sister B. Consolata Ferrero³⁸⁰

---

[378] Maria Valtorta, *Autobiography*, op. cit., p. 379. These are*:* Myriam de G., *Vingt-deux ans de martyre, Biographie, Lettres, Sermons* [Twenty-two years of martyrdom, Biographies, Letters and Sermons] *(1874-1921),* Librairie Catholique Emmanuel Vitte, Lyon 1927; Myriam de G., *Ventidue anni di martirio* [Twenty-two years of martyrdom], Edizioni Carroccio, Milano 1934. This text, although crowned by the Académie Française, is now almost forgotten and therefore unknown.

[379] *Maria Valtorta, Autobiography,* op. cit., Appendix, p. 434. These are: Francesco Olgiati, *Sillabario del Cristianesimo* [The Syllabary of Christianity], Vita e Pensiero, Milano 1924 (This text of dogmatic catechesis, made for the female youth of *Catholic Action*, is still being sold, obviously in updated editions) and Francesco Olgiati, *Il sillabario della morale cristiana* [The syllabary of Christian morality], Vita e Pensiero, Milano 1924.

[380] cf. Benigna Consolata Ferrero, *Vademecum proposto alle anime religiose* [The Counsellor proposed to religious souls], Scuola Tipografica della Divina provvidenza, Como 1917. It is a pocket booklet of the inner phrases received by this pious woman. It received the imprimatur of the bishop of

(*Vademecum proposed to religious souls*), or on anything which had struck me, perhaps even a flower or a star, or a thunderbolt, or a word I had heard... My poor meditations of that time are still visible! A few lives of saints: Bernadette, Don Bosco, St. Thérèse of the Child Jesus, St. Francis of Assisi; a few biographies of good people: Mattei, Agostini, Moscati, St Pius X, and so on. Since I have been serving Jesus as an instrument, I have no longer been reading anything. Since 20 March 1946, Father Migliorini has had the list of books I own or have owned."[381]

The already mentioned John van Ruysbroeck (1293-1381), a Flemish priest and mystic, a Blessed, called *Doctor Admirable*, is a recurring name in Maria Valtorta. His work *Nozze Spirituali* [Spiritual Wedding] which she had, was almost certainly the source of other citations, some of which were left anonymous[382]. "I love the Belgian mystic very much because I really understand him..."[383]; "When speaking of the gift of piety, my Ruysbroeck in his chapter on the gifts of the Holy Spirit says..."[384]; "Ruysbroeck is quite right in saying: 'The soul that has been in the presence of Christ feels sweetness, and from this sweetness arises a chaste enjoyment, which is the embrace of divine love'"[385].

During the drafting of the most important texts of Maria Valtorta, we find also these references: "The other day, I was reading in the booklet that You sent to Marta, a passage of the Meditations on the '*Little Way of St. Thérèse*' and to be precise, the one titled: '*All for the souls and nothing for me*', all references are unknown"[386]; the missal; the

---

Como on 1 October 1917. The radical nature of this writing resonates in Valtortia's life and work.

[381] *Maria Valtorta, Autobiography,* op. cit., p. 407. The description of the studies done — and also of those that had been discontinued — and the list of the books she owned are reported in an appendix that Maria Valtorta added after 20 March 1946 (cf. ibid., p. 435).

[382] ibid., Footnote p. 59.

[383] ibid., p. 119.

[384] ibid., p. 395.

[385] ibid., p. 258.

[386] Maria Valtorta, *Lettere a Madre Teresa Maria 1*, op. cit., p. 300. This is the letter dated 28 October 1946.

Holy Bible[387]. From 1949 there are also: *Invito all'Amore, scritti di Suor M. Josefa Menendez* [Way of Divine Love, writings by Sister M. Josefa Menendez], and *Le Rivelazioni* [Revelations] of A.C. Hemmerich (Anne Catherine Emmerich)[388]. Not many, although very significant and typical of her time. However, five of them are predominant and contributed to shaping Maria Valtorta's personal spirituality. (1) *The Bible,* translated into Italian and with brief notes by Father Eusebio Tintori, OFM. (2) *Story of a Soul,* by St. Thérèse of Child Jesus, Doctor of the Church. (3) *The Imitation of Christ* by Thomas à Kempis, or by an anonymous medieval. (4) *Spiritual Wedding* by Blessed John van Ruysbroeck. (5) *Vademecum proposed to religious souls* by Sister Benigna Consolata Ferrero. We must conclude, once more, that between the library in the Valtorta's house and what she wrote, there is such a huge abyss that can only be passed with a direct intervention by God.

The great and small clergy of Viareggio

Father Migliorini was the first and true spiritual director of Maria Valtorta and, after him there were none, at least not at his level. His forced transfer to Rome and the simultaneous human break-up caused unbelievable discomfort to Maria. To understand what really happened and why Father Migliorini's superiors came to the decision to send him to Rome for good, with the order to never come back to Viareggio, we need to say something that will explain, in part, what happened.

In that terrible post-war period, the Archbishop of Lucca was Msgr. Antonio Torrini[389]. The situation in Italy in general, and in

---

[387] Maria Valtorta, *The Book of Azariah*, op. cit., p. 10. This is the translation of E. Tintori O.F.M., Pia Società San Paolo, 1935. [Not in the English edition]

[388] Maria Valtorta, *The Little Notebooks*, dated 28 January 1949, op. cit., pp. 186-8.

[389] Msgr. Antonio Torrini (Pomino, 30 August 1878 – Lucca, 20 January 1973) was a Bishop from 1928 until 1958, when he was given Msgr. Enrico Bartoletti as coadjutor. He was a great Marian devotee who twice consecrated the city of Lucca to the Sacred Heart (1938, 1943) and was not afraid to oppose the political regime in power at that time. So he was neither lukewarm nor lacking in devotions.

Lucca and its province in particular, was a very confrontational one: anarchism, communism, and a fierce anticlericalism were widespread; the Church and the clergy were accused of all sorts of evil and hypocrisy. Led by Togliatti, the communist party had chosen the policy of Gramsci: power would be obtained by means of culture, not by a coup as was more frequent in other countries. Although ingenious in its essential falsehood, the communist propaganda managed to unite under the same category of 'fascist', 'fascism', 'Nazi-fascism' anyone who seriously opposed it and all those who for any reasons spoke or declared themselves anticommunist. The trap smeared people who had nothing to do with those ideologies and who had come out of the war defeated[390], and were, as communism itself, a relic of the past. Many Catholics became obsessed with trying to avoid being put in that category at all costs[391]. But Lucca[392], the hometown of St. Gemma Galgani and St. Zita, and Viareggio with its St. Curatino (St. Antonio Maria Pucci, 1819-1892), among the neighboring Massa, Carrara, Pisa, and Livorno, were an exception and endured even the most slanderous insults. Anyway, the fear of an atheistic and anticlerical tyranny was very strong. Along with the

---

[390] Those who lived through those years know it very well. But suffice it to say that even John Ronald Reuel Tolkien, with his fantasy novels (primarily *The Lord of the Rings* which started the genre), at the beginning of the Italian publications of his books, was segregated into those categories.

[391] Msgr. Cristoforo Arduino Terzi was the bishop of Massa and Carrara (the diocese at the time was called Apuania) from 1934 to 1945. He had to be moved for the sole reason of being displaced in Lunigiana as ordered by the occupying troops, and for not contesting as the Communists and anarchists of the time demanded. Certainly, he was not a fascist in the proper sense, but he was considered by the winners to have been at least a crypto-fascist, and the Holy See replaced him with Msgr. Carlo Maria Boiardi (bishop from 1946 to 1970) who, as a young priest, had helped Catholic partisans in his parish of Borgotaro in the province of Piacenza.

[392] "Lucca is a healthy environment, but also has a closed religious' tradition. Thus Prof. Don Lenzi (historian of the Church of Lucca) defines Lucca's religiosity: "very devotional, individualistic, scarcely liturgical, founded on religious sentiment, rather than on the knowledge of the data of the revelation". The clergy, pastorally active and generous, is culturally firm, unaware of the most recent developments in biblical and theological sciences". *http://www.diocesilucca.it/documenti/Bartoletti_icle_Mons_Gianneschi.pdf*, consulted 16 December 2015.

accusation of fascism, there was also the older accusation of religious fanaticism, typical of whoever decidedly opposed the anticlericalism of the intellectual stars: socialists, communists or liberals. This accusation was also greatly feared.

To all this must be added a strictly and subtly inter-ecclesial motive. The 'mystical question'[393] debated at academic and world level, and ended in the early 1930s, had not yet fully entered in the life of the Church. There were still a lot of clergymen who acted based on 'mystical coordinates', which were in fact antiquated. We must wait until the Second Vatican Council, celebrated between 1963-1965, to really shake things up, although not even that was enough. In the past, the 'mystical question' had divided the two ways of praying: the ordinary and the extraordinary (or mystical). The ordinary way was for everyone; it consisted of various devotions, sacraments and penitence; it consisted of widespread vigils and fasts, catechesis, etc. It was called the ordinary or ascetic way[394]. The seminaries brought up a clergy with this mentality and consequently, no one looked at this way from a different perspective. Anything that touched on paramystic or on tangible mystics was prejudicially seen as something suspicious. Apparently, the debate ended around the 1930s, but it was only with the Second Vatican Council that the new and true vision really circulated: the universal call to sanctity of the *Lumen Gentium*[395] called everyone to a mystical life. Freedom and Grace worked together for the good of the individual. A connection between the individual and the Grace of God would have done the

---

[393] cf. Giuseppe Paparone O.P., *La teologia mistica in Padre Garrigou-Lagrange* [Mystical theology in Father Garrigou-Lagrange], in "*Sacra Doctrina: monografie*" [Sacred Doctrines: monographs], Edizioni Studio Domenicano, Bologna 3-4 May-August 1999, pp. 11-53.

[394] Subtly important for their dissemination were the Spiritual Exercises of Saint Ignatius of Loyola. The Jesuits stressed its ascetic value, distrusting, like everyone else, mysticism. So, when they held the Exercises for six or ten days, they only held the first week of the four weeks present in the booklet, omitting the other three weeks. The ascetic compression was thus highlighted against the mystical value, which instead is the real keystone of this type of spiritual exercises.

[395] cf. Dogmatic Constitution *Lumen Gentium [A Lght for all Nations]*, n. 40.

rest. Charisms, therefore, did not constitute a problem any longer[396]. If there were any, they only had to be acknowledged. The problem was how to discern carefully. Hence, during the late mid-1940s, the normal feeling of priests and bishops was still the same. This also explains the attitude of Msgr. Antonio Torrini towards Maria Valtorta. Marta Diciotti described the episode: "She ardently wished to speak to the Archbishop of Lucca, Msgr. Torrini, on his post-war pastoral visit to this town, and to the parish church of San Paolino. I do not recall the exact year, but no doubt it was between 1945 and 1949, during his pastoral visit in Viareggio… 'The Archbishop is coming and … if you would be so kind as to bring him here… Oh, I would love to talk to him! Yes, I would like to talk to him. Maybe if he talked to me… we could clarify many situations, and things could even change'. […] Father Rocchiccioli, then, with a quiet mind, found it natural to tell his bishop: 'Look, Your Excellency, there is a parishioner… so and so…' and he gave a few explanations. The Archbishop gave no reply, as if he had not even heard what his prior had said. The latter, the following day, naturally came back on the subject and made the same request to his superior, who curtly replied: 'I do not go to anyone and do not do anything. And, seeing as you insist, instead of leaving tomorrow morning, I am going to leave tonight. And tell that person who would like to speak to me, that she should not create fanaticism around her because if there is fanaticism, there will be sanctions. Serious sanctions.' You can imagine how poor Father Rocchiccioli felt on hearing that reply… Discouraged, disappointed, downcast, he told poor Maria… (She) looked up and said: 'Fine! If up until now a stranger or a person I barely know has been able to come into my house, starting from today they will no longer be able to enter. And also, very few among those I know and I am friendly with, will be able to come'"[397].

---

[396] The birth of the most diverse ecclesiastical movements during the post-council is proof of this.

[397] Albo Centoni, *Una vita con Maria Valtorta. Testimonianze di Marta Diciotti*, op. cit., pp. 55, 56. A complaint from the Bishop from two or three years before must be added here: his attending physician, Dr. Nieri confided directly to Maria: "Monsignor Bishop is shocked to have been the last to know, and to have known second-hand, while from the beginning he should have been made aware as Head of the Diocese. And he

So there was a total and prejudiced closure on the part of Msgr. Torrini, without the possibility of appeal; or at least, it appeared so because there are some people who give different views. Among these, Mother Teresa Maria said: "Someone told me that they heard from a priest that Msgr. Torrini reads the 'Dictations' and he likes them! [...] Does this mean there is hope?"[398] But a few months later someone told Maria Valtorta: "His Eexcellency the Archbishop said that they are diabolical writings because he has compared them with the words of the Church and they 'do not conform' (?)"[399]. However, sometime later, Maria Valtorta received this information from Father Migliorini: "As for the Archbishop of Lucca, I can tell you that if he had found even one single mistake, he would have put it in the diocesan Bulletin. If he has not done that, it is because he has realized that the content is good. I also know that in the Seminary of Lucca, there were many discussions about some files handed over by the Archbishop, but I have never heard that they were considered heretical. Quite the opposite!"[400] The most obvious conclusion seems to be that the Archbishop could not believe that God gave someone that special charism. The fear to even seriously consider the problem put to him by his loyal assistant, Father Rocchiccioli, had completely overwhelmed him. Rationalists and devotionalism allied, had won once again.

Father Migliorini between mystic and paramystic

There is so much to say about Father Migliorini due to his relationship with Maria Valtorta. To sum it up, we can write that what

---

disapproves of the spread of these supernatural writings without approval" (Maria Valtorta, *Lettere a Padre Migliorini*, op. cit., p. 114). This error made by Father Migliorini (but not by Maria Valtorta who was ordered to keep silent and to hide) in his communications to Msgr. Torrini may have been one of the causes of the bishop's closure towards her.

[398] Maria Valtorta, *Lettere a Madre Teresa Maria 1*, op cit., p. 56. This is the letter dated 5 February 1946.

[399] ibid., p. 156. This is the letter written by Maria Valtorta and dated 10 June 1946.

[400] ibid., p. 181. This is the letter from 21 June 1946.

had started very well, ended in a very tragic way[401], generating such a misunderstanding that only Paradise will be able to resolve. In comparison, of course, there is the extreme difference between the spiritual guidance of Father Germano for St. Gemma Galgani[402]. As strong and precise as Father Germano was, Father Migliorini was in comparison, shallow and with no tactics. The feeling of spiritual superficiality is obvious: it already showed in the comparison with Fr. Berti. After all, his life as a passionate and active missionary does not show him as having a profound knowledge of mystical life with charismatic gifts, as with Maria Valtorta. On the contrary, the impression we have in light of the events we know is that of a good person of goodwill, but who did not have a global vision or the depth

---

[401] Maria described her detachment from Father Migliorini in many passages. Among them: "Father Migliorini no longer understands me ..." (Maria Valtorta, *Notebooks 1945-1950*, op. cit., dated 20 April 1946, p. 254); "And you, Romualdo, have not been a Father or Director for my instrument [Valtorta], but a *stepfather and tempter* [...] You – a Father for Maria? No. You were. Soon after, very soon, Satan ensnared your paternity and altered it. He changed it from spiritual into material - you became good only at earthly things. Then, with Satan tightening his cords around you, you also stopped being paternal even to the creature's flesh, and man aged to become just sour, harsh and biting. You – a Director? No. I had to rectify the rudder and sail of this poor soul because your conduct was a north wind changing its course and causing it to crash into the rocks of certain forms of knowledge and disappointments which I wanted to spare her so as not to cause scandal for this child who is little John. This child who had a steadfast faith that every Priest was another Christ. Another Christ! If I had been like that, I truly would not have attracted to Myself even the meek Andrew and the loving John! If I had been as you are, I truly would not have attracted to Myself children or sinners or Gentiles. And doesn't it scald you like a burn to tell yourself, 'I *destroyed the work of my Lord,* which had brought the Belfantis back to the Church and the Priesthood?' Peter at least wept over the scandal he had caused the night I was captured, to the point of forming creases into his cheeks. But you!" (ibid., dated 31 October 1947, pp. 435-6).

[402] cf. For example Maurizio Iandolo, *La direzione spirituale e l'esperienza mistica: il caso di santa Gemma Galgani e dei suoi direttori spirituali* [The spiritual direction and the mystical experience: the case of Saint Gemma Galgani and her spiritual directors], Facoltà Teologica dell'Italia Centrale, Firenze 2015 (doctoral dissertation).

or height of what was going on, and of the importance of what he had to handle. The result was chaos, and in the end, a total break. To reply in advance to the doubt that could arise after reading some of Jesus' dictations on Father Migliorini, it must be noted that in *Notebooks 1943*, on 26 November, Jesus dictated: *"And in truth I tell you that Father Romualdo [Migliorini] is really a 'son' for my Mother, and my Mother is really a 'mother' for him. Not all his companions are like him under the clothing, which makes them equal. It is the heart that is different. And it is the heart that is everything.* In his, there is no malice; there is no pride; there is no hardness; there is no humanity involving the senses and the mind. As he laid aside the ordinary clothing of men to take on sacred garb, so he has stripped himself of humanity to become exclusively the servant of his Lord, the bearer of Christ, the light and voice of God and of my Mother and his"[403]. On 21 January 1946, in a dictation full of elements for holy discernment, Jesus had praise for him and then a warning: "In you, immortal child, there must not be pain because I instruct you on something. You belong to my array: the array of those lacking malice who at heart are defenceless against the crafty world and Satan, extremely crafty in his works. It is a glory. But it is also a continuous danger. And I give special help to these defenceless ones precisely because they are such, so that they will not be deceived by lying appearances. (…) Romualdo, be careful with the multicolored glistening which dissolves into mist! I always leave light and concrete, orderly, clear elements. Watch out for the false saints who are more injurious to My triumph than all the open sinners. The holy supernatural exists. I inspire it. It should be accepted and believed. But let every jar upon which there is written 'Oil of Supernatural Wisdom' not be accepted at first sight – or every closed book upon which there is written 'God is here'. Be sure that a hellish stench does not emerge from the former, and heretical formulas do not emerge from the latter"[404]. On 23 February Father Migliorini was warned again: "Romualdo, why do you reproach Me for not having been clearer? And what more did you want? Don't you know that I am Charity? Have you still not felt the *infinity* of this love, which is

---

[403] Maria Valtorta, *Notebooks 1943*, op. cit., dated 26 November p. 508;
[404] Maria Valtorta, *Notebooks 1945-1950*, op. cit., 21 January 1946, pp. 178, 180.

my essence and which, by paternally supporting its creatures' wishes and protecting some imprudent acts by them which are not real sins [...] for the constant purpose of making the soul a masterpiece, becomes everything to everyone, if only it can help, console and save?"[405]. At the end of the same dictation, the cause of the problems is revealed: "And, besides.... How can you say I didn't advise you concerning Dora? I said, 'Father *should limit himself* to performing the functions of his ministry, and nothing more' -that is, Confession and Communion, for you cannot refuse to administer them to a Catholic who is not excommunicated. I said, 'Go to the Bishop.' I definitely said so! If the Parish Priest was failing in his duty towards a tormented soul, it was right and proper for there to be someone to force him to concern himself with the matter. And to obtain this, someone was needed who would speak. And what's wrong with that? I said, 'Father should greatly insist on Confession and the Eucharist,' for the more she feeds on it, the better it will be for her soul, which on its own has less resistance than seaweed in a ditch. But I also said, 'Father should be *very* vigilant regarding pride and deceit.' A *very* revealing sign. But I also said, 'Father should leave everything and concern himself only with Maria and the dictations.' And I permitted the disturbing demonic apparitions on 30 December and thereafter. And I provided the tremendous dictations on Satan, the clear dictations on the differences between true mystics and doubtful or completely false mystics"[406]. So, Father Romualdo was at first praised for his purity of intentions and his 'spiritual childhood', and then he was warned with a series of teachings. But in the end, he was confused by the experiences with several charismatic people and for doing something so reckless to cause his dramatic transfer[407] to Rome and a void in so many people who trusted him. We could argue that it was a 'classic' example of successful temptation. St Ignatius, in the rules for the discernment of souls of his *Spiritual Exercises*, writes: "It

---

[405] ibid., 23 February 1946, p. 213.

[406] ibid., p. 215.

[407] The reality is the fact that he was literally chased away and deprived of his whole apostolate in Versilia. The Curia of Lucca and the superiors of the Order joined forces, and for his imprudence that caused disturbances in the Diocese, he was expelled with the obligatory command to never set foot in Viareggio again.

is typical of the evil angel, who turns into *sub angelo lucis*, to enter with a devoted soul and to exit with himself; that is, to insert good and holy thoughts, consistent with that person, and then, little by little, to cause their exit, dragging the soul in his occult imposture and perverse intentions"[408]. Ribadeneira, one of the early companions of St. Ignatius', mentioning the founder's thought, comments as follows: He offers "to the pious things that apparently look godly; and he does not enter all of a sudden and impetuously, but little by little, treading carefully, until he wins the will over, and finally he jumps into the souls, taking full possession of them"[409]. Father Migliorini probably did not know the *Exercises* by St Ignatius. In any case as a Servite, he was not supposed to know them, or to put them into practice, or to live up to them. He certainly did not have them as the measure of his behaving cautiously. Having said that, to put it simply, he should only have practiced humility, charity and caution to do everything right. Unfortunately, the opposite happened; the supernatural warning: 'Father should beware of pride and falsehood' which fell on deaf ears, and Father Migliorini ended up ruining himself, and causing many others terrible pain and disappointment.

Why is Father Migliorini in Rome?

The material causes, the real motives were, in fact, two. The first was the fact that Father Migliorini had to discern the mystical charism of both Maria Valtorta and Dora Barsottelli[410]. In this pitiful story –

---

[408] Ignazio di Loyola, *Esercizi Spirituali. Ricerca sulle fonti*, op. cit., p. 413.

[409] ibid.

[410] The presence of Dora Barsotelli di Camaiore (nothing more is known) and her actions greatly upset and embroiled Maria Valtorta, not only the person involved, but also for the things she said, and for her excessive interest in Father Migliorini (cf. Maria Valtorta, *Notebooks 1945-1950*, op. cit., dated 18 April 1946, p. 250; Maria Valtorta, *Lettere a Padre Migliorini* [Letters to Father Migliorini], op. cit., p. 99). A whole dictation was dedicated to Dora Barsottelli of Camaiore (LU) and how she was different to Maria Valtorta (cf. Maria Valtorta, *Notebooks 1945-1950*, op. cit., 19 December 1945, pp. 124-9. In the beginning, both had the calling, albeit differently; then the Enemy and the environment led Dora (whom Maria Valtorta did not believe much, believing her to be deceiving and misleading to others) to deviate, confuse gifts and inventions. An emblematic phrase

confused and forgotten by now – entered also with their own contradictions, Sister Maria Gabriella (Emma Federici), the Mother Superior of the Poor Daughters of the Holy Stigmata of St. Francis (known as the Stigmatines) of Camaiore, and Sister Maria Rosa Gatti, herself a Stigmatine[411]. Maria and Dora knew each other, and the latter had sometimes visited the former[412], even though Maria had received a precise order from Heaven: "You must neither get to know that woman, nor go near her"[413]. The characteristics of the two women were in fact very different, as were their attitudes. Maria Valtorta was reserved, almost a recluse, frank, with a 'clear, masculine, St. Catherine-like'[414] style, and with the order from Heaven to remain completely anonymous[415]. Whereas Dora Barsottelli was available to everyone, or at least to many[416]. But there

---

can be identified: "Well then, pray for her who will have *so much* to suffer, *so very much*, poor Dora! Support her. She is a sister. *May she not be lost! May having been called not be harmful to her!*" (ibid., p. 129).

[411] cf. Maria Valtorta, *Lettere a Padre Migliorini*, op. cit., pp. 124-5.

[412] ibid., p. 99.

[413] ibid., pp. 131-2.

[414] ibid., p. 132. This is how Maria Valtorta defines herself in a letter to Father Migliorini.

[415] It is explained in the dictation of 18 July 1943: "In regard to Father, I am very, very pleased that he should use my words for himself, for his soul, for his preaching, for the guidance and comfort of other souls, whether or not they are priests. But he must not reveal their source for the time being" (Maria Valtorta, *Notebooks 1943* op. cit., 18 July, p. 176). And in the dictation of 24 September 1944, the Voice rewrites what has already been said on the subject: "No one should know you as a writer of my thought, except for two or three privileged persons ... Later, when I will [reveal it] and no one can harm you anymore, the name of the little voice will be known. By then, you will be where human pettiness cannot arrive and where human wickedness cannot act" (Maria Valtorta, *Notebooks 1944*, op. cit., 24 September, p. 573).

[416] Here is an example reported by Maria in the letter dated 20 April 1946 written to Father Migliorini: "That day, Eroma Antonini had come to my house to tell me that the 'voice' [Dora Barsottelli] was speaking to the Parish, in the presence of all the Mencarini family and other people, about me to the point of sending me a greeting and by giving out my address etc., etc." (Maria Valtorta, *Lettere a Padre Migliorini,* op. cit., p. 135).

was something that annoyed the clergy and Father Migliorini's superiors: the messages of the two women, real or alleged, were circulating freely and widely among people[417]. However, in the case of Maria Valtorta, this happened due to the private initiative of Father Migliorini's himself[418], contrary to the orders of the authors of the messages, and is therefore responsible for very serious abuse. In the case of Dora Barsottelli, it was the normal and desired course of action. And there was a lingering suspicion regarding Father Migliorini, described as follows: "He became increasingly excited about those writings (by Maria Valtorta) to the point that he recklessly started distributing them in typed booklets… which would later acquire the name 'birdseed'. It also appears that Fr. Migliorini boasted about the nature of 'divine revelation' in these pages, which, detached from the context of the whole works, could be provocative in their originality"[419]. When the diffusion of the writings, the reputation that surrounded them, and the rumors about the consultations (with regard to Barsottelli only) became annoying and dangerous at the risk of fanaticism, to use the words used by Msgr. Torrini – for the good name of the Diocese and the Servite Order, Father Romualdo's superiors, in agreement with the Bishop of Lucca, sent him away and forced him to move to Rome[420] with the order of

---

[417] cf. ibid., pp. 112-4, letter dated 11 April 1946, from Maria Valtorta to Father Migliorini, who had already been in Rome for some days.

[418] Several times, Jesus asked for silence and non-diffusion (cf. Maria Valtorta, *Notbooks 1943*, op. cit., 13 August, p. 234ff.).

[419] *L'Opera di Maria Valtorta e la Chiesa* [The Works of Maria Valtorta and the Church], "Bollettino Valtortiano" op. cit., n. 23 – January-June 1981, p. 90. This article is not signed but it can be deduced that it was written by Dr. Emilio Pisani, editor-in-chief of the newsletter. Italics are ours.

[420] In the letter written on 6 April 1949, Maria wrote to Mother Teresa Maria: "F.M. [Father Migliorini] has been under investigation by the H.O. [Holy Office] for three years due to M. Gabriella and Dora Barsottelli from Pieve di Camaiore who were directed by him against the advice of God…" (Maria Valtorta, *Lettere a Madre Teresa Maria 2*, Centro Editoriale Valtortiano, Isola del Liri (FR) 2012, p. 193). On 1 July 1946, she wrote: "F. M. was punished for having 'exalted and exalting souls' and namely for having thrown himself with his full weight into the Dora Barsottelli case. I said it was dangerous! Yes!!! The remedy, or at least an improvement for me and the Work, would be that he hands over all control to others, because

residing there and to never go back to Viareggio, not even for holidays[421]. So from 17 March 1946, Maria Valtorta was left alone and forsaken. To a series of questions she put in a letter to Father Romualdo to which he replied that: "What was required of me did not include our writings"[422]; "I tread carefully before handing over a page"[423]; "I have been allowed to communicate with you, to go on writing and to handle these writings"[424]. In the meantime, he apologized: "I know I am inept and good for nothing. I am only sorry for having caused pain"[425]. And he ended with a declaration of cautious behavior: "I would like to assure you that from now on I will act with caution"[426]. Maria Valtorta had by then a belief from which she could not deviate, caused by his behavior and by that of the man who substituted him in the handling of her writings, namely, Father Berti: "The person who makes my case seem unreliable is he, who has always believed all the false cases"[427]. About a month later, Father Migliorini tried to patch things up, although it is not typical of the clergy to make a U-turn, except for macroscopic mistakes (as in the case of the Blessed Rosmini Serbati[428] as a prime example). Maria

---

it is he who makes my case unreliable and he is the one who has always believed in all false cases" (Maria Valtorta, *Lettere a Madre Teresa Maria 1*, op. cit., p. 189).

[421] "Father [Migliorini] came back this morning at 4 and came to me at 9. He returned only to leave again definitively. He will leave early in the week, as soon as possible. I still do not know the extremes that caused this order which deprives me, at the end of my life, of the Priest who knows me as a soul and as a spokesperson" (Maria Valtorta, *Lettere a Madre Teresa Maria 1*, op. cit., p. 84. A letter from Maria dated 17 March 1946).

[422] ibid., p. 116.

[423] ibid.

[424] ibid., p. 117.

[425] ibid.

[426] ibid., pp. 116-8. The letter of 15 April 1946. It is interesting how terms – inept and good for nothing – are used that are not spiritual, but psychological or voluntary. Perhaps he would have needed a greater spiritual sensitivity, which would have allowed him see everything in the light of humility, so as not to act imprudently.

[427] Maria Valtorta, *Lettere a Madre Teresa Maria 1*, op. cit., p. 188.

[428] "Blessed Antonio Rosmini was a profound thinker – 'one of the six or seven great intellectuals of humanity' according to Manzoni – and author of

Valtorta wrote: "F.M. (Father Migliorini) has written, sending requests for all the places where he has worked. But I immediately replied saying that it *would have been* more appropriate if the request had come from others rather than from him[429]. And I waited for his reply before handing it over to the respective Superiors. There is nothing for you, since F.M. is already in possession of your letter of certification. He wants to submit all the documents requested, containing declarations on 'how he preached, *directed, advised, if he ever used words that might incite disobedience, rebellion, exaltation, or if he instilled religious ideas that were not strictly in accordance with religious perfection, or with the evangelical doctrine of the Holy Mother Church*'. And, 'for how long he had been coming into the community, how often and in what way (through exercises, retreats, sermons, confessions, etc.), what they thought of his ministry, what good or evil he brought, and how had he behaved with the nuns'. Poor Father!"[430]. Maria Valtorta was unable, in any case, to prevent the tragedy of loneliness, which led her to write in mid-June: "Distressed, embittered, and filled with doubt about everything and everyone, and even the blessed Voice, because of the behavior of certain men regarding the Work, I felt determined to offer resistance to what I had come to think was a diabolical trick"[431]. Jesus then tried to console her, but men attacked her again: on 12 July 1946, she was told that the Father General of

---

numerous works, the complete edition of which, edited by Città Nuova, has now reached 44 volumes, but will see about eighty when it is finished… a further judgment expressed by the Holy Office. It has judged 40 propositions taken from Rosmini's works as erroneous and, with the Post obitum decree (of 1887, published only on 7 July 1888) condemns them. Only on 1 July 2001 – 146th anniversary of the death of Antonio Rosmini – did the 'Note' of the Congregation for the Doctrine of the Faith come out, signed by the then Prefect Cardinal Joseph Ratzinger, which rehabilitated these forty propositions" (in: *http://www.rosmini.it/Objects/Pagina.asp?ID=197*, consulted 10 October 2018).

[429] Noteworthy is Maria Valtorta's ability to give prudential advice.
[430] Maria Valtorta, *Lettere a Madre Teresa Maria 1*, op. cit., p. 99, Letter dated 17 April 1946.
[431] Maria Valtorta, *Notebooks 1945-1950*, op. cit., 17 June 1946, p. 272.

the Servite Order of Mary had given the order to stop taking the Eucharist to her[432].

The situation with Father Migliorini precipitated in a horrible way: Maria Valtorta discovered that he was a cheat, a liar; a person who had damaged her[433] and her Work, which at the time was still being drafted. Her doubts about him became very strong and so did the insinuations that had been weighing on her heart. Mother Teresa Maria was her spiritual confidante, practically a close advisor to whom she confided heart-to-heart about an atrocious doubt: "Mother... I cannot be silent any longer about a thought which has been tormenting me for months, seeing all this... condescension, indulgence and more in F.M. (Father Migliorini) towards Miss Federici and her company: that he has disrespected her and therefore it suits him to be overindulgent; that he, in short, is afraid that she may speak and say something against F.M. You know... so harsh with me and so... soft with her!!! God have mercy of us all!"[434]

The pieces left behind

Time went by slowly and the relationship between the two improved until it was almost calm again, though it never went back to what is was at the beginning. Some letters describe various episodes of life in Viareggio and Maria's wish to obtain the *imprimatur* of the Holy See. Father Migliorini had helped also financially because the two members of the Valtorta household – Maria herself and Marta Diciotti – lived exclusively on the rent of the small upper part

---

[432] Maria Valtorta knew pain and suffering in very serious ways and yet here she added: "I almost die of it" (ibid., p. 274). It is difficult to understand the attitude of the Servite Order of Mary, who threw out the baby out with the bath water, without any discernment and without distinction of the true 'culprit', who was Father Migliorini and not Maria Valtorta.

[433] cf. Maria Valtorta, *Lettere a Madre Teresa Maria 1*, op. cit., pp. 296, 309, 322, 335.

[434] ibid., p. 274. We wish to clarify that Maria Valtorta was not gossiping, but it was as if she were speaking in confession to a priest, as if to reveal a temptation and to be certain that what was thought was wrong.

of the house and on the few alms they received[435]. Poverty, due also to the constant need of medicine, was extreme, and in these years, Marta Diciotti's loyalty was as extreme as it was moving. But starting with the letter of 16 November 1949, the relationship with Father Migliorini stopped: he wrote that a 'Voice' had told him that for years she had been bad-mouthing a priest – namely, Father Migliorini himself – and after various reproaches, he abruptly and peremptorily ended the letter: "With this letter, I mean to step out of the material scene of your life, although you will always be present in my mind..."[436]. Maria Valtorta drafted a letter, never sent, in which she replied to the accusations, pointing out: "Do not concern yourself with the Voices with a capital V. They have nothing to do with this"[437]. Adding other details of a pointless argument, the editor of the text annotated that Maria Valtorta 'in the margin left blank at the beginning, wrote: *Letter which I did not send in the end, as I thought it was pointless. Silence is the hardest lesson...* for some people! '[438] In the last letter of 6 October 1952[439], Father Migliorini confirmed, without reiterating the previous argument: "That the content of these writings (the Work of Maria Valtorta) is obviously too ultramundane (far beyond this world)"[440], and it therefore comes from Heaven and is not the result of Maria Valtorta's imagination. He died on 10 July 1953. Five days later, Maria Valtorta wrote: "I regret that Fr. Migliorini died without seeing the Work published for the triumph

---

[435] For example: "You will remember how I had already been in dire straits since 1945. One can easily think that after three years, my problems have increased despite the fact that I sold the piano and other objects, moreso for having been left without any income from January to July in 1948 because of those two wretches [spiritists] that I had to send away from my house because, perhaps, out of an excessive sense of morality and, above all, out of respect for the One who has come down to us, I could not have allowed them to continue living under my roof after having learned of the truth about those two" (Maria Valtorta, *Lettere a Padre Migliorini,* op. cit., p. 176).

[436] ibid., pp. 182-4.

[437] ibid., p. 185.

[438] ibid., note 79. A revealing a yet distressing end.

[439] cf. ibid., p. 194.

[440] ibid.

of which he worked and suffered so much"[441]. Jesus then appeared to her adding sweet words of eternal salvation for him, but also of reproach: "because he went against my clear and repeated orders, he did not merit seeing its completion"[442].

Mother Teresa Maria, the Carmelite

Father Migliorini, who had spiritually guided Maria Valtorta from the end of 1942 until March 1946, had moved to Rome where he was substituted in part by Father Luigi Lopalco[443]. Yet the spell had been broken: for better or worse, no one was ever as important in the life of Maria Valtorta, as she said herself, almost screaming in writing: "Enough! Enough with directors! I had one, unfortunately, and I have had enough... And then! Can you ever impose a director on me?"[444] The sentence coming right before this one is spiritually disconcerting: "I talked of the second visit by Fr. Benedetti (a Servite Friar himself) charged with the task of collecting the third year (the typed pages of the third year of Jesus' public life that I had just completed) and of becoming my Spiritual Director, and this on the order (?) of Father Migliorini"[445]. Here we have a glimpse of what Father Migliorini meant by spiritual direction. It was, however, typical of the past, where the guided person was more a slave than a

---

[441] Maria Valtorta, *The Little Notebooks*, op. cit., 15 July 1953, p. 227-8.

[442] ibid., p. 228. "He wanted to do things by himself, deaf to the reality that his work was different to mine. So because of this, he died before seeing the Work finished. I do not tolerate pride, rebellion and disobedience. I will give him a reward for his life as a priest, but also a punishment for his obstinate will, contrary to mine" (ibid.).

[443] Father Lopalco Luigi Maria of Jesus Crucified was a Passionist. He was born in Francavilla Fontana (Brindisi) on 28 August 1888 and died in Orbetello (Grosseto) on 30 March 1967. We only have four quotes attributed to him; very little is known about him, and his importance for Maria Valtorta must not have been extraordinary, even if she wrote that she will keep "a memory of peace and justice" of him. (Maria Valtorta, *Lettere a Madre Teresa Maria 1*, op. cit., p. 191) and that it was Jesus himself who sent him to her (cf. Maria Valtorta, *Notebooks 1945-1950*, op. cit., 19 March 1946, p. 233).

[444] ibid., p. 295.

[445] ibid.

free and responsible person, and this shows the theological limits behind this behavior. After all, if it is true that there was true commonality with Father Migliorini, it is also true that Maria Valtorta had always been, thanks to God, rather independent. She wrote to Mother Teresa Maria: "*I have never had any Director.* Always and only confessors to whom, just in case, I submitted the offers that I received... from I do not know where. Certainly not from me, poor soul, and that I immediately accepted because I have never been afraid to give God what He would be grateful for. And generally, I was told: 'Be careful, it is serious! It could cause you pain, fatigue, etc, etc. You must not overdo it!' You must not overdo it!!! Jesus did overdo it for our sake! He had himself killed with those terrible tortures! Can His love be considered exaggerated? And if He did not exaggerate immolating Himself that way, can we consider our always *relative* immolations exaggerated? I did not feel the need for a Guide. Everything has always taken place between me and Him, clearly and surely. I proceeded, led by the hand [...] and, making no resistance, I moved up and up, without even realizing how high I was, higher and higher!... I looked and I look at Him and I see nothing else... His smile is the thread pulling me. My Sisters? No. Not even them"[446]. Mother Teresa Maria was not her 'director of conscience', rather a loyal and silent listener-advisor-friend. No easy matter, although the writing style she used in her letters to Mother Teresa was very similar to the honesty-clarity-truthfulness she used in the *Autobiography*.

So, Father Migliorini's tasks with regard to Maria Valtorta were shared: Marta Diciotti typed up the writings written by hand by Maria

---

[446] ibid., pp. 130-1. Mother Teresa Maria replied on 20 May, saying: "We will wait patiently for the hour marked by the Lord. I do not know the Priest of whom you are speaking because here, we must only deal with an ordinary Confessor, a Franciscan, and with an extraordinary confessor, a Carmelite. And with others in writing, with the particular Director. You have always had the Holy Spirit as a Guide, but I instead since the age of 13 have always been directed by a Priest because I am smaller and lower... but I am very happy, and I recognize a merciful grace from Jesus for my poor soul... Even if His sufferings came from the devil, channeled as they are for the good of souls and of the Church, they are blessed by God. It is bad for the devil if he contributes to such great good!" (ibid., p. 134).

using a fountainpen; the spiritual side had Father Lopalco, Father Pennoni and a few passing Servite Friars as points of reference – though no longer as widely and intensively as with Father Migliorini. There were also two brand new figures: a Carmelite nun, Mother Teresa Maria – the Mother Superior of the Convent of Camaiore – who acted as spiritual confidante, spiritual aide, and spiritual advisor; and Father Corrado Maria Berti – a Friar Servant of Mary himself – who, despite assisting Maria Valtorta with her writings in every possible way, he never was her spiritual director.

A new arrival

On Monday 30 September 1946, after a long wait and late as was his custom, Father Corrado Maria Berti of the Friar Servants of Mary arrived for the first time to the Valtorta house. A professor and founder, along with Father Gabriele Maria Roschini of the Pontifical University Marianum, he did not substitute Father Migliorini, but helped Maria Valtorta until her death, in trying to make the Holy See approve her writings and in finding a printing house ready to bear the cost of the printing process. He was also the first to create theological explicative annotations to the first published texts.

At first glance, this is how Maria Valtorta judged the meeting: "At 4pm on Monday, Fr. Berti came. At last! I had just finished eating and I was going to lie down, exhausted after a 4-hour-long crisis... My impression? *Excellent*. Young: 36-years-old, humble despite being knowledgeable, pious and *frank*. He did not deny the faults and responsibilities of either the General or of others. I clearly expressed my thoughts, reminding him of the note I already sent you, and I also showed it to him. He said: "You see, you cannot write: Author Jesus Christ. You are certain of this, but others...'. I took the Vademecum by Sister Benigna Consolata and I said: 'The Lord has been saying to behave this way for 40 months. There is the example' and then I took the book by the Stigmatized of Mese, I showed it to him and I made him read the preface, written by the Bishop only 18 days after the death of Sister Tommasina[447]. And I also made him read a few pages

---

[447] This is in reference to Sister Tommasina Pozzi, born in Trevano (CO) in 1910 and died in Mese (SO) on 4 November 1944, a mystic with

of the book itself, in reply to some silly objections. They are the pages of a theologian, and they contain writings by another great French theologian about our phenomena. He was left... numb by both my note and the two books, and he took notes"[448]. This was the start of a partnership that continued well beyond her death (12 October 1961), and stopped only with his own death, although his archive cannot be consulted to this day[449] - even now that his secretary is also dead, who was the depositary of everything. In any case, we must ask who Father Berti was and what part he had regarding Maria Valtorta and the drafting of her Work.

Father Corrado Maria Berti

"Born in Florence on 17 March 1911, he entered the Order of the Friar Servants of Mary in 1926 and he was ordained a priest in 1934. After graduating with honors in Philosophy at the Pontificio Collegio Urbano de Propaganda Fide [Pontifical Urban College for the Propagation of the Faith] in Rome, he attended an ordinary course of Theology at the college of his Order in Rome and then the University course of Theology in Leuven, Belgium. A Professor of Dogmatic-Sacramental Theology at the Pontifical Theological Faculty 'Marianum' from 1939, and Secretary of the same Faculty from 1950 -1957, he held official positions in the fields of discipline, of studies and historical-liturgical research. He produced several publications and worked at the Second Vatican Council as an anonymous contributor as requested by some Council Fathers. His work in teaching and in research went hand in hand with preaching and, above all, with the tireless apostolate among patients in the hospitals in Rome (at the Forlanini, then at San Gallicano for 23

---

the stigmata and who was perpetually in a struggle, even physically at times with the devil.

[448] ibid., p. 280.

[449] Even the small part of the correspondence that is in the Valtortian Editorial Centre's possession is currently not available. The clear feeling is that, for one reason or another – and no one knows exactly why – Father Corrado Berti had fallen into a strange form of ostracism. I repeat that it will not be possible to shed full light on the life of Maria Valtorta until all that exists is published.

years, and finally at San Camillo)"[450]. So on 30 October 1946, he set foot in Valtorta's house, changing his life as a priest forever. Father Migliorini had probably already told Maria Valtorta about him, if on 18 March 1946 she was able to write: "that other priest who teaches a course on the Sacraments"[451]: Father Berti alone had this qualification. From that point, Father Berti had already started writing[452] to Maria Valtorta, but she did not meet him in person until 30 October and started the relationship that became a constant one between the two of them. Although the relationship with Father Migliorini was first one of spiritual trust, and only later of help with the gift that Maria Valtorta had been granted, with Father Corrado Berti, she never had the former, but she had the latter for the rest of her life. As it is impossible to consult Father Berti's personal archive (held and still kept secret by his secretary's nephew), what can be known comes from Maria Valtorta's letters and from the recollections of Dr. Emilio Pisani published in the volume *Pro e contro Maria Valtorta*[453]. Although Maria Valtorta spoke from the heart, saying what she knew about him, we cannot say the same thing of Dr. Pisani's writings who as a young man had collaborated with Father Berti, breaking away from him at a later stage. So much so that in the short text that records Father Berti's recent death, Pisani

---

[450] "Bollettino Valtortiano", op. cit., n. 23 – January-June 1981, p. 91. He was remembered like this at the time of his death by Dr. Emilio Pisani of the Valtortian Editorial Centre.

[451] The context is this: "My angel tells you, Father, that the Holy Masses for the 'voices' are to be read and known only by my Superiors, and should not be disseminated for any reason, to anyone, until after my death. Accordingly, except for you, and of course, the Father General, the Procurator General, and the other priest who teaches the course on the Sacraments (if you agree). No one else should be familiar with them in Rome or elsewhere! (Maria Valtorta, *Notebooks 1945-1950*, op. cit., 18 March 1946, pp. 232-3).

[452] cf. ibid., p. 275. This is in reference to the text from 12 July 1946.

[453] Emilio Pisani, *Pro e contro Maria Valtorta*, op. cit. A part of the written exchange between the two is in the possession of the Centro Editoriale Valtortiano. After having asked one of their managers in May 2018 the reason for this confidentiality, it was explained that Dr. Pisani does not consider it useful to the purpose for which Heaven had given visions to Maria Valtorta.

could not avoid this criticism: "Perceptive and wise, yet stubborn and touchy. To handle the work by Maria Valtorta alongside him was both pleasant and difficult. For a long time, we have been his devoted subordinates; then, whilst owing him a lot, we started to oppose some of his subjective opinions and tactics. Yet, his presence has been providential all the same, and his actions will not appear to have been purposeless. There will be many occasions to speak about him, so we shall see that, not having to confront each other on earthly matters, we shall be able to get better acquainted"[454]. Time had not prevented it from coming up although in the end, the sand had entered the wheel of their relationship. Despite the final disagreements, however: "Father Berti was the director of the Valtorta case for thirty years"[455]. The real motives for the serious breakup remain undisclosed for the time being. Still, thirty years are a lot, as are the events. The story of Father Corrado Berti and Maria Valtorta was very intense and has not been fully clarified yet. The breakup with Emilio Pisani made sure that he was gradually banned from the publication of the Work by Maria Valtorta. His comments, his prefaces and even his skills as a university professor were forgotten and maybe were even made to be forgotten. But his contribution remains intact, for good or bad: two aspects that remain, in any case. We must point out from the start that the criticism of Prof. Corrado Berti cannot go down to the level of his religious role or quality of his religious role, but it must remain at the level of his actions as a professor and as a participant in the life of Maria Valtorta. He was not her spiritual director, nor her confidant: the part which he was involved with was her Work, her writings.

Light and shadow in Father Berti

Whoever picks up *The Gospel as Revealed to Me* today may perhaps believe that the subdivisions, the order, and the titles are obvious and made by Maria Valtorta. This is not the case. The first edition of the fundamental work – *The Poem of the Man-God,* published in Italian in four volumes between 1956 and 1960 – presented two serious inadequacies. On the one hand, it collected the manuscripts typed by

---

[454] "Bollettino Valtortiano", op. cit., n. 23 – January-June 1981, p. 91.
[455] Emilio Pisani, *Pro e contro Maria Valtorta,* op. cit., p. 17.

Father Migliorini and Marta Diciotti without comparing them with the hand-written text by Maria Valtorta, producing a text cut up and full of mistakes, even serious ones[456]. The second limitation was the typographical choice of ignoring the starting of a new line after the paragraphs, resulting in a text which was difficult to read and required excessive attention on the part of the reader, making it almost inaccessible to simple people. These editorial choices, due to the need of keeping the cost of printing low, and to make as few volumes as possible, were very limiting. Even the title was very controversial and in the end *The Poem of the Man-God* was chosen[457]. The second edition makes it clear from the start that the editing had changed. In fact the editor was Father Berti, who had a university academic mindset. He and a very young Dr. Emilio Pisani spent a summer on the beach in Viareggio, collecting the writings, comparing the typescripts with the autographed notebooks of Maria Valtorta, and with a real masterstroke, they ingeniously multiplied the line breaks after paragraphs, as we can still see in *The Gospel as Revealed to Me*. On top of that, he also wrote a sober, theological comment with many biblical references. The result was ten volumes in Italian in all, with an undeniable big capital investment on the part of the publisher; subdivided into 652 chapters, long, and easy to read for everyone. For that time – it was 1961 (for the first volume) and 1967 (by the time the tenth and last volume was printed) – it was a real masterpiece of publishing and editorial professionalism. The only serious flaw was

---

[456] cf. The introduction written by Dr. Emilio Pisani in which he tells the story of the first and second edition. Maria Valtorta, *Il Poema dell'Uomo-Dio* [The Poem of the Man-God], op. cit., vol. 1 pp. XXXIX-XLVII. [Not in the English edition]

[457] "The Work was now about to come to light with its first volume and we were still looking for a more suitable title, without a doubt having to put aside the one indicated initially by the writer: *The Gospel of Jesus as revealed to little John*". It was then that Prof. Nicola Pende, admirer of the Work since 1948, suggested to call it *The Poem of Jesus*, a title that immediately after the appearance of the first volume, had to be transformed into *The Poem of the Man-God*, at the insistence of a publishing house that included among its publications, a book of poems whose title coincided with ours" (ibid.).

the choice of the author for the Preface[458]. Father Berti probably wanted to give the text an aura of modernity and authority too, so that it could reverse the fact that the first edition, published anonymously, had been put on the Index. The choice fell on Prof. Luciano Raffaele, Secretary of the Italian Parapsychological Society: in other words, on a convinced and practicing spiritist[459]. This

---

[458] Thus recalled, Marta Diciotti: "It was Professor Pende who, in agreement with Father Berti, thought that the fate of the Work could be revived on the pretext of the scientific interest that the 'Valtortian phenomenon' aroused. So, in this respect, he proposed it to the Italian Society of Parapsychology, which revolved around its Secretary General, Dr. Luciano Raffaele" (Albo Centoni, *Ricordi di donne che conobbero Maria Valtorta*, op. cit., p. 277). Confusion between "science" and mediumism called "mediumistic science" is still widespread today. It goes without saying that keeping in mind the distinction, and keeping the two fields well separated, is instead essential for the good of Maria Valtorta and the Work itself.

[459] This is in part what he wrote: "There was a moment in my life during which I felt, deep down, that too narrow and unnatural boundaries were imposed on research and experiences carried out with traditional scientific methods, and that the spectacle of existences, which reveals itself with a wonderful explosion on the planet in which we live, was only partially able – through the contribution of sensations which are limited to the five channels of perception known so far – to form mankind's common patrimony of the knowledge of reality. So it was that I became attracted to, and have dedicated myself to, the studies of the phenomena that fall within the Parapsychology research area. [...] I was comforted and supported in this new trial by the examples and experiences of scholars and scientists of worldwide importance, such as Richet, physician and physiologist, 1913 Nobel prize winner; Crookes, eminent chemist and physicist; Lodge, James, Lombroso, Luciani, Tamburini, Patrizi, Morselli, and others; who, were the first to defy the disbelief of their prejudiced colleagues, their ridicule and even the ridicule of the followers of the official science of the time, and who wanted and knew how to bring to the attention of the world, unexplained and yet undeniable facts of para-super and abnormal nature. But soon I realized that, after the explorations of those great investigators of truth, [...] they became sterilized by academic controversies, without any longer making concrete investigative contributions, nor shedding light on new experiences on appreciable phenomena. [...]. I wanted to say these things so that the very interest I have in this work has meaning and

obviously does not detract from the goodness and beauty of the text by Maria Valtorta, and yet it was a huge mistake for someone who wanted to be fully accepted by the Church. The mistake was fatal because with that long preface, it categorized the text as a spiritist text which was therefore unacceptable for the Church and, in fact, this caused a terrible split. The Church and theologians categorically rejected both the text and the author, whereas those who were far from the theological issue, who followed the 'reasons of the heart' and therefore devotionalism, appreciated them enormously[460]. The risk was already present because it was a 'private revelation'[461]. In a situation where there were a huge number of similar cases – but false ones – the Index caused a real split. On the one side were those devoted to Maria Valtorta but who fell into the trap of devotionalism and were only interested in the gesture of love from Heaven. On the other side were the theologians who expected a rational-scientific elaboration, even of the data deriving from a private revelation[462]. Unfortunately, due to their style and content, the writings of Maria Valtorta would have required a long time to be studied and proven.

Father Berti in a trap

Maria Valtorta, talking openly with Mother Teresa Maria, spoke of two details that shed some light on Father Berti. In the letter of 19 September 1946 while the Prior Father Migliorini was absent, she

---

justification, which I do not hesitate to define this Work as a monument of immeasurable scientific, as well as artistic value, to which the minds and the investigative tools of scholars from all over the world will soon turn, who are currently poured into the various disciplines that contribute to forming the embryonic scientific nuclei of Parapsychology" (Maria Valtorta, *Il Poema dell'Uomo-Dio*, op. cit., vol. 1 pp. IX-X). [Not in the English edition].

[460] Not for nothing is *The Gospel as Revealed to Me* widespread and translated into more than thirty languages today (Taken from a private conversation with a member of the Centro Editoriale Valtortiano).

[461] This is obviously the opinion of the writer, who is waiting for the Church to confirm it.

[462] Opinion and working hypothesis of the writer, who is awaiting a thorough study by the Church and therefore hoping for a change in the positions expressed officially.

wrote that: "There were séances in the Convent of St. Andrea!!!"[463] It is not known who had told her that, but we cannot rule out that the author of this scoop had been Father Mariano, a very chatty and naive Servite Friar[464] who told Maria Valtorta another piece of news – that Father Berti had been found guilty of modernism[465]. This second detail relates to Father Berti's notes on *The Poem of the Man-God*, where there was an effort to appear academic and in-step with the times[466]. We must not, however, jump to conclusions; as the historical documents of Father Berti are not yet accessible, so it is hard to tell whether these two details are true or not. Father Mariano's talkativeness itself would make us believe they are true, but we must be very careful. It may be added as confirmation, that after the death of Maria Valtorta – and only after this – Father Berti was not afraid of proposing and getting the preface accepted to the whole Work by Prof. Luciano Raffaele, Secretary of the Italian Society of Parapsychology and therefore, a genuine spiritist. The Work was thus

---

[463] Maria Valtorta, *Lettere a Madre Teresa Maria 1*, op. cit., p. 264.

[464] It seems that Father Mariano De Santis was fast to insinuate, to ask nosy questions or to spread strange secrets. For this reason, it is good not to take this news for granted. For example: "But yesterday Fr. Mariano told me with tears in his eyes that the Order is in great decline and that defections are an everyday occurrence, not only with the leaving of the priesthood but with the passage to the secular, rationalist camp, and perhaps also to the communist… And it seems to me that this says a lot…" (ibid., pp. 170-1); "Fr. Mariano is a good guy, but of a nosiness greater than that of ten idle women… and he would storm me with questions" (ibid., p. 185); "Sunday came and he stayed for two hours… and, as usual, he slipped into a discussion about spiritism. They are all low, very low tests in order to find me guilty…" (ibid., p. 228).

[465] "The other Fr. Mariano told me yesterday, in passing, that at the beginning of his teaching career, Fr. Berti was reproved and condemned by the H.O. [Holy Office] for 'modernism'. And it is precisely to Fr. Berti that Jesus makes me send the dictation of 3 February (For the Holy Father) in which the dictation speaks precisely of modernism which, by the way, I do not even know what it is and of what it consists… Aren't these coincidences that make you reflect?" (Maria Valtorta, *Lettere a Madre Teresa Maria 2*, op. cit., p. 40).

[466] cf. for example Maria Valtorta, *Il Poema dell'Uomo-Dio*, op. cit., vol. 1 Notes pp. 69-70. [Not in the English edition].

published with this preface, both important and 'cumbersome'[467]. So, we must limit ourselves to simple conjectures, albeit supported by some facts. Father Berti knew that the Church condemned spiritism[468], but he probably believed that spiritism was scientific, though certainly not a Galilean science[469]. It is also possible that deep down, he shared the same ideas as Luciano Raffaele; namely, that spiritism was a superior possibility given to science for a better understanding in every field of knowledge, in the hope of widening human possibilities through this so-called science. Had he successfully demonstrated that spiritism was one of the causes of the countless and very detailed visions of Maria Valtorta? Clearly, that kind of science – although rebuked by scientists – could it have universally become a chance to further explore science itself as well as Catholic canonical Revelation? The confusion he must have had

---

[467] cf. Maria Valtorta, *Il Poema dell'Uomo-Dio,* op. cit., vol. 1 pp. IX-XXXVII. In the note on p. X, Dr. Luciano Raffaele is called a "fervent scholar". And Dr. Emilio Pisani is the one who: in the "Introduction [...] wanted to establish the scientific criteria of the new edition". Who Dr. Luciano Raffaele was exactly, was clear to everyone. Nor was he in any way hidden or kept silent, but rather used as a person of honor, given that on the inside title page of the first volume, there is the explicit subtitling: "with a preface by Dr. Luciano Raffaele, Secretary General of the Italian Society of Parapsychology". [Not in the English edition].

[468] There was a negative response by the Holy Office on 24 April 1917 on spiritism communications, later confirmed by the Catechism of the Catholic Church: "All forms of divination are to be rejected: recourse to Satan or demons, evocation of the dead or other practices that are wrongly believed to 'reveal' the future [...] and recourse to mediums, conceal a will to dominate time, history and finally men and, at the same time, a desire to make the hidden powers advantageous. They are in contradiction to the honor and respect, combined with a loving fear, which we owe to God alone" (n. 2116).

[469] Spiritism would be considered scientific if it would use the scientific method. Galilean science demands rigorous experiments and reproduces them at least potentially; something not possible in spiritism, in which there is no real experimentation or reproducibility of phenomena, and therefore there is no real scientific basis (Cf. AA.VV., *PARA Dizionario Enciclopedico,* op. cit., Entry: *Spiritismo e Spiritismo scientifico* [Spiritism and scientific Spiritism], pp. 931-40).

in his head and his lack of knowledge of spiritism – its history, facts, and doctrines (plural)[470] – led him to support a theory impossible on every level. And by the way, forgetting that even the ancients knew of the possibility of contacting the spirits[471], but as soon as Galilean science started to be applied, that pseudo-science ceased to exist, and scientists always avoided using it. The affinities between spiritism and necromancy were well known[472], but these too, were swept aside by Galileo's followers. He must have been deceived and led astray by the scientific and theological wealth of the writings by Maria Valtorta[473]: two fatal mistakes. Maria Valtorta never had any doubt in censoring spiritism, but as soon as the Church got a hint of spiritism, it was forced to confirm the indexing of the writings[474]. And so, first Father Migliorini and then Father Berti, were discredited in the eyes of the Church.

Preparation for printing

Among the various attempts to publish the Work, there was also this episode reported by Maria Valtorta herself: "...that I consent to the highest levels: clandestine printing (?) and present it then in the

---

[470] cf. Maria Teresa La Vecchia, *Antropologia paranormale. Fenomeni fisici e psichici straordinari*, op. cit.

[471] Even the Bible speaks of it, for example in the episode of Saul which evokes the spirit of Samuel by the sorceress of Endor (1Sam 28:7ff).

[472] It is true that spiritism is a particular strand of doctrine and practices, however magicians, witches and sorcerers have always used spiritism as theories and practices to package the various alchemies they use (Cf. Massimo Introvigne, *Il cappello del mago. I nuovi movimenti magici, dallo spiritismo al satanismo* [The magician's hat. The new magical movements, from spiritism to Satanism], SugarCo, Milano 1995).

[473] Father Berti made this splendid statement, perfectly acceptable: "Therefore, those documented and splendid pages [...] are to be explained in the light of the interpretation that the Experts will give to the complex Valtortian phenomenon, when they are aware of all the necessary or useful elements for formulating a dispassionate, adequate, scientific judgment (Maria Valtorta, *Autobiografia*, op. cit., p. XI-XII). [Preface not in the English edition].

[474] This is the writer's personal conjecture, however, supported by subsequent events.

United States to an Ordinary (a bishop) and have it approved (?!) etc., etc. This was all madness and rebellious which I refused because I *do not rebel*. The *reason why* is foolish: the approval even from Spellman (bishop of New York from 1939 then cardinal in 1946) would then be annulled and it would be condemned to the Index for rebellion and extorted, fraudulent approval etc., etc., by the Holy Office III *because it is a scam* (sic) to receive money from lay people, then lose it and have to destroy the printed volumes..."[475]. Maria did not sign the document which Father Berti had drafted, and which would have served this expropriation. So this attempt resulted in nothing too. The idea was a little over the top because it was unfeasible on every level, but the desire to publish and to have the go-ahead of a bishop made the imagination run wild, which in the end, would turn this into a nightmare.

Among other things, there was also the attempt to set up a company that would manage the printing house for the publishing of the writings by Maria Valtorta. Marta Diciotti mentioned this: "How busy Father Migliorini and Father Berti became in having the writings published! The effort they made! At one point, they even planned to find a publishing house. But I do not want to go into too much detail here, as it is not right. I think that Father Berti will do that himself when he collects testimonies"[476]. It was Michele Pisani of Isola di Liri, in the province of Frosinone, who solved the printing issue. He was a publisher who had dealings with the Holy See and had been contacted by a very dear friend. "Having been made aware, supported and encouraged by the advice and pressures of competent people, I bravely undertook the significant task with enthusiasm"[477]. And thus, between 1956 and 1959 the first edition of what is now titled *The Gospel as Revealed to Me* was published. Regarding the publishing of the first edition of what was *The Poem of God*, it seems only right to clarify a very important point: we must give credit to the providential

---

[475] Maria Valtorta, *Lettere a Madre Teresa Maria 2*, op. cit., p. 194.

[476] Albo Centoni, *Una vita con Maria Valtorta. Testimonianze di Marta Diciotti*, op. cit., p. 355.

[477] Maria Valtorta, *Il Poema dell'Uomo-Dio* [The Poem of the Man-God], Tipografia Editrice M. Pisani, Isola del Liri (FR) 1959, p. V. This is from the reprint with the modified title of *Il Poema di Gesù* [The Poem of Jesus]; both of which were published anonymously.

intervention of Tipografia Michele Pisani [Printing House] and then of Dr. Emilio Pisani, owner of the Centro Editoriale Valtortiano [CEV, Valtortian Editorial Centre] who inherited all of Valtorta's writings. It is right to remember that without the hard work and risks they ran taking on this task, every piece of writing would have probably ended up in some dark cellar at the Vatican where it would have been forgotten forever. It is very likely that without Mr. Pisani, this would have happened in view of the biased hostility of the Holy See at the time. Therefore, it is only right to give thanks for the hard work and the risk incurred, and this should be done all the time and by everyone around the world who reads the writings by Maria Valtorta. All the rest – everything concerning the printing times, the prices of the books, the completeness of the texts, the formats used, the editions, the translations, the titles of the publications – can and must be discussed, praised or even severely criticized[478]. But none of this can come in the way, not even slightly, of the fundamental element: Heaven has given Maria Valtorta several gifts, but without those who accepted the inheritance and then published it, thus giving everyone the chance to be able to read it and study it, no one could easily access it.

The two autobiographies

The sources that help us get to know Maria Valtorta are not many. Until April 1943, we have the *Autobiography*. It was requested by her spiritual director, Father Romualdo Migliorini, and written for him. With an unusual openness of mind and heart, she described herself intimately, sparing no details. She was not writing for the world or for ordinary people, as they used to be called, but to be read spiritually by Father Migliorini alone, and therefore to give a fundamental tool on which to be able to grow even more in union with God. She was not showing herself up out of vanity, complacency, self-commiseration, justification, or pride; her purpose was exactly the opposite: to be known in order to ascend to perfect humility, well

---

[478] For example, the claim, decidedly excessive and meaningless, improper, and worthy only of painful tears over the person who printed it, for "considering himself also heir to her 'thought'" ("Bollettino Valtortiano", op. cit., n. 91 – January-June 2016, p. 1).

aware that she was still far from this goal, and also in order to reach the peak of immolation in imitation of Jesus Christ. The following events – already described in part – show that Father Migliorini did not fully understand because he could not decipher and penetrate God's design for him. The same thing can be said of Father Berti and of the Friars of the Servants of Mary: they did not understand God's design for them. Anyway, at the time when Maria Valtorta wrote her autobiography, many other people did the same, some out of romanticism, some to justify their actions, and some to boast about it later. Diaries, biographies and memoirs were already commonplace in the 19th and 20th centuries. And during the war, there was no General or politician who did not hope to write what, at the end of the conflict, would be the memoirs of a war which was won. Obviously, it was not always like that because where there is a winner, there is also a loser; but in the meantime, diaries, reports and memoirs have literally filled the shelves of libraries. We can see that some of these, although detailed, are partial and conceal a few aspects of the people involved. Maria Valtorta did something extremely special and different: she needed a guide along the paths of the spirit because she acknowledged that she did not have the necessary tools. As the ascent towards God is a very narrow ridge and she was not ready for it, she felt the need for a guide who, in possession of the right knowledge, would have been able to help her. We can also say that she wrote about herself in order to be better, faster and guided. She knew the passage from the Gospel well: "Enter through the narrow gate. For wide is the gate and broad is the road that leads to destruction, and many enter through it. But small is the gate and narrow the road that leads to life, and only a few find it!"[479] So towards the end of 1942, she had decided to have a spiritual director – at the age of 45 and with her health outlook of having only two years left before her death. She made this decision, although this was difficult for her because it meant giving up a bit of herself to follow the requests of another. She already had the cross of her mother Iside and she already had her serious illnesses: one might have thought that this was enough, but she wanted to follow what Jesus had already told her heart, and that was her own immolation. So we must be clear:

---

[479] Mt 7:13-4.

Maria Valtorta did not write her own memoirs, nor the diary of her life, nor the story of her life, but she described her intimate life and all the external events that had made her become what she was.

The text stops at April 1943. Then, following the departure of Father Migliorini, there is another source - the letters, which now allow us to piece together, although not everything, much of what happened afterwards. An equally important element lies in the fact that at least a part of the countless letters appear to be the continuation of the previous autobiography. Mother Teresa Maria had become her best friend, spiritual advisor and confidante, so the letters between herself and Maria Valtorta are very revealing. As well as this, the sources for the years after 1943 are also part of: *Notebooks 1945-1950*, the memoirs of the 'familiar' Marta Diciotti, and the memoirs of a few acquaintances. From these documents, we can extract much, but not all of the necessary information, because of the already-mentioned issue of the letters of Father Berti, which have not seen the light yet and no one knows whether they will ever be published in their entirety[480], even though we can reasonably assume they contain important information and facts (given that everything is important, even the smallest details).

The breakup with the Friar Servants of Mary

At the start of 1947, Maria Valtorta realized that she was near to completing the draft of what would become her main Work[481], *The Gospel as Revealed to Me*. This realization is well documented in the letters which she exchanged with Mother Teresa Maria[482]. There is, however, something disconcerting, and it is the attitude of the Friar

---

[480] Perhaps it contains information that is not wanted to be made known now. In fact, one may get the impression that it has been somehow kept secret. However, one must be confident that the future, sooner or later, will do justice to everything that has happened.

[481] She herself, "little John", was aware of her role in transmitting what had been given to her, but without wanting to take authorship that she did not have: the term "Work" should not be confused with that used to define the work of a novelist.

[482] For example, cf. Maria Valtorta, *Lettere a Madre Teresa Maria 2*, op. cit., pp. 43, 54, 85.

Servants of Mary towards Maria Valtorta, as an Order. In January 1949, Maria Valtorta wrote[483] to the Carmelite, adding a few more details regarding what had caused the complete break: "What adds to my sorrow for the unjust decree[484], *is the near certainty,* based on proof[485] that is in my possession, that *plotting alongside the laity and the H.O.* [Holy Office] *etc., are the very Fathers* [Servants of Mary], *who have always sought to publish the Work without approval, and as a 'human Work'.* They even wanted to call it 'scientific' due to its style: 'mediumistic' (that is, of spiritist origin), thus dishonoring me on a human level as well as on a spiritual one, and making me look like a spiritist who saw and heard what I described in the book by means of séances (satanic ones because to me, anything to do with mediums or spiritism, call them what you want, is satanic). The Servite Friars have been insisting for months that I give the publishers the go-ahead to publish the Work in any way… And I have been saying *'no'* for months"[486]. The peak of the break is dated 8 May 1949; Father Berti wrote: "It was a humiliating day for me: Maria, surrounded by a group of laypeople, allowed [or wanted?] the documents which had spontaneously tied her to us [Friar Servants of Mary] to be torn up"[487].

Comparisons

To understand the seriousness of what happened and its even greater consequences, we must know and compare two historical examples, which happened before and after the lifetime of Maria Valtorta.

The first is the famous event of the apparitions of the Sacred Heart of Jesus. We are in 1673 in Paray-le-Monial, France. Following

---

[483] It is actually undated, but the editors place it between the letter of 29 January 1949 and that of 15 March 1949. Cf. ibid., p. 178ff.

[484] cf. ibid., p. 165.

[485] Unfortunately, they are not published. It is therefore unknown what evidence this is in reference to.

[486] Maria Valtorta, *Lettere a Madre Teresa Maria 2*, op. cit., pp. 179-80.

[487] Maria Valtorta, *Autobiografia prima*, op. cit., p. XI note 24. [Not in the English edition].

the terrible Thirty Years' War, Jansenism[488] arose in France and within the Catholic Church. Without going in much detail, it is important to say that Jansenism was a heresy but at the same time it was a theological, moral, ecclesiological-disciplinary, social, and political heresy. These five aspects turned into an anti-Roman nationalism called Gallicanism; but the most obvious aspect, at least for us, is the moral one. Jansenism was a system with an absolute moral rigidity at its centre, which instead of educating souls to love, it weakened charity. "Many are called, but few are chosen"[489] was interpreted in the most rigorous way. Also misinterpreting St. Augustine, Jansenists came to affirm that original sin had cancelled free will, so everyone was destined to go to Hell, but the merciful God would save a few intended ones. Many adhered to this rigoristic turn, such as the mathematical genius Blaise Pascal, who expressed it well in his *Pensées* [Thoughts][490]. Even the liturgy was affected by it: often, the tabernacle was doubled[491] with one placed high up to indicate the distance and the relative moral purity needed to get close to it. The most affected Sacraments were those of Confession and the Eucharist: penitents were often denied absolution and were advised to take Holy Communion only rarely. Divine Mercy was so incompatible with Divine Justice that it almost disappeared. Jansenism affected the Christian life of the ruling classes and paved the way to rationalism, which resulted in the French Revolution first, and then in the Napoleonic Wars. As in all things, there were also positive aspects, but these were used to make people blind, diverting them from a true Catholic life. Jansenism made everybody grow a sense of moral rigorism, and even those who did not feel it were influenced by it. The reaction came through the private revelations

---

[488] Cf. Françoise Hildesheimer, Marta Pieroni Francini, *Il giansenismo* [Jansenism], Edizioni San Paolo, Milano 1994; Marie-Emile Boismard, *All'alba del giansenismo* [At the dawn of Jansenism], Piemme, Casale Monferrato (AL) 2000.

[489] Mt 22:14.

[490] Blaise Pascal, *Pensieri* [Thoughts], Fabbri Editori, Milano 1998.

[491] For example, two towns in the diocese of Massa Carrara – Pontremoli, Antona and Pariana, have this liturgical layout of the two tabernacles in the parish church: one high, dominant and almost unreachable, and one low for daily use.

of the Sacred Heart: Saint Margaret Mary Alacoque[492] on 27 December 1673 was ordered by Jesus to make mankind aware of His love through the adoration of His Sacred Heart. Her spiritual director, the Jesuit, Claude de la Colombière, on realizing that this veneration was ordered by the Lord, set about to promote it with the help of his confrères. The success of this veneration was due to the Jesuits, who succeeded in making it known everywhere, not even disdaining to use it against Jansenism. They even modified the Catholic liturgy, establishing the liturgical solemnity of the Sacred Heart. The Jesuits, through St. Margaret Mary's confessor, St. Claude de la Colombière, managed to impose the veneration of the Sacred Heart on all Catholics.

The second event, the one which took place after the death of Maria Valtorta, concerns the devotion to Divine Mercy. When Communism had been in power in Russia for 13 years, Fascism in Italy for 9 years, and two years before the National Socialist Party had absolute power in Germany, St. Maria Faustina Kowalska (born Helena Kowalska, Glogowiec, 25 August 1905 – Krakow, 5 October 1938), had the private revelations on Divine Mercy on 22 February 1931 and the vision of the image we all know about[493]. In the face of unimaginable amounts of violence and hatred, God replied with a new form of devotion, with an even greater amount of mercy. To start with, on 28 November 1958, this devotion was indexed as false by the Holy Office (today known as the Congregation for the Doctrine of the Faith). The sentence ordered the removal of any image representing it from every church and chapel, and this way, it

---

[492] Verosvres, 22 July 1647 – Paray-le-Monial, 17 October 1690. She entered the Monastery of the Visitation of Paray-le-Monial on 25 May 1671. The Order of the Visitation of Holy Mary was founded by Saint Jane Frances de Chantal and by Saint Francis de Sales in 1611 (cf. Valerio Lessi, *Margherita Maria Alacoque. La santa dal Sacro Cuore* [Marguerete Mary Alacoque. The saint of the Sacred Heart], Paoline Editoriale Libri, Milano 2014).

[493] The most widespread image of the Divine Mercy refers to the restoration of the original painting, which modified – among other things – the face of Jesus (see *https://it.aleteia.org/2018/10/03/perche-the-vatican-has-prohibited-the-dissemination-of-the-diary-of-santa-faustina*, consulted 8 January 2019).

seemed that everything had been put to rest. But in 1978, the future St. John Paul II was elected Pope. With incredible willpower, he removed every condemnation of this devotion and of its image. On 30 November 1980, he issued the Encyclical (*Dives in Misericordia*) on Divine Mercy, on 18 April 1993 he beatified Faustina Kowalska, and on 30 April 2000 he inscribed her among the saints. And finally, he modified the liturgy designating the second Sunday of Easter (which had been celebrated as the Sunday *in albis*), as the Sunday of Divine Mercy. Here too, a single person who had been granted special mystical gifts had been supported to spread the message by someone prominent and authoritative who accepted and spread the new devotion. Interestingly, Maria Valtorta already knew[494] the devotion to Divine Mercy as a private revelation, and she made use of it. When she entered silence, at first she continued to write the formula taught by Divine Mercy 'Jesus, I trust in you', covering whole prayer cards with this phrase[495].

The Servants of Mary had begun very well, to the point of convincing[496] Maria Valtorta to join their Third Order, complete with the religious clothing and profession (31 March 1944). This wonderful atmosphere continued until December 1945, then the suspicions and the warnings began: "But tell Father [Migliorini] this: Satan did not lose his powerful intelligence [...] but uses it for evil

---

[494] "Make me, I–Mercy known, and make my prayers dictated to Sister Maria Faustina known to as many people as you can. Every soul you bring to Me-Mercy raises your level of glory. If you knew the torrent of graces I pour out on those who pray to Me-Mercy! Make, make, make me known, and every year, from Good Friday, always a fatal day for you, to the second Sunday in Easter (in albis), recite the Divine Mercy Novena in order to bring back to Me all those who are remembered in it" (Maria Valtorta, *The Little Notebooks*, op. cit., dated 26 May 1953, p. 213).

[495] Albo Centoni, *Una vita con Maria Valtorta. Testimonianze di Marta Diciotti*, op. cit., photo n. 16.

[496] To celebrate Holy Mass in her sickroom, Father Migliorini proposed this trick to her, and she accepted (cf. Emilio Pisani, *Pro e contro Maria Valtorta*, op. cit., p. 38).

rather than for good as he would have used it if he had remained an archangel"[497].

Rejected

Jesus reminded the Servants of Mary of the gift bestowed, urging them to go on and lay down guidelines for the publication and the distribution: "To the Order, to which my Charity decided to grant a gift and a mission in times as these, when antichristian darkness is rising and makes the souls blind, and the fevers of the cursed doctrines penetrate and kill, while the flock I have mercy on is dying of hunger and cold, thus to the Order of the Servants of my Most Blessed Mother do I speak [...]. My Will, expressed clearly and constantly since the beginning of the Work – and Romualdo knows it – is that my Word is to be known, spread and used by the consecrated and the faithful while the instrument must remain unknown until after her death. The pen of a writer is never celebrated, not even because of the silly enthusiasm of the crowd. But the writer is celebrated. Maria is my pen. Nothing more. I am the Writer. The Thought is mine. I can therefore make of it what I please. [...] Arise, you who are sleeping! Arise, you bashful! This is not the time for sleeping. Do I have to be the one who shouts at you, who are sleeping while the boat is rocked by the wrecking waves: 'Arise or you will die'? Do I have to be the one who says: 'Make your faith stronger'? Let it not be so. Look at how many die or are seduced because the only bread they have is poisoned by all sorts of heresies or are seduced because they are deafened by the voices of the false apostles serving the Beast... *Look for an endorsement which will defend and ensure the Work. Look for it now and do not stop until you find it.* Publish the evangelical cycle, which consists of three parts: (I) the conception, birth, childhood, and wedding of Mary. (II) The Annunciation, conception, birth, childhood, adolescence of myself. (III) The three years of evangelical life [...] *Do not mince words. I want a definite approval. The spokesperson must remain unknown.* She does not demand [anything else] and you cannot deny her what she asks for: that the Work is published with all the guarantees; that the Order supports her

---

[497] Maria Valtorta, *Notebooks 1945-1950*, op. cit., dated 28 January 1947 p. 338.

spiritually and not only with the ecclesiastical assistance of a Father who administers the sacraments to her as to any other Catholic person, but also with the spiritual and moral guidance of a Father, one of the best [...]. And that the Order supports her materially, too. You are in the presence of the continuous miracle of a finite human being, who produces because I want it so. But *My* miracle must not undo *your* charity [...]. Therefore, I *want* a Father, Father Romualdo, to stand-in here where the spokesperson lives, with the first copy of the manuscripts which, after being corrected by the spokesperson, will be sent to Rome, then to Romualdo who will continue the work. I approve of Fr. Corrado [Berti] helping Romualdo [Father Migliorini] in the research and correction of transcription mistakes. *Be aware that even a small error can produce a sentence against the dogma and the doctrine*[498]. So read, read again, and compare, so that you do not allow those who are against it to find mistakes [...] And be solicitous. The spokesperson is like a light fading out. Act. Act as the others act. Act with justice and charity, as the others act with injustice and anticharity. Act at once. From the manner and the time period in which you act and do what I want, and what charity requires regarding the spokesperson, your preparation, your faith and your obedience will be manifested: the countenenace of your spirit will be seen"[499]. But on 2 April, there was the terrible break up. "As from today, the Friar Servants of Mary by order of the General and the Provincial Fathers (given at the Provincial Chapter held in Florence

---

[498] An example of an error and a correction "In the hours of exhaustion, very extreme for some time, I scroll down a few pages of the typescripts, and I discover errors in the copy that have also escaped my correction. So, in the dictation from 27 August 1944 (Life of the Virgin) on p. D 1041, you wrote the word schiava [slave] on the 52nd line. Mind you that the word is schiva [reserved]: s-c-h-i-v-a. Writing 'slave' distorts the whole meaning of the sentence, and it almost becomes an insult instead of what is considered praise in the supernatural Word" (Maria Valtorta, *Lettere a Padre Migliorini*, op. cit., p. 121).

[499] Maria Valtorta, *Notebooks 1945-1950*, op. cit., dated 2 June 1946, p. 272. The text has been shortened for editorial reasons. Maria Valtorta continued to write on this point for a long time and, if it is true that the recrimination was profound, she never lowered herself to insult or seek revenge.

between the 20 - 24 June) cease to bring me the Eucharist. So I am left without the Sacraments... and I make no comment"[500]. And five days later, all that Maria could write was: "But charity is dead in them. And I die from their dead charity"[501]. Just as had happened with St. Margaret Mary and the Jesuits, and as it would happen with St. Faustina Kowalska and St. John Paul II, so it happened with Maria Valtorta and the Servants of Mary: "The Order to which my Charity wished to grant a gift and a mission". But they, the Servants of Mary, had rejected it.

Maria Valtorta did not trust them anymore, any of them. In 1949, she came to the point of having the Order issued with a formal warning: "I have legally warned the Servite Order not to make use, or allow the use of my Work contrary to the decrees of the Holy Church, not because I doubt that members of the Order could rebel. I have never heard words about them, other than words of deep respect for and obedience to the Holy Church. And if others by some design of theirs said the opposite, they would be lying and should be prosecuted for defamation in court. [...] I am only worried that some ill-doing by others could embitter the Church towards me, and have punitive sanctions applied to me, which would make me die in the anguish of the ninth hour and without the Mother (Church) by me in my agony. I do not worry about anything else with regards to myself. But with regards to the Church: *I do*. I would suffer terribly if the gift that God has bestowed which is also for the good of the Church and rejected by the Church itself, its enemies could cast aspersions on it"[502]. The passage is subtle: it was not a matter of orthodoxy on the part of the Order, but only a possible misuse of its texts by third parties against the Church. Maybe she could perceive a spiritist deviation lying in wait, something that would in fact happen, after her death. As a matter of fact, the most serious charges – but also wrong and caused by an unjustifiable personal ignorance of the

---

[500] Maria Valtorta, *Lettere a Madre Teresa Maria 1*, op. cit., p. 189, letter dated 2 July 1946.

[501] ibid., p. 191.

[502] Maria Valtorta, *Lettere a Mons. Carinci* [Letters to Mons. Carinci], Centro Editoriale Valtortiano, Isola del Liri (FR) 2006, pp. 44-5.

matter by those who made them[503] - came both against her and her writings, so her action was fully understandable. Anyway, God's design was thwarted. We want to believe that God will act in a different way to arouse enthusiasm in mankind, perhaps with new workers, or new congregations, or something else which we do not know yet. For the time being, the road is closed and it is still dark.

The Gospel is completed

The 'fight' with the Servites and, in particular, with Father Migliorini actually continued until his death. With the Servants of Mary, relationships took a turn for the worse and Maria Valtorta became very harsh with both Father Migliorini[504] – 'the ineffable'[505] but also 'the clown'[506] – and the Order: "I want to see what he has

---

[503] cf. Pier Angelo Gramaglia, *Maria Valtorta. Una moderna manipolazione dei Vangeli*, op. cit. With the justification that, at the time, some of her most important works – including her correspondence – had not yet been published.

[504] For Maria Valtorta, Father Migliorini's spiritual situation was serious: "You see? I am more afraid for Fr. M. [Father Migliorini] than his brother [who suicided]. Because Fr. M. has resisted the Will of God and resists it out of pride by being a consecrated person and having received many lessons from the Master. He is precisely 'dead' for J. C. [Jesus Christ] and with him, many of his other confreres" (Maria Valtorta, *Lettere a Madre Teresa Maria 2*, op. cit., p. 31).

[505] ibid., p. 36. If to some pious person the words of Maria Valtorta seem excessive, Father Berti in note 16 of the first edition of the Autobiography, recalled "Jerome's insults against Ruffino, with which the saint honored the monk with the title of 'pig who grunts, whose doctrines are 'Grunianae familiae stercora' [The Dunghill of the Grunian family]. Perhaps, some, will not like that we have lowered ourselves to sucj details: but we have retained it as necessary for those who will later, want to understand the personality of Maria Valtorta and explain the phenomenon. Moreover, we are happy: we took the opportunity to compare her, albeit timidly and modestly, to a great Saint and a great Doctor of the Church: St. Jerome!" (Corrado Berti, in Maria Valtorta, *Autobiografia prima*, op. cit., p. IX). [Not in the English edition].

[506] Father Migliorini and Father Berti sought to contact the Pope and, for this reason, prepared a memorandum. Regarding this, Maria Valtorta blurted out: "Even if the wait for the Holy Father is long, just do it well!

the courage to propose and tamper with. And then he will hear from me! Father Migliorini must be thinking that I am giving in. Instead, I am now made of hardened steel! I demand that they leave me in peace. I do not want them to do anything any longer. They have done enough harm to the Work and the creature. Enough"[507]. She never gave up hoping for repentance and better times, but Father Pennoni caused even more sorrow in Maria Valtorta when he told her that Father Migliorini did not believe her any more[508]. Here we find an inexplicable ambiguity in Father Migliorini: on one side, he no longer seemed to believe Maria Valtorta, therefore her writings should not have meant anything any longer to him, inasmuch as they were only human, of her own creation, and nothing more. But at the same time, he seemed to fear that they might end up in the hands of others, as if he were afraid of losing a treasure.

The letter of 8 April 1947 to Mother Teresa Maria is a cry of joy: "After writing a notebook of 408 pages in nine days (!) and having suffered my agony from midday on Friday until yesterday (although yesterday it was jubilation, but 1,914 years ago, it was the fatal Friday, and Jesus wanted me to commemorate it with Him), today I can take up my pen and… take a holiday. I spend it with You. *I have completed Jesus' mortal life*. So, I could say: I have finished. But Jesus told me that when I […] resurrect from the fatigue of the past few days, during which *I wrote for at least seven hours a day*, sometimes even nine (and such tiring and sorrowful pages!), He will dictate the *few* facts from

---

Do you feel that Father Migliorini is a clown? Now he doesn't want any more damage! Yes, No; no, yes! Will this block the way for H.H. [His Holiness]? Of course. He feels that his stunts are rising in the air! What's more, he likes the news that he will also be part of the Papal audience… He shows off that he's the 'spiritual director of the spokesperson'. He let everyone know who he was!!! His pride is his ruin!!!! (Maria Valtorta, *Lettere a Madre Teresa Maria 2*, op. cit., p 50).

[507] Maria Valtorta, *Lettere a Madre Teresa Maria 1*, p. 332.

[508] "Pennoni unwillingly said: 'F. M. [Father Migliorini] previously believed it but now he no longer believes that it is a supernatural work and therefore…'. I understood it on my own that he no longer believes in it, but this information is always valuable. Pennoni also said: 'I am afraid you want to get rid of us or to turn to others'" (Maria Valtorta, *Lettere a Madre Teresa Maria 2*, op. cit., pp. 17-8).

the Resurrection to the Ascension, and then I will be able to say: 'I have completely finished the Work'"[509]. Maria Valtorta seemed to be in a hurry[510] to finish the complete draft of every part of *The Gospel*. In fact, she continued writing, adding small fragments and only finished on 27 April 1947. The following day, she informed Mother Teresa Maria: "Extremely busy copying up the reasons for the Work, added as a farewell to it, *which I finished yesterday at Pentecost* [...] By him [Father Benedetti, Prior of the Servants of Mary of Pisa] I will have a visa affixed[511] on the completeness of the Work and a signature, in order to assure that the Work remains in the form dictated and enlightened by God without any human adjustments, which every writer usually makes to refine the writings before sending them to the publisher. My work will not be published, who knows for how long, but that does not matter - it is good that we do it this way"[512]. As a matter of fact, it was published in due course, but followed by the fury of the Holy Office. The pages written by Maria Valtorta are 13,193 in total, 11,000 of which describe the public life of Jesus Christ; something like 90 notebooks written quickly and by hand, with no revisions whatsoever[513]. The anxiety which transpired from the letters written up to that point to Mother Teresa Maria, slowly subsided. A few days later and much more relaxed, she was able to write: "I told Marta: 'If Mother Teresa Maria is re-elected, I will ask her for 12 funeral mementos for me'. I would not need any more,

---

[509] Maria Valtorta, *Lettere a Madre Teresa Maria 2*, op. cit., p. 79.

[510] "Oh! If it weren't for the fact that *The Gospel* needs to be finished, how I would like to die!" (ibid., p. 38. This is the letter dated 8 February 1947). Again, on 30 April, she expressed the same desire: "Both Jesus and I have a great desire to... reunite in Heaven, and the contemplation of Earth could also be short... Meanwhile last night, I really thought I was going to die and not even have time to say: 'My Jesus, mercy!'. My heart is whistling and bubbling like a poorly closed boiler, or too tightly closed, and it could burst from moment to moment. And then there are all the rest of my other ailments" (ibid., p. 95).

[511] She said it was signed on 30 April (ibid., p. 97).

[512] ibid., p. 93.

[513] cf. Emilio Pisani, Introduction to Maria Valtorta, *Il Poema dell'Uomo-Dio*, op. cit., p. XXXIX. Cf. Emilio Pisani, *Catalogo dei quaderni autografi di Maria Valtorta*, op. cit., p. 72.

but I would like them in that style... I must get everything ready because... I hope I will not remain down here for long... I really want to always see the Blessed Virgin Mary *forever*, to touch Her crown in Heaven"[514]. Maria Valtorta was afraid to die before she could complete the writing, but she was wrong because once the work was complete, she still had 14 years of hard physical and moral suffering. She might not have the thorn of writing for the moment, but a double problem arose: typing everything up and getting it ready for printing. It seemed easy enough, almost trivial, given the presence of the author, but it was very hard work with mistakes and omissions, so much so that Maria said: "Is my final call nearby? It would be a shame because I still have so much to copy, and Marta *does not want to go on*: another sorrow to add to the all the other ones! I wish I had put *everything* in order and then..."[515]. Marta Diciotti had turned from being a cleaning lady into a *factotum* (a handy-woman) around the house and her closest collaborator; she typed up her letters and her manuscripts. But oddly enough – so to speak – she could not keep up with the writer! The sick woman, always in pain and agonising, seemed to have more physical resources than Marta, who was healthy!

Not only *The Gospel*

Maria Valtorta not only wrote the *Autobiography* and *The Gospel as Revealed to Me*, but much more[516]. It is necessary, however, to make a distinction between what has already been published and what has not. Leaving aside the various extracts, the published works are: the *Autobiography, The Gospel as Revealed to Me, Notebooks 1943, Notebooks 1944, Notebooks 1945-1950, The Little Notebooks*[517]*, The Book of Azariah,*

---

[514] Maria Valtorta, *Lettere a Madre Teresa Maria 2*, op. cit., p. 102.

[515] ibid., p. 115.

[516] For a complete list of published texts – including extracts from the main writings – you can consult the website of the publisher-heir-holder-of-copyright: *http://www.mariavaltorta.com*.

[517] On page 4 of the third Italian edition, the publisher reports: "First Edition [2006] with some writings on the Tomb of St. Peter. Second Edition [2012] without the writings on the Tomb of St. Peter re-presented with additions in an extract. Third Edition [2015] the writings on the Tomb

Lessons on the Epistle of Paul to the Romans[518], *Letters to Father Migliorini, Letters to Monsignor Carinci, Letters to Mother Teresa Maria 1, Letters to Mother Teresa Maria 2.* [These four books of Letters are not available in English] There is also the commentary to the 'first four chapters of the Apocalypse', but this can be found in *Notebooks 1945-1950*.

There is a real uncertainty about the texts not yet published; for instance, the 'secret lessons' which Maria Valtorta mentions in *Notebooks 1945-1950*[519]. These are intimate directions – which do not go beyond 1950 – dictated to Maria Valtorta by Jesus and perhaps by her Guardian Angel, Azariah. Maria Valtorta mentioned them on 7 January 1947 (and on other dates)[520], saying that by the order of Jesus Himself, these dictations would not be reported anymore. This suggests that the secret lessons were written up to 13 October 1946, but they have certainly not been published – yet.

Maria Valtorta forged relationships with various people, also important ones. This suggests that there may be some documents that prove this– and hopefully, they have been stored. Instead, we do not have official information about the archives of Father Romualdo Migliorini, which should contain notes, cards, memos, letters to various religious and lay figures, preparatory writings for publishing, and other things. We only know about the letters in this archive, published in the homonymous text[521] that he wrote to Maria Valtorta. Even more important is the history of the archive of Father Corrado Maria Berti. Having died as a true Servite, he cooperated – from 1946 and practically until his own death on 15 December 1980 – at first with Maria Valtorta and then with her heirs, of whom he was for many years also an advisor and guide, obviously in a completely

---

of St. Peter are found in the appendix". In reality, the text also contains other documents not present in the two past editions and this is not reported. For example: from pp. 55-68, the documents are new. The first edition in English was only published in 2022.

[518] Maria Valtorta, *Lezioni sull'epistola di Paolo ai Romani* [Lessons on the Epistle of St. Paul to the Romans], Centro Editoriale Valtortiano, Isola del Liri (FR) 2007.

[519] Maria Valtorta, *Notebooks 1945-1950*, op. cit., dated 7 January 1947, p. 317.

[520] ibid., dated 31 January 1947, pp. 344-5.

[521] Maria Valtorta, *Lettere a Padre Migliorini*, op. cit.

disinterested way. These documents[522], in total or in part, should have been handed down to his private secretary and, now that he is dead, to his heirs. However, they seem to have been sealed, perhaps also because of unclear contrasts which took place. It is public knowledge that after years of cordial relationships and fruitful collaboration, the story between Father Berti and Dr. Emilio Pisani ended in misunderstandings and arguments[523]. This disagreement is also evident through the removal of theological notes in the Preface of *The Poem of the Man-God* written by Father Berti himself, without making a separate booklet out of them (as many expected and still do). Whereas the notes to the present edition of *The Gospel* have been compiled by Dr. Emilio Pisani, published by the Valtorta Editorial Centre, and as a separate volume[524]. Without going into their personal story or deciding who was right or wrong, what is clear is that the memoirs of Father Berti are indispensable to better understand Maria Valtorta, what really happened, and the human and spiritual environment in which she lived. This is the main reason why we insist so much on the necessity to publish absolutely everything relating to her. There is also the case of the indefatigable and meritorious Prof. Albo Centoni[525] who did not personally know Maria Valtorta, but

---

[522] "He, with notebook in hand, took note of everything" (Emilio Pisani, *Pro e contro Maria Valtorta*, op. cit., p. 35).

[523] Dr. Emilio Pisani himself testifies: "For a long time, we have been subjected to him with devotion. Then, although we owed him a lot, we began to oppose the subjectivism of some of his opinions and tactics" ("Bollettino Valtortiano", op. cit., n. 23 – January-June 1981, p. 91).

[524] Emilio Pisani (editor), *Note all'opera di Maria Valtorta con indici tematico e biblico* [Notes on the Work of Maria Valtorta with thematic and biblical indexes], Centro Editoriale Valtortiano, Isola del Liri (FR), 2001.

[525] Born in 1914 in Altopascio (LU) and died in Viareggio on 28 April 2003. A professor of letters, he taught for ten years in Hungary while also studying authors of mysticism. On returning to Italy, a colleague gave him a copy of *The Poem of the Man-God*. He admired it and he did not understand the indifference of the local clergy in the face of such a marvel. He did not meet Maria Valtorta, but only Marta Diciotti in 1974, and became enthralled by her. As a man of great culture that he was, he understood that it would be very serious to lose the testimonies of those still alive. He was not satisfied with short statements - he wanted to detail as much as possible what had happened in the life of Maria Valtorta. Using a tape recorder – a

who read *The Poem of the Man-God* from 1974 and got excited about it. So he had the brilliant idea of using an audio recorder to interview the women who lived in Viareggio and its surrounds that had met Maria, starting with her *family member* Marta Diciotti. Out of these recordings, two books were published ten years apart and with great difficulty, compiled by Prof. Centoni himself: *Una vita con Maria Valtorta* [A life with Maria Valtorta] in 1988 and *Ricordi di Donne che hanno conosciuto Maria Valtorta* [Memoirs of Women who knew Maria Valtorta] in 1998, both published by CEV (VPC). The rest of this fundamental material has not been published and we can only hope that it will also, sooner or later, see the light[526]. The missing documents are an altogether different matter. In the second volume of letters to Mother Teresa Maria, there are time 'gaps' which reveal the absence of some letters; so there could be some missing in the first volume too, albeit in a less obvious way, for a total of about 200 letters. On top of this, there is no trace of the novel *Il cuore di una donna* [The Heart of a Woman][527], which Maria Valtorta wrote before

---

brilliant idea – he made the people who spent time around Maria Valtorta, and who would have never written a line, speak for as much as they could. It can be assumed that, apart from someone like Father Ubaldo Coppi, a Franciscan from Viareggio, he found himself facing a wall. But he persevered and today we have a part of those testimonies available. He talks a little about himself in Albo Centoni, *Una vita con Maria Valtorta. Testimonianze di Marta Diciotti*, op. cit., pp. 18-22. His greatest effort must have been the harmonization of what was recorded. Translating what was previously recorded into comprehensible, correct and explanatory Italian must have been an improbable effort.

[526] The Valtortian Editorial Centre has affirmed: "The unpublished material is for now, kept in our archive" ("Bollettino Valtortiano", op. cit., n. 66 – July-December 2003, p. 263).

[527] "'Burn everything. You must only be known as a writer of my Work'. So I, always obedient to Him, burnt that masterpiece. An obedience that cost me a lot, and which still weighs on me. However, the Will of God must always be done, whatever it is, whatever it costs!!! (This undated text which we have placed at the end, was written on a little piece of paper inside an envelope, on which Mother Teresa Maria of St. Joseph, a discalced Carmelite who was a great confidante of Maria Valtorta, had written: 'Piece of paper of Maria V. about her novel: *The Heart of a Woman*, and some lines by Marta. Marta's lines on another piece of paper are as follows: 'Various

anything else, and which her heirs said was burnt according to her wishes before she died and before becoming absent from this world. Another missing writing is the list of books in the Valtorta household. In *The Book of Azariah,* there is a reference to the books in Maria's tiny domestic library. Her Guardian Angel Azariah praised her for compiling a list of them, also including those books that she had lent and had not been returned yet[528]. Towards the end of the *Autobiography* (pp. 406-7), there is a sort of book list, almost a summary, but nothing more. Scattered here and there within the other writings, are references to single texts[529]. But in *The Little Notebooks,* a collection of 'the writings by Maria Valtorta – unpublished until 2006 [sic] – written on loose sheets of paper and bundles of sheets'[530], there are no traces of this important list. The heirs of Maria Valtorta and of Marta Diciotti have published the list of the original notebooks in a small volume with a table of contents[531]; this publication is obviously a good thing, but the official list of books in the Valtorta library is still missing.

A problem which may seem trivial, but is serious, arises in the analysis, even a superficial one, of *The Gospel as Revealed to Me.* As no scientific editorial methods were adopted [for the Italian edition] – notes, for instance, have been made using asterisks in the margins;

---

correspondence and her message about the order to burn her book *The Heart of a Woman* which I didn't want to burn and therefore still exists, unknown to her. Marta Diciotti 15 February 1962'. The voluminous manuscript was then delivered to the Publisher Emilio Pisani with the following letter: 'Viareggio 15 August 1978. *Dear Emilio. I entrust the manuscript of The Heart of a Woman to you. It should have been destroyed, as Maria told me, but I did not do it. You who have the means to burn it, can do it when you want. However, before my death. Marta Diciotti"* (Maria Valtorta, *the Little Notebooks,* op. cit., undated pp. 247-8. Maria Valtorta speaks of her novel in her Autobiography, in just a bit over halfway through the first chapter of the seventh part (cf. Maria Valtorta, *Autobiography,* op. cit., pp. 392-3).

[528] cf. Maria Valtorta, *The Book of Azariah,* op. cit., p. 35. This is the commentary on the readings on the third Sunday of Lent of the old missal, dated 24 March 1946.

[529] For example, cf. Maria Valtorta, *Autobiography,* op. cit., p. 59; Maria Valtorta, *Notebooks 1945-1950,* op. cit., dated 8 september 1945, pp. 107-8.

[530] Cf. Maria Valtorta, *the Little Notebooks,* op. cit., p. 9.

[531] Emilio Pisani, *Catalogo dei quaderni autografi di Maria Valtorta,* op. cit.

and the subdivision of the verses within each chapter is editorial and therefore questionable – there is no clarity, and it is impossible to make precise references. The impression is that one aims at readability but presenting it as a novel rather than as a scientific illustration of the Gospel. One could object that all these observations are trivial, even worthless. Why then waste time with such minor details? Are there not more important things at stake? The answer is simple: it is not true that they are worthless, minor details. Before the judgment of the Church, nothing is worthless. Even her shopping lists would be important, as proof of the poverty and the destitution, of the winter chill and the summer heat in which Maria Valtorta lived. Even these, then, should be made public and available for study. The example has not been chosen at random: in the *Carnets de Tamanrasset* [Notebooks of Tamanrasset] by Blessed Charles de Foucauld, there are also the daily shopping lists[532], and practically a whole volume is dedicated to these apparently futile notes. This information is important also in the case of Maria Valtorta.

So much written work!

At this point, it is important to give an explanation to those who do not understand why Maria Valtorta and her writings have not been accepted by the Church yet. The point of view wants to be – presumes to be – that the Church wants to know everything, absolutely everything, to avoid making human mistakes, to examine and give a dispassionate judgment. After all, it is obvious that the Church demands, and will demand knowledge and a scrutiny of every possible material regarding Maria Valtorta: even the smallest thing must be examined before making any serious analysis regarding her heroic life. This is the ecclesiastical approach, obvious and foregone. The process of the beatification of Maria Valtorta is at a standstill, frozen, for the simple reason that even today, not everything has been published and made public. And this keeps any analysis by the

---

[532] cf. Charles de Foucault, *Carnets de Tamanrasset 1905-1916* [The Notebooks of Tamanrasset 1905-1916], Nouvelle Cité, Paris 1986. Blessed Charles lived the last 15 years of his life in extreme poverty in Tamanrasset, a poor village on the edge of the Algerian Sahara.

Church from starting. And any official sanctity only comes later. In addition, we must understand that it is only the Church that judges and decides - no one else. It is the Church that sets the rules. Neither the number of translations nor the copies sold have any value in demonstrating orthodoxy and personal sanctity. Our desires, feelings and laziness – not to mention our conceit and a know-it-all attitude – are insignificant at best, or even sins at worst. What is the distribution during the years of the writings by Maria Valtorta? In other words: has the number of written pages been uniform, year after year, or were there periods when her commitment was stronger?

This is a general chart of the amount of work done by Maria Valtorta during the various years. Horizontally are the years 1942-1955; vertically is the total number of written pages; in the grey area are the different texts. It is a general, schematic representation showing the curve of intensity and quantity of work over the years. After an almost insignificant start in 1942, there was the beginning of 1943 with dictations only; there followed a strong increase in 1944, besides which were the visions, and this year was also marked by the discomfort for her of the evacuation to Sant'Andrea di Còmpito. In 1945, the writings increased even more because there were, at the same time, dictations, spiritual letters to Mother Teresa Maria and visions. The effort peaked in 1946, with the drafting of dictations, visions, and letters to Mother Teresa Maria and to Father Migliorini; there also started the dictations of her Guardian Angel Azariah. The year 1947 continued with the same rhythm until the end of April. From May onwards, the visions decreased with the completion of *The Gospel*. In 1948 the writing work decreased; it was mainly the *Lessons on the Epistle of St. Paul to the Romans* written during the first six months. The work further diminished in 1949, followed by a peak in the final months of 1950 when, in a different style, she wrote the comments to the first four chapters of the Apocalypse, which later ended abruptly. The fragments of *The Gospel* of the years 1952, 1953, 1954, maintained the usual style; the letters to Mother Teresa Maria never really stopped, but many of them – about 150 – were lost or burnt [!] by the nun herself.

These letters aside, there are 13,193[533] notebook pages, written by hand using every available space. *Catalogo dei quaderni autografi di Maria Valtorta* [The catalogue of the handwritten notesbooks of Maria Valtorta] contains a few pages of her notebooks at the end. They remind us, visually, of the authors of the glorious Soviet *samizdat*[534], bravely written during the hell of the ruling Communist Party, making use of every available blank space. Regarding Maria Valtorta, this only shows the poverty in which she lived. We must stress that the scale of the contents of *The Gospel* alone was mentioned by various authors: between January 1944 and April 1947, she wrote 90 notebooks with about 11,000 handwritten pages; not a novel, written in one go, with no real historical-geographical references, but of something incredibly precise. The initiator of these discoveries wrote: "Now, even in possession of an exceptional biblical knowledge, of unlimited documentation and many years of preparation (all things that Maria Valtorta did not have), it is undeniable that no human being, albeit erudite, could have written of their own initiative, the manuscript works left behind by Valtorta"[535]. Is this a unique case of

---

[533] Emilio Pisani, *Catalogo dei quaderni autografi di Maria Valtorta*, op. cit., p. 72.

[534] For example, cf. http://www.italian-samizdat.com/2017/11/samizdat-e-tamizdat.html and, in general, also http://www.russiacristiana.org, consulted 19 October 2018.

[535] Jean-François Lavère, *The Valtorta Enigma*, op. cit., p. 285. Father Berti wrote: "Very lively intelligence ('oracle of the class'), remarkable culture (high school curriculum, twenty months of selected readings), tenacious memory ('phonographic record') and kept in operation ('Gospel... by heart'), extraordinary sensitivity ('transmitting stations', 'wires', or 'receiving antenna'), empathy ('engagement', 'spousal') with Christ (in the sense of: Galatians 2:19-20), singular charisms ('dreams', 'visions', 'words', 'caresses', etc.). These are the main elements that explain the great Valtortian phenomenon and, in particular, the Work *The Poem of the Man-God*" (Maria Valtorta, *Autobiografia prima*, op. cit., p. 232 note 132) [Not in the English edition]. This language seems to investigate any qualitative diversity, but remains ambiguous, almost excluding the supernatural intervention of God, which instead should be explicitly emphasized. All the characteristics reported here would have served no purpose to Maria Valtorta if, in her life, there had not been a direct divine intervention.

the writer Maria Valtorta? Yes and no. Historically, there have been very prolific writers. Isaac Asimov, a writer born in Russia but a naturalised US citizen wrote 500 fantasy novels, some extremely successful. The whole work is breathtakingly large and inventive, but they are fantasy novels: pure invention, which despite being tidy and coherent has at its base a sometimes purely hypothetical science. There are large written works also in the esoteric, spiritist and *New Age* worlds: Helena Blavatsky, who co-invented theosophy, wrote an impressive number of texts[536], same thing for Tommaso Palamidessi and his *Archeosofia* [Archeosophy][537], written in five large volumes; then there are the spiritist texts of 'Circolo 77' [Circle 77] [538], with a disproportionate number of published pages; *Un corso in miracoli* [A Course in Miracles][539], a *New Age* text and many more. The Catholic world also has similar examples of extremely prolific authors. Just think of the 36 volumes of Luisa Piccarreta, the mystic of Corato (Bari)[540]. So, in this regard, Maria Valtorta was not a unique case at all. But it was a unique case if we look at it from the Galilean-science viewpoint. It is undeniable that her writings are an act of love from Heaven for mankind of the 20th-century and beyond. However, without their extraordinary scientific depth, their value would be limited to whoever has the gift to receive it. Instead, since scientific coherence 'signs' the writings, everyone can surrender to Love, if they wish, regardless of their cultural background.

---

[536] Helena Petróvna Blavatsky, *La dottrina segreta* [The Secret Doctrine], Edizioni Teosofiche Italiane, Vicenza 2003. This consists of eight volumes of approximately 2,500 very dense pages. To these we should add *Iside segreta* [Secret Iside] of roughly the same size.

[537] Tommaso Palamidessi, *Archeosofia* [Archaeosophy], Edizioni Archeosofica di S. Palamidessi & C. s.n.c., Roma 1989.

[538] cf. *http://www.cerchiofirenze77.org/Libri/Libri%2077.html*, consulted 19 October 2018.

[539] *Un corso in miracoli* [A Course in Miracles], Gruppo Editoriale Armenia, Milano 1999.

[540] A strange situation regarding her texts is that they are all published by Edizioni Segno (Tavagnacco, Udine). However, the publishing house did not have the consent of her heirs. The Editrice Gamba (Verdello, Brescia), which is the official heir of Piccarreta, has not yet published anything.

The tortures of Maria Valtorta

Leaving aside the external events like the war, the fight between Maria Valtorta and her body was huge, it was gigantic. We must keep this firmly in mind, otherwise we risk playing down her struggle to write. Whoever has been ill – and we have all experienced illness in one way or another – knows that even just feeling a bit weak, having a headache or a 'simple' toothache makes it impossible to have a clear head. The huge number of elements of a various nature, which Maria Valtorta had to manage at the same time, is not compatible with the state of her health. No one would be able to do it, especially not that way, with simplicity, without mistakes, without a rewrite, with precise places, people, and times. It is right to stress this: her state of health did not consist of a few recurring colds; but of serious and debilitating illnesses. Maria Valtorta had offered her life to help Jesus convert and save mankind; she did it several times, offering herself up to Divine Justice. And the good Lord had taken her seriously. Furthermore, her health makes us think of an external and superior intervention that helped her. The starting point of her physical suffering is without a doubt the iron bar blow to her lower back in 1920, which eventually left her bedridden and subsequently experiencing terrible suicidal thoughts[541]. The tears caused by the various illnesses never dried up. In her *Autobiography*[542] there is an amazing description: ", Seeing that I often cried for fear of losing her [her mother Iside], the doctor told me: 'Just thank God! I bet you will get better if your mother dies. Think of yourself!' But she was my mother. She is my mother. She did not do anything to be loved. On the contrary, she did everything to kill even the most stubborn love. But I still love her, I always love her. I am the only one who loves her. In the past it was me and father. Now it is only me. Without that little peace that I used to have before, eating even less and worse food than usual in order to make ends meet with the little money that mother gave me, I would leave her the best cuts of meat and generous wines, rare fruit and refreshing drinks. I would strain my ears at night to hear if she moved, being reproached even more than usual, and hearing Marta being reproached *all the time*. The sorrow in seeing her

---

[541] Maria Valtorta, *Autobiography*, op. cit., p. 169.
[542] ibid., pp. 410-2.

suffer were all further blows to my already hurt body. Since then, I have gotten worse than I have ever been in almost ten years. I developed new illnesses, which added to those already present: neuritis with a stabbing pain, so intense that I begged the doctor to make me die. I resorted to covering my face with a very strong tincture of iodine to make the trigeminal, which was driving me crazy with pain, go numb. I could not relieve these discomforts with any painkillers because of my heart problems. The neuritis was joined by a pachymeningitis which made me as cold as a mummy. The smallest movement made me scream. My kidneys deteriorated and the chronic cystitis became more complicated with a pyelocystitis which culminated in kidney and bladder hemorrhages. The peritonitis worsened causing intestinal occlusion. The pleurisies grew on the right-hand side where some painful adhesions formed. In the very cold December 1940 while Marta was away for a few days, I suffered a lung congestion which got worse and worse with all the various relapses I have had since then as I had no hot water bottles left, and no heating"[543]. Maria Valtorta remained a born fighter, and so she was able to write: "I accept my five illnesses, and I agree to accepting another five, another ten with all the torments, but I only ask to be left in my own house where Jesus has done so many things for me and which is sacred to me for His sake, for the house was given to me by Him, and my parents died here"[544]. Her illnesses became seven[545], and the vision said to her: "The valid proof that *it is not you* who is writing by your own reflection and knowledge: it is offered precisely by the sentences introduced between the lines and the visible corrections observed in the dictations. They are caused *by the physical and sometimes mental weakness* of the sick spokesman, oppressed by seven chronic diseases which sometimes flare up again, entirely or in part, bringing about mortal suffering and weakness in the writer. *The external disturbances in the environment* for the spokesman, make writing in those environmental conditions neither peaceful nor

---

[543] ibid.

[544] Maria Valtorta, *Notebooks 1943*, op. cit., dated 2 November, p. 445. Also in Maria Valtorta, *Notebooks 1944*, op. cit., dated 25 November, p. 623.

[545] Maria Valtorta, *Lettere a Madre Teresa Maria 2*, op. cit. p. 92, letter dated 18 April 1947.

comfortable."[546]. But to Mother Teresa Maria, her confidante and spiritual friend, she listed the serious illnesses that plagued her: "*The spine*: the pain starts from the cervical vertebra and extends to the whole spine, increasing and reaching the maximum pain where I was hit: the lumbar area. *The heart*: myocarditis with *very strong* systolic murmur, a dilated heart beyond measure, the outcome of exudative pericarditis. (Borraccini said that my heart was healthy and only its functionality was compromised. Not!...). Lungs and pleura: right lung: silent while breathing with rattling, hissing, and crackling in the whole area. Left lung is less obstructed but with a baseline tendency to become like the former. Outcome of pleurisies are stronger on the right-hand side than on the left where at present, there is a pleural crisis in progress. The fluctuation that I can feel on the left hemithorax is caused by an effusion which alternatively forms and reabsorbs. *The Liver*: twice as large as normal. It goes beyond the thoracic arch by four fingers. The gall bladder is very painful and hard. *Abdomen*: active pain which prevents palpation of the right-hand side of the abdomen where there is the presence of a hard, large mass. The left-hand side is soft and painless. (At this point, Father Berti was sent away in order to proceed with the gynecological examination). *Gynaecological examination:* tumor on ovary cyst which has penetrated the uterus from the right ovary and is advancing. This has caused peritonitis, adhesions, inflammation of the colon, and appendicitis, which are merged and squeezed by the timorous mass. And that is it. I think I have enough"[547]. According to Dr Ezio Bocedi

---

[546] Maria Valtorta, *Notebooks 1945-1950*, op. cit., dated 6 December, 1947, p. 446. On 8 March 1949, she wrote to Msgr. Carinci: "On the 17th of this current month, I will have been sick for 29 years, and on 18 December 1948, it will be 16 years that I have been a prisoner of the sickness that nails me to my bed. I have lost all my savings in this long illness; I do not have the means to cure myself as I should, and to live the life that even my seven diseases would impose. I never complained about anything" (Maria Valtorta, *Lettere a Mons. Carinci*, op. cit., p. 42).

[547] Maria Valtorta, *Lettere a Madre Teresa Maria 2*, op. cit., pp. 125-6. Note the subtle humor at the end. In her 1943 autobiography Maria said that at that time she had gotten "over 13,000, I say thirteen thousand..." injections (Cf. Maria Valtorta, *Autobiography*, op. cit., p. 353). Starting from when she

of Carrara (Massa Carrara) her clinical picture was that of someone in agony all the time[548]. And yet, despite all these serious physical problems, Maria Valtorta did not let any of them stop her, and went on writing tiressl for the glory of the Father, of Jesus and for the salvation of mankind.

A less-known thing is this remark by Eroma Antonini: "Despite her great pain (because she did not take morphine, as she did not take any type of drugs, nor calmine, and on this we totally agreed as I did not take them either, or to be precise, I did not take them during the years of my illness), Maria was lucky because she was able to sit up in bed"[549]. In these few words, we can see to what extent Maria Valtorta accepted and wanted to unite herself with the crucified Christ. Self-immolation was no joke to her.

Marta Diciotti also testified that despite being seriously ill, Maria Valtorta was never scruffy: "To Maria, her body really was a temple for the Holy Spirit. She cared for it as for a gift from our Maker, a precious gift, the value of which we must appreciate, but without any exaggeration, idolatry, so frequent especially among women. Her body to her, was above all, a way to reach spiritual fullness, to reach that maturity and purification necessary for the conquest of Heaven, of bliss [...]. She loved cleanliness, but she was not manic about it; she loved beauty and she was very sensitive to it, but she did not concede anything to frivolity and silly feminine vanity. She was able to appreciate and taste the delicacy and goodness of food, but she did not indulge in it, but only to the extent necessary for keeping her strength up to be able to work and survive, but never overdoing it with abstention, fasting and penitence"[550]. Whoever goes today to her house-museum, will find it in the same condition of order and cleanliness as it was when Maria Valtorta was alive. The only thing missing today is, obviously, "the pungent smell of medicines and

---

had suffered the assault on her lower back, that is an average of more than 1.5 injections per day.

[548] A statement that was made several times verbally in public meetings and to the microphones of Radio Maria as already reported in note 225.

[549] Albo Centoni, *Ricordi di donne che conobbero Maria Valtorta*, op. cit., p. 115.

[550] Albo Centoni, *Una vita con Maria Valtorta. Testimonianze di Marta Diciotti*, op. cit., pp. 151-2.

disinfectants mixed with the sweet scent of talc"[551], which reflected her diseased state and the way she was looked after.

On the political barricade

Maria Valtorta felt like a Carmelite and a recluse[552]: she regarded the size of her bed as the fencing wall of her own Carmel. As she had a good sense of humour, she was able to joke about it: "[I am] Sister Maria of the Cross, a discalced Carmelite of a *very closed order*... More closed than this! For 13 years, I have been occupying the same space that I will occupy once dead: 2 square or cubic metres, whatever you wish to call it: my bed"[553]. From Good Friday 1934, she was bedridden inside a small room. Until 23 April 1943, visits were infrequent due to her infirmity. Afterwards, when even Heaven asked her to live in total enclosure and following the Bishop of Lucca's denied visit, she shut herself off from the outer world even more. One might wonder what she could have done that was socially or politically relevant in such a state. Had she had a background such as Franklin Delano Roosevelt – already an active politician and later a victim of a serious form of polio, who despite this, became the President of the United States of America? She may have been able to do something too, but in her condition, no contribution was possible neither was it required. And yet, if we scratch the surface of

---

[551] Testimony of Flora Antonioni in a tabloid article published on 11 July 1959 in the newspaper 'Il Tempo', with the horrendous and disparaging title: "The Bible of the antipope Clement was written in a trance by a madwoman". (From the cutout of the newspaper without the page number.) The female journalist managed to overcome the Marta Diciotti's barrier and enter the small room.

[552] The reason is also this: "I have not made you a public prophet because the public would invade your seclusion and you need to need seclusion. A strict seclusion, but also one with freedom; more than you would get if attracting vast, special attention to you as a prophet, resulted in having to take the prudent or cruel step of putting you in a convent" (Maria Valtorta, *The Little Notebooks*, op. cit., p. 131).

[553] Maria Valtorta, *Lettere a Madre Teresa Maria 1*, op. cit., p. 25. "I will pray for those aspiring to Carmel ... I ... a discalced Carmelite for 12 years (!?) And a recluse of love. I don't know when I will make ... a bundle" (ibid., p. 52).

her life a little, we may find and learn something. Before she was left permanently bedridden during her life in Viareggio and despite her mother Iside – who *was decisive* and a great fan of Fascism and of the Duce – Maria Valtorta had been a member, brave and fearless, of *Catholic Action*. When the Fascists closed the organization's offices, she was the one who faced the events because everyone else panicked and left all duties to her[554]. Her aversion to Fascism and Nazism[555] first, and to Communism later, has always been clear, ever since they were in power and not just when they were relegated to the *scrapyard of history*. Marta Diciotti gave a lucid, curious and at the same time cheerful description: "When in 1938 the first signs started to show, which became more frequent and ominous in 1939, she used to say: 'Oh, yes! These two with their actions will lead us to a horrific war'. [...] And her mother with her monocle dangling from a black cord worn as a necklace, hitting the newspaper which she was reading and commentating with her magnifying glass, would exclaim: 'Nonsense! Never! This man, Mussolini, he knows what to do and what needs to be done. If this man says so, it means that it is the right thing to say and do. But... you! You are always a prophet of doom!' And Maria: 'I pray to the Lord that I'm mistaken! But unfortunately, if you live long enough, you will see for yourself - that great man of yours is just a little man. Pray to the Lord that you may soon die and take me away with you, or else you will see what those two cronies will do. Let us hope neither of us shall still be here, or we shall have to go through the mill'"[556]. Then the horrific war came and stayed for a year in Viareggio, which was the starting point of the famous Gothic Line.

---

[554] cf. Maria Valtorta, *Autobiography,* op. cit., pp. 299-300.

[555] "It seemed to me that you [Albo Centoni, with whom Marta Diciotti is talking] had something to say about the two Mussolini brothers, Arnaldo and Benito. I don't remember if we have already written about it. Do you remember? I think so. However, Maria's thoughts on the two were as follows: she felt sympathetic towards Arnaldo and said: 'He was a just man. In fact, as long as he was alive, the other did not do a lot of nonsense." Then when Benito Mussolini went with Hitler, she said: 'It is now over for us'. Nevertheless, for certain things, she appreciated him" (Albo Centoni, *Una vita con Maria Valtorta. Testimonianze di Marta Diciotti*, op. cit., p. 272).

[556] Albo Centoni, *Una vita con Maria Valtorta. Testimonianze di Marta Diciotti*, op. cit., pp. 337-8.

Eventually the war ended, and the post-war period began with all the choices that the Italians had to make. And Maria Valtorta took sides, at great risk to her life. We do not have any particular memories of 2 June 1946[557] except for very broad foresight regarding future events which years later, she mentioned to Msgr. Carinci: "The Divine Author together with several prophesies have now taken place: on the fall of the monarchy, on the preservation of the Vatican City despite Hitler's contrary opinion, on the invasion of our whole country, on mass deportations, on the collapse of morality, as well as on the misuse of minerals enclosed by the Creator inside the globe for *good purposes*, and extracted in order to build instruments for the destruction of mankind and of despair for the souls. She said that He was giving these writings: *to fight* the anti-Christian doctrines which would spread around the world after the war; in preparation for the advent of Communism or religious persecution; for man's freedom of thought which God himself respects; and *to help* mankind endure the terrible trials of the future of even more horrific wars, without dying of despair"[558]. After all in 1946, the drama of the break-up with Father Migliorini and the relative consequences were still too fresh in her mind for her to look at that day's events with much attention, even though she read the newspaper every day. We can see the sign and the worry of what could have happened on 18 April 1948: the Italian people had to decide whether they would become a satellite of the Soviet Union or remain free with the West. What Maria Valtorta cared about was the religious and Catholic side of the matter. Her stance had therefore deep religious roots because on one side, there was imposed state atheism and on the other side, there was religious freedom. As the communist-led popular front seemed to be preponderant, which had prevailed in the choice of a republic, even the last vote became decisive and it was necessary to remain unflinching. Freedom had to be defended at all costs, even at the cost of one's life! On 17 April "Immediately after Holy Communion which I offered for the elections, and my Viaticum in case I died on my way to going to vote, I say to Jesus: 'I offer you my life and even

---

[557] Voting day for the people's choice between Monarchy and Republic.
[558] Maria Valtorta, *Lettere a Mons. Carinci*, op. cit., p. 90, letter dated 24 July 1950.

renounce seeing the Work published, provided the Communists don't win'"[559]. Maria Valtorta really risked her life, as she went to vote on a stretcher. "It was election time and as 18 April was a Sunday, she told him (Msgr. Carinci, the Prefect of the Sacred Congregation of Rites): 'I am going to vote on Sunday'. He advised her against it, saying: 'Beware what you do'. And she added: 'No, no, Monsignor, I have to go, and I will go'"[560]. The fear was great for many because of the possible consequences, some of them even boarded up their homes, weapons in hand[561]. Maria regarded the victory of freedom as a gift from God, and as such, she always defined it.[562]. Maria

---

[559] Maria Valtorta, *The Little Notebooks*, op. cit., p. 108. But Jesus did not accept the offer: "But this time, no. My Will is something else" (ibid.).

[560] Albo Centoni, *Una vita con Maria Valtorta. Testimonianze di Marta Diciotti*, op. cit., p. 399.

[561] "The free world is in suspense; the Peninsula is at a crossroads. Italy does not only have Stalin's troops in Trieste; The largest and fiercest Communist Party of the West is found within its borders: 2 million members, 50 thousand cells, 50-100 thousand armed (the Red Volanti and the Gap had gone on a rampage, eliminating with impunity a hundred priests and other political opponents). [...] 18 April was the *redde rationem* (day of accountability). Togliatti, who scornfully called De Gasperi Chancellor von Gasper, had promised him that – in the aftermath of the victory – he would have kicked him out of the Interior Ministry. Especially in the red regions, 'the leaders (of the Front)' says Andreotti 'had brazenly threatened revenge and pitchforks'. In this climate of fear, violence and intimidation, the Italians had to choose the future of their country. "An event of historical importance," said Churchill. "The whole election campaign," wrote De Felice, "seemed aimed at a dramatic choice of regime." The result will be amazing, surprising, unique in the history of Italy" (cf. *http://www.europaoggi.it/content/view/1502/94/*, consulted 18 October 2018).

[562] "Having obtained democratic freedom from the Italian people, they also wanted to vote on 18 April 1948. And then, commenting on the results, he said: 'Here, the Italians had a great gift from the Lord. We hope that they will understand its profound meaning and treasure it for the future. These words, which in the ear of many may seem those of a naive bigot, had instead a conscious and accentuated vein of melancholy, because she had experience with human nature, and certainly had no illusions about it. She knew the value of freedom, indispensable for the true growth of man, and she feared that the Italian people, unaccustomed by many years of

Valtorta's courage never failed, not even in politics. She never compromised with communism, ready to show it to the point of paradox: "Rather than being ruled by the communists, it would be better for Italy to be pulverized by the Atomic bomb"[563]. Maria Valtorta knew very well what was going on in many countries, and that is why she fought at the risk of her life so that this would not happen to her own country as well[564]. She offered the Lord prayers and tears, sacrifices and penitence, so that Italy would not fall into the abyss. We might wonder what the political model was that she adhered to. Perhaps, if we could make an external reference, it would be that of Don Sturzo[565]. He was a priest but involved in politics since his youth. In 1919, he founded the Italian Popular Party, clearly Christian and anti-state, and as a determined opponent of Fascism, he had to remain abroad until the end of World War II. Once back in Italy, he joined the Christian Democratic Party and always opposed the advent of Socialists to power. He died in Rome in 1959. However, it is not right to compare Maria with him because Maria Valtorta did not need a political party to support. She only had a strong Christian wish for Italy to remain a Catholic country. Social atheism – in any form – was what she feared and what she strongly opposed. This attitude grew stronger when Heaven started to reveal itself to her. In any case, even in politics she could not show any signs of weakness[566].

---

dictatorship, would not be able to make good use of it and would not have sufficient awareness of both its great value and of its fragility" (Albo Centoni, *Una vita con Maria Valtorta. Testimonianze di Marta Diciotti*, op. cit., p. 379).

[563] Maria Valtorta, *Lettere a Mons. Carinci*, op. cit., p. 94.

[564] "And in these terrible times, in which Communism increasingly advances its tentacles like that of an infernal octopus that throttles the Good in the nations that it, openly or subtly, invades" (ibid., p. 37).

[565] cf. Marco Invernizzi, *Il movimento cattolico in Italia dalla fondazione dell'opera dei congressi all'inizio della seconda guerra mondiale (1874-1939)* [The Catholic movement in Italy from the foundation of the work of Congress to the beginning of the Second World War (1874-1939)], Mimep-Docete, Cassano con Bornago (MI) 1995.

[566] It is interesting to note that the term "resignation", with all that it means, is very present in all her writings. However, "resignation" can only occur before an invincible evil or if there is no longer any possibility of action. This is the meaning of the word. Throughout the Valtortian work

Marta Diciotti's recollections

Due to their bedridden lives, their contemporary environment, their serious and several illnesses and the gifts they received, Maria Valtorta, Luisa Piccarreta (23 April 1865-4 March 1947), Marthe Robin (13 March 1902-6 February 1981), and Alexandrina Maria da Costa (3 March 1904-13 October 1955) are very similar[567]. They spent years and years in bed, totally dependent on other people's love, and having to make do with very few or nothing at all. All four of them, although in different ways, made their own lives an 'immobile Journey'[568]; they all lived with small things, despite having been granted great gifts. Maria Valtorta had a good witness, Marta Diciotti, and thanks to the tireless help of Prof. Albo Centoni – without whose hard work everything would have been lost forever – we have today, the memories of many small-great-indispensable things which took place in her small but beloved bedroom. Not everything has been typed up in current Italian, but within what has already been printed, we have a great deal of news and legitimate curiosities. So we can follow Marta Diciotti in some of her recollections in order to better understand Maria Valtorta.

First, her discretion: "Maria did not like talking about herself and she was especially reluctant to open up with regards to her inner life. She was very shy about this and closed in on herself like a

---

the term "resignation" is used at least 40 times and always in a positive way. Pain is also accepted within this term. For this reason, in chapter 83 it is also said: "'Is pain not always evil?' 'No, my friend. It is an evil from a human point of view, but from a supernatural one, it is good. It increases the merits of just people who accept it without despairing and rebelling, and they offer it, as they offer themselves with resignation, as a sacrifice to expiate their own imperfections and the faults of the world, and it is a redemption for those who are not good" (Maria Valtorta, *The Gospel as Revealed to Me*, op. cit., vol. 2, p. 44).

[567] Maria Valtorta also mentioned several times Sister Josefa Menendez (1890-1923). However, despite being a great mystique, she did not have a story similar to the other people mentioned (cf. Josefa Menendez, *Invito all'amore* [Invitation to love], Editrice Shalom, Camerata Picena (AN) 2015. Cited in: Maria Valtorta, *The Little Notebooks*, op. cit., pp. 181-3).

[568] Jean Jacques Antier, *Marthe Robin. Il viaggio immobile* [Marthe Robin. The motionless journey], San Paolo Edizioni, Milano 1994, pp. 186-8.

hedgehog"[569]. This attitude was in part natural to her and in part it came from Heaven's request not to reveal anything before everything had been completed. Marta explained: "As she was so shy and so strongly reticent about her intimate spiritual life, she was obviously the least-suited person to give rise to fanaticism and to want it around her. That's right, if she had been less strict and had claimed: 'I can see the Lord... He speaks to me... He shows me... He orders me...' and so on, you can imagine what would have happened within these walls, out there in town... and so on"[570]. This discretion – which is not present in the letters to Mother Teresa Maria due to the confidence and spiritual openness already mentioned – may arguably have further increased after the refusal by Msgr. Torrini to go to her house during a pastoral visit[571].

Maria Valtorta did not write whenever she wanted or whenever she could, but whenever Heaven requested or demanded it. "Maria told me many times: 'I do not know where the Lord will take me today, what He will dictate to me, what He will show me and make me describe'... And in fact, often, in the morning, I would see her there, washed and all tidy, at work because she had always something to do on hand - some sewing or crocheting; not knitting because the movements involved in that task made her back pain worse. When I saw that she was not writing... 'Well, what now?'. As if to say: 'Does the Lord not need you today?' And she: 'I do not know whether He will want me today... Let's wait and see. I may even have a day off today...'"[572]. Then, at a time not decided by her, she would start writing without a break: "Sometimes many hours went by when Maria, all caught up in her task, did not stop writing. And of course, as I knew where her mind and her heart were, I did not dare disturb her: I did not bother her, even if I needed her. So, I would come back here, with all the things that needed to be done, and that made mornings fly!"[573]

---

[569] Albo Centoni, *Una vita con Maria Valtorta. Testimonianze di Marta Diciotti*, op. cit., p. 59.
[570] ibid., p. 60.
[571] The story is recounted in ibid., pp. 55-6.
[572] ibid., p. 61.
[573] ibid., p. 63.

This simple fact, which seems very small, is further proof that she was not the one who wrote her story. As already mentioned, it was not even a matter of strange evocations or altered states of consciousness: Marta would have certainly mentioned them and anyway, they would have been visible in the details of her daily life. We should also emphasize Maria Valtorta's industriousness, as she was always ready to do something practical or to read, always ready to write and never prone to laziness and idle sleep.

From the statements of Marta Diciotti, we have a portrait of a clear-headed, pragmatic woman, perfectly normal despite her illnesses and the terrible trials of her life, a realist beyond measure, even a decision-maker, full of common sense and not in the least trapped in a past from which does not return. She said: "I never saw in her any pettiness or small-mindedness. On the contrary, despite her spontaneous simplicity, I often perceived in her soul such amounts of greatness and generosity that took my breath away in astonishment. She was always right... and (to my childish annoyance, sometimes) she was never wrong!... even when she arrived at making those statements all by herself, and when she made them after being enlightened from Above. Without a doubt, she constantly lived ... in high spheres, with her mind, heart, and her whole self turned towards her immense Love. And yet, she kept her feet firmly on the ground, meaning that her observant eyes and her subtle mind could see reality's infinite miseries very well, especially the moral ones. No, her capacity for discernment was not attenuated or obscured by false idealisms, by misleading illusions. She could look the sad truth in the face, denounce it with honesty and fight it with strong-mindedness"[574].

The radio

Against her mother Iside's will, the arrival of the Belfanti family who evacuated from Reggio, Calabria, also brought the arrival of the radio. "This huge appliance remained here... it remained on that bedside table by Maria's bed... until later, in 1950, she was given a new one, which is still in her bedroom now. Yes, it is small, but it is also short-wave; and she liked that because she could listen to the

---

[574] ibid., p. 84.

Vatican Radio which broadcasted on short-wave. She listened to the programs of that radio station: she regularly listened to the Rosary, to church services and especially to the Sunday Mass. If there was something religious on, she would not miss it[575]. But she did not disdain non-religious programs if they were serious and of artistic value. She could not stand jazz music, or those flippant silly songs"[576]. She, who *listened* virtually daily to the voices from Heaven, also appreciated these small earthly things, just like that 'short-wave radio'. At the time, there were no independent radio stations[577] or Radio Maria[578], but only the national RAI, which could be listened to on 'medium wave' and on three channels in *frequency modulation*. On the rest of the waveband there was just a crackling sound. A piece of the world entered the Valtorta household, but in a filtered way, so that it would not cause any distraction whatsoever: the 'short waves' allowed her to follow the Vatican Radio and listen to the voice of the Pope. It must be noted that even in the case of the radio, the strictly religious and Catholic dimension of life was her constant goal and listening filter. In 1952, the experimentations with television technology resumed, and on 3 January 1954, a national television broadcast began. Television is always very attractive to a bedridden patient. There is pain, of course, but also boredom and a sense of uselessness: television could alleviate at least the latter ones. In fact, a few friends of Maria Valtorta's, moved by compassionate love, would have liked to buy her a television set, but Maria Valtorta was clear about this: "With regard to a television, she said: 'No, I do not want it because they could broadcast something about Palestine and then someone could think that it was easy for me to describe scenes and landscapes, as can be found in the Poem' despite the fact that when she was offered one, she had already written everything

---

[575] ibid., p. 98. "Fr. Lombardi, the great Jesuit speaker, holds a radio sermon every Monday and Wednesday (red network stations). I listen to them. How I wish you could listen to them too! If I were there, perhaps in the farmer's house, I would turn the radio up completely to let you listen…" (Maria Valtorta, *Lettere a Madre Teresa Maria 2*, op. cit., p. 50).

[576] Albo Centoni, *Una vita con Maria Valtorta. Testimonianze di Marta Diciotti*, op. cit., p. 98.

[577] They began in 1974.

[578] It was founded in 1982 in Arcellasco d'Erba (CO).

concerning the Holy Land. Indeed, around Christmas and Easter, they would have broadcast programs on the life of Jesus... and she would have certainly watched them, interested as she was to see and know... But no! She did not want to give some sceptics the chance to make malicious remarks. So, the television did not enter this house until 18 December 1964, when Maria had already been dead for three years. I bought it and registered it in my name"[579].

It would have been very easy for her to fall into this *trap* and justify herself, but it did not happen. The illnesses of Maria Valtorta afflicted her body, but not her psyche: here her good health and normality were whole[580].

The telephone, the dog and the hen

The Valtorta household had another little-noticed electrical appliance: the telephone. Unfortunately, we do not have precise information; Mrs Maria Teresa Mencarini – a privileged eyewitness of those years, although after such a long-time memories get muddled – remembered that the telephone was installed in the second half of the 1950s; maybe it was linked to the widow's pension after her father's death. But this statement cannot be true because the pension was only granted in 1961 and the money only arrived on 18 September of that same year[581], one month before Maria Valtorta left this world. The telephone probably arrived at the beginning of 1950 because Marta Diciotti recalled this episode: "Despite all good intentions, the bell would ring, or (after 1949) the telephone would ring... and she would cry: 'There goes our peace!... ' But ready, with

---

[579] Albo Centoni, *Una vita con Maria Valtorta. Testimonianze di Marta Diciotti*, op. cit., p. 99. For the whole theme, cf. Franco Monteleone, *Storia della radio e della televisione in Italia. Un secolo di costume, società e politica* [History of radio and television in Italy. A century of customs, society, and politics], Marsilio Editori, Venezia 2001⁵.

[580] Also, thanks to this fact, it is evident that the criticisms of psychiatric and psychological pathologies are nothing. The case raised in Pier Angelo Gramaglia, *Maria Valtorta. Una moderna manipolazione dei Vangeli*, op. cit. is completely worthless.

[581] Albo Centoni, *Una vita con Maria Valtorta. Testimonianze di Marta Diciotti*, op. cit., p. 186.

a sense of calm and patience, she would face the unexpected"[582]. Marta also mentioned that Maria did not like the telephone much[583] and Mrs Mencarini confirmed that she only used it when Marta was away, to know who was knocking at the door and to beg for some indispensable help as she was bedridden. In any case, during the time in which Maria Valtorta wrote, there was no telephone, and this fact eliminates any suspicions which the critics may have.

Maria Valtorta loved animals, the company of which she always enjoyed. This friendship always proved to be useful to her, from many points of view. For example, the little dog which was given to her by Dr. Lapi paid her back by saving her life during a serious cardiac arrest. Marta Diciotti said: "That is how it went: I put the dog in Maria's bedroom, closed the door and went out to do some shopping. That little dog, realizing that her mistress was feeling unwell, jumped up and down so much that it managed to pull the handle and open the door. When I came back home, I found the dog by the entrance door, barking nervously and alarmed: 'Woof, woof, woof, woof!' 'What is wrong with you?' I said needlessly because I had already realised that something exceptional was going on. That is why, instead of going straight to the kitchen without thinking of Maria, which would usually happen as I had always many things to do, I burst into her room and saw at once that the situation was very serious. Speed in that case was of the essence and decisive, and I always remembered that rescue due to the intelligence and affection of that beautiful pet, so dear and so good"[584]. There is also a photo of this dog in Marta's arms[585], and there is also a photo of Maria and her cat Ninetto[586]. This lovely relationship with her pets was however totally realistic and anti-ideological. Also shown is Giacomino, 'a house-trained sparrow, one of the many found in the vegetable garden, or fallen from the nest or injured. It was a sparrow whose feathers she stored as a memento, […] along with the teeth of Toi

---

[582] ibid., p. 266. Cf. Albo Centoni, *Ricordi di donne che conobbero Maria Valtorta*, op. cit., p. 119.

[583] Albo Centoni, *Una vita con Maria Valtorta. Testimonianze di Marta Diciotti*, op. cit., p. 85.

[584] ibid., p. 124.

[585] ibid., p. 524, photo n. 4.

[586] ibid., p. 531, photo n. 15.

(the milk teeth replaced during dentition), and the whiskers of Ninetto and Ninetta, which she kept in her parents' little wedding box [...] Someone may smile, a little baffled by this sentimental behavior of an old maid [...] Giacomino was a sparrow, which Maria herself mentions somewhere, because I remember reading it. But with the sparrows (as I said, we wound find one in the vegetable garden from time to time), came the pigeons, the chickens, the canaries, the dogs, the cats, and so on. Yes, a lot of these little creatures came because Maria loved to be surrounded by them"[587]. However, Maria was not an animal activist (a term only developed today) and she was not dominated by these small but great friends: "Among those hens there was one which did not lay eggs, it was barren. It would often go to Maria to pay her a visit. She would look at it and say: 'Couvage, couvage, unless you want to end up in the cacciatova'. [Translator's note: "couvage" instead of "courage" and "cacciatova" instead of "cacciatora" - a popular Italian way of speaking jokingly, swapping the "r" for the "v" to sound more French]. No, Maria did not have any qualms about eating them: if she did not have to kill them herself... she said: 'It is a silly pietism. After all, they were born for this purpose, so it is useless to dwell on it. If they are not mistreated, because really... to mistreat them, no! And they must be kept as animals: not to buy, as many do, this and that or some special and expensive food. No, they must eat well, but as animals. They must be fed according to how hungry they are, but with their natural food: they must not be spoiled, nor must they be made to suffer with insufficient or unhealthy foods which could make them weak or sick'. And if they got sick, if they hurt themselves in some accident, she cured them with compassion or she had them treated, if necessary, with generosity and humanity. She loved them and they knew that, and they clearly paid her back; but she was not soppy in her affection. And of those which could be eaten, she said: 'After all, nature wants it when their time has come...'"[588]. She loved animals, of course, but never as much as mankind.

---

[587] ibid., p. 459.
[588] ibid., p. 435.

Radiesthesia

We have already mentioned Father Berti's oversensitivity towards anything paranormal. He made use of spiritists and radiesthesists, which Marta regarded as 'childish actions and mean expedients which make me smile and, to be honest, disgust me a little and make me sad'[589]. Quite often, there seemed to prevail in him a certain irrationality- he who was a Professor of Sacramental Theology at the Marianum Faculty of Theology in Rome. Marta Diciotti also reported these episodes: "Yes, some experiments of Radiesthesia were carried out on... the Writings. And there were several radiesthesists. There was one, perhaps the first one, I do not know, whish made a clear distinction between the person who dictated and the person who wrote. And perhaps he or someone else, I do not know, said that these two were both alive (Maria had not died yet. Jesus, well... I do not think there is anyone more alive than He is since He rose from the dead). This experiment was also repeated after her death: and then the result was that the person who dictated was alive and the person who wrote was dead. [...] Among them was a Jesuit priest, Father Bortone, who was very excited about the Writings"[590]. Without going into too much detail, there is no need to bother the CICAP (Comitato Italiano per il Controllo delle Affermazioni sulle Pseudoscienze) [Italian Committee for the Investigation of Pseudoscience Claims][591], to understand the approximation of radiesthesia. Admittedly, there is no risk of preternatural infiltrations as in spiritism[592]. In any case, a mystical situation must be discerned by means of mystical and similar theological sciences. The risk of

---

[589] ibid., p. 313.

[590] ibid., p. 312. This was his conclusion: "For him, the Writings are sublime, so much so that they cannot be compared to anything else in the genre" (ibid., p. 360).

[591] cf. *https://www.cicap.org/n/icle.php?id=275315*, consulted 20 October 2018.

[592] Cf. Egon von Petersdorff, *Demonologia* [Demonology], Mondadori, Segrate (MI) 1990. A rather complete picture of spiritism with a desire to be impartial and a remarkable bibliography is found in: Simona Cigliana, *Due secoli di fantasmi* [Two centuries of ghosts], Edizioni Mediterranee, Roma 2018.

making mistakes using the *pendulum* – both positive and negative ones – would be far too great. But Father Berti had a soft spot for these worlds and so he also involved a few radiesthesists to have (pseudo) confirmation that Maria Valtorta was only the pen and not the author of the texts she wrote[593].

The cold

Maria Valtorta was very sick, but there was always the possibility of getting worse for a period if she was not careful about catching even a simple cold. And back then, the discomforts were much worse than nowadays. Marta explained: "At that time, we did not have paper tissues". Consequently, the rest was rather distressing. "It was a spectacle that could have even been hilarious in its excessive visual drama, had it not been extremely worrying. As Maria had runny eyes and a runny nose, and she sneezed so violently all the time that I could hear her from the kitchen, I was scared because I realized that she shook and jolted to such an extent that it was dangerous for her sickly heart"[594]. Maria Valtorta's *normal* pathological situation was so bad that any possible remedy for a simple cold could have greatly harmed her. So she had to fight "without taking any medicine which could have given her some relief, albeit temporary. At best, if she did take anything, it was half a tablet of Aspirin by Bayer"[595]. Perhaps the best remedy was the prevention implemented by Marta: "When the very few people showed up at the door to visit Maria, I always asked, before letting them into her room, whether they had any relatives with the flu or even just a cold. And in that case, I apologized and did not let them in"[596]. So, this was something else that the Lord

---

[593] Dr Emilio Pisani wrote: Father Berti "one day, let it slip that sometimes it happened that he would to mistake a fantasy for reality. So, it was then that I began to be wary of his every report". Emilio Pisani, *Pro e contro Maria Valtorta*, op. cit., p. 28. Can this explain his yielding towards the paranormal? It is certainly a possibility.

[594] Albo Centoni, *Una vita con Maria Valtorta. Testimonianze di Marta Diciotti*, op. cit., p. 393.

[595] ibid.

[596] ibid.

granted his beloved Maria, ensuring that the self-immolation of her mystical body was full and total[597].

A new Evangelization

Maria Valtorta was ahead of her time, not because of her gifts for prophecy or foresight, but simply because she acted with common sense. She could have focussed on her terrible pain, spending her time crying over her own misfortunes. But she did the opposite: she talked of a 'new evangelization'[598], of a 'new, full evangelization'[599], of an 'extreme evangelization'[600], long before Pope St. John Paul II first spoke about it[601]. The evidence provided by her 'family member' Marta Diciotti is clear: "I think that she would have liked the Church of today, as it has emerged from the Second Vatican Ecumenical Council, to be completely open to every need. [...] She would have liked all this. This liberalization would have been congenial to her

---

[597] cf. Col 1:24.

[598] Maria Valtorta, *Notebooks 1945-1950*, op. cit., p. 566-7. This is the text and the context: "At that time [...], darkness will fight with the light, bestiality with the spirit, the Satanic with the surviving children of God, Babylon with the Heavenly Jerusalem, and the lusts of Babylon – the threefold lusts – will overflow like stinking, uncontainable waters, seeping in everywhere, even into the House of God [...]. In that time of open separation between the children of God and Satan, in which the children of God will reach a spiritual power never before attained, and those of Satan, an evil power so vast that no mind can imagine what it will really be like, the new evangelization will come, the full new evangelization, which for the time being is going through its initial awakening, exposed to opposition. And it will work great miracles of conversion and perfection. And there will be great efforts by Satanic hatred for Christ and the Woman. [...]. With new means, in the right way and at the right time, the final evangelization will be carried out, and those who yearn for Light and Life will have them, full and perfect, and provided through a means known only to the two Givers, by Jesus and Mary" (ibid.).

[599] ibid.

[600] ibid.

[601] This happened on 9 June 1979, in Nowa Huta, a district of Krakow, on his first trip to Poland.

because she was more open in her thoughts"[602]. And "She was too honest, too ready to find the lies of others, and to tell the truth without fear. In short, she was not very diplomatic"[603]. That is why she was not afraid to use every possibility to have the Lord on her side. "Father Sostegno Maria Benedetti of the Servite Order… enrolled Maria in the 'Misericordia' [Mercy] association because in the statute of that Association, there was a rescript that allowed all associates… the possibility of having Holy Mass celebrated in the room where they lay sick. This Father… had her enrolled in that association not so much for a spiritual adherence to it, but so that she could take advantage of this privilege, of this benefit. And so, this dear Servite Friar would leave Pisa where he was the Parish Priest of the church of St. Anthony, and with his small suitcase he would come to bring the Lord into this house, celebrating Holy Mass to Maria's great joy"[604]. Her practical sense went also beyond her own person. Charity often consists of looking at man with no other expectation. What happened was that "Fr Mariano played hard to get on Sundays, blaming ecclesiastical authorities because Paola was able to walk, etc., etc. I replied: 'Oh, go on! Just be happy to give souls your God!' I am so happy to see them so faithful and loving in the Eucharistic Jesus. But the Fathers do not understand anything. Poor Jesus!"[605] How can one not see in this the application of the evangelical that "The Sabbath was made for man, not man for the Sabbath"[606]?

Paranormal?

Keeping now to one side the unique gift that made Maria Valtorta known to the world, namely the visions and the dictations, which are clearly mystic gifts for their content, we can however answer the question whether she had received other gifts from Heaven, which were perhaps less visible and less well-known.

---

[602] Albo Centoni, *Una vita con Maria Valtorta. Testimonianze di Marta Diciotti*, op. cit., p. 420.
[603] ibid., p. 419.
[604] ibid.
[605] Maria Valtorta, *Lettere a Madre Teresa Maria 1*, op. cit., p. 297.
[606] Mk 2:27.

To signify the life of Marthe Robin, the French mystic who died in 1981 after spending 53 years bedridden, completely paralyzed (25 March 1925 – 6 February 1981), the formula 'immobile journey' was used[607]. As already mentioned, Maria Valtorta was referred to by various terms, such as 'Little John'[608], 'Sister Maria of the Cross'[609], 'Little Violet of Jesus' or 'Violet of Jesus'[610], and 'Writer of My Thought'[611] to which we could also add *'convict of the pen'*[612], as she described herself, or even 'God's pen'[613]. The terminology used somehow defines or sums up the gift or charism she had received. In every mystic – using the term in its popular meaning, not the academic or scientific one of 'a person gifted with special charisms which are very particular and not obvious'[614] – there is not only one gift. There may be one which is more evident than others, one which we could describe as being more characteristic and distinguishing, but this is usually accompanied by other gifts.

This is true also for Maria Valtorta. In fact the Grace of God is not a dense liquid or hot air; the Grace is God Himself who transpires in man. So, depending on how God transpires and on how a single person (and people) reacts, the way in which sainthood is attained, varies. Pope St. John Paul II (1920-2005) stirred huge crowds, yet he remained deeply humble; St. Francis Xavier (1506-1552) and St. Frances Cabrini (1850-1917) crossed oceans to announce the Gospel; St. Thérèse of the Child Jesus (1873-1897) received the charism of

---

[607] Jean Jacques Antier, *Marthe Robin. Il viaggio immobile*, op. cit.

[608] Term used often. It is found, for example, in: Maria Valtorta, *Notebooks 1943*, op. cit., p. 296.

[609] *Maria Valtorta, Lettere a Madre Teresa Maria 1*, op. cit., p. 333. Maria Valtorta would very often sign her letters in this way when writing to the Carmelite.

[610] Maria Valtorta, *Autobiography*, op. cit., p. 313; Maria Valtorta, *Lettere a Madre Teresa Maria 1*, op. cit., p. 231.

[611] ibid., p. 225

[612] Maria Valtorta, *Lettere a Madre Teresa Maria 2*, op. cit., p. 34.

[613] Massimo Cuofano OSSM, *http://www.santiebeati.it/Detailed/91766.html*, consulted 21 October 2018.

[614] It is the common way of describing a mystic. By a 'mystic' it refers, for example, to a person through whom miracles occurs, or to whom Our Lady or Jesus appear and speak.

sainthood, apparently without paramysticism, while St. Pio of Pietrelcina (1887-1968) lived immersed in it. St. Vincent de Paul (1581-1660) encouraged outpourings of charity in his own time and in the following centuries[615]. And what about Maria Valtorta? First, we must make a distinction between natural gifts that are biologically inexplicable, and those granted by Heaven. This writing by Maria Valtorta in 1921 (when she was 24) is emblematic: "In that early summer of 1921, I did not need to sleep to notice strange events. I had the sensation that very long threads, *or* something of the sort, were coming out of my fingers and were hurled into the space. And that these had hooked up with other similar threads coming from Mario. Not only that, but in addition to feeling that our spirits had become fused in a communion which no obstacle or human wickedness could impede, I also felt that the distance was constantly shrinking [...]: the threads were going out from me and returning to me after having found him and bringing him back to me. Was it perhaps the soul's faculties issuing forth in rays through the ether, in search of his soul to tell him that I was dying with desire for him? Goodness! Who knows? These are mysteries we shall never fully understand as long as we live."[616]. This is a *natural* gift, in that it is not due to a mystical state: it is by no means mysterious and falls under the paranormal[617], there is no need to resort to paramysticism. In truth, nobody really knows anything about its causes or requirements because it has characteristics typical of the paranormal: it is not foreseeable, not manageable, and it is transitory. It is almost impossible to create the repetition of a certain paranormal event. Spiritism wants and looks for *mediums* who – through special

---

[615] "Everything socially relevant, that in the last three centuries the Church has known to have built, finds in Vincent de Paul its precursor and teacher" (Antonio Sicari, *Nuovi ritratti di santi* [New portraits of saints], Editoriale Jaka Book, Milano 1991, p. 83).

[616] Maria Valtorta, *Autobiography* op. cit., p. 199. The passage was written in 1943.

[617] Defined as "relating to psychic or physical phenomena that cannot be rationally explained". An emblematic case of paranormal natural gifts is represented by the figure of Gustavo Rol (1903-1994), a psychic from Turin (Cf. Remo Lugli, *Gustavo Rol. Una vita di prodigi* [Gustavo Rol. A life of wonders], Edizioni Mediterranee, Roma 2008).

techniques, sometimes even very simple ones – reach a *trance* state (or at least an altered state of consciousness[618]), but from then on, they cannot do anything else. It is those who are on the other side in the spirit world[619] who decide the *game*. We can make several assumptions, but we basically do not know its real origin or all its possibilities: as they usually say: 'they are natural gifts'. In any case, they always need techniques, but even these do not work all the time.

Another natural gift was Maria Valtorta's power of observation. Marta Diciotti defined it this way: "Attentive: always attentive and… very careful, especially when she spoke. So, I think I am not mistaken when I say that her penetrating ability to understand the outside world was equaled and maybe exceeded by her capacity for introspection, reflection, and meditation"[620].

Her memory itself was way beyond the norm. Maria described it this way: "I was less than three-years-old but I remember my memory emerged very early. Even recently, I have reminded mother of her dresses at that time and events of those days which she had forgotten on account of their insignificance"[621]; "Oh, I remember! I remember everything, even the most insignificant things. Could I fail to recall what I have repeated interiorly, in thought, thousands of times? I could repeat to you all the letters I have written. They are engraved in my mind as if it were a Phonophore record, just like his letters are engraved in my heart"[622]. Theology has always explained that grace fine-tunes and improves the natural qualities of a person. This truth is present also in Maria Valtorta: her natural gifts were enhanced, as we can see in *The Gospel*.

---

[618] AA.VV., *PARA Dizionario Enciclopedico*, op. cit., p. 944.

[619] Cf. Egon von Petersdorff, *Demonologia*, op. cit.

[620] Albo Centoni, *Una vita con Maria Valtorta. Testimonianze di Marta Diciotti*, op. cit., p. 309.

[621] Maria Valtorta, *Autobiography* op. cit., p. 26.

[622] ibid., p. 228.

The supernatural

Above this natural *level*[623], the spiritual level started to rise. We must avoid pelagian[624] attitudes where the natural, human correspondence, becomes stronger and more important than the action of God and therefore, of his Grace. In Maria Valtorta, there were two particular gestures made at different times, but both strong and serious that were necessarily caused by Grace and only afterwards, was there the collaboration and correspondence of Maria herself: the offering of herself to Merciful Love[625] and the offering to Justice and Love[626]. These came from God and provided that Maria accepted them, they are mystical gifts. Then one might wonder whether the treacherous act she suffered on 17 March 1920[627] had been allowed by God in view of a much greater good. To the Devil, who wanted to destroy prematurely the Work that God was creating, the Creator himself replied with an even greater and more beautiful *harmony*, capable of keeping the original plan and including also the artfully created disharmony. It can be said that Maria Valtorta, with

---

[623] This refers to everything related to the carnal part of man.

[624] "Christ with his sacrifice has not cancelled any sin but has simply set a good example for humanity. [...] To save oneself, no special grace is needed, only good will and good works. Grace is not given freely but according to merits" (Battista Mondin, *Storia della teologia. Volume 1* [History of theology. Volume 1], Edizioni Studio Domenicano, Bologna 1996, p. 339).

[625] "In the evening, in the room I am in now, with my heart pounding, I read my act of offering, kneeling on the floor. And I have been renewing it every day since then. Since that day, sorrows have come raining down upon me. But if man were granted [the ability] to cancel the time transpired, and I were to return to 28 January 1925, the day I received those books, *I would do what I have done over again*" (Maria Valtorta, *Autobiografia*, op. cit., p. 254).

[626] "I felt the act of offering blossom in my heart just as I had wriiten it and pronounced it on 1 July [1931], the feast of the Most Precious Blood. What lovelier day could I choose to unite myself to the Victim whose Divine Blood flowed forth entirely to placate the Father's justice? And what name could I have chosen for myself, from that moment, more beautiful than 'Maria of the Cross?" (ibid., p. 300).

[627] This is the aforementioned strike to her lower back.

these two 'yeses' faithfully kept until her death, played her part to allow this new divine correspondence[628].

This resulted in another mystical gift: 'the immolation'[629] which Maria Valtorta made of herself in imitation of Jesus Christ for the salvation of souls. And the ultimate meaning of the word 'immolation' was annihilation or martyrdom. Jesus asked for her immolation-annihilation-martyrdom to save those souls which through their own fault would have become lost, and – incidentally – this is exactly where Maria Valtorta shows her personal sainthood and her adherence to Jesus Christ. All the possible gifts included in paramysticism are not part of a person's sainthood; the heroism of a Christian life, which shows the sainthood of a particular person, reveals itself through its persevering desire to be united with Jesus by doing what He did, that is by following him – in an almost endless variety of ways – on the path of the cross for the salvation of as many souls as possible.

Immolation, in turn, has other paramystic consequences, almost never equal to others. Marta Diciotti added this story to her memoirs: "When I next provided the service of washing her, I saw this large bruise which did not seem to reduce, heal or go away. 'Bah! Is this hematoma ever going to heal? Do you keep bumping into something?' And she replied: 'No, I will tell you...' So she was forced to give me the true explanation, and I found out that it was a whipping of supernatural origin, which she had received from God as a grace. She had not flogged herself, getting the bruise that way"[630].

---

[628] A similar thing is poetically described in: John R.R. Tolkien, *The Silmarillion*, Allen & Unwin, London 1977 (the title of the chapter is "Ainulidalë. The music of Ainur").

[629] "To give oneself to Jesus is to enjoy and suffer. This is what many do not understand and are shocked that we suffer. But we suffer precisely because we have given ourselves! And this is also what keeps many souls from giving themselves. They are afraid. They do not think that if immolation is painful to the human creature, the fusing with Love is always beatific to the spirit. How many lights! How many lights come from the continuous firing of sparks of love between God and the soul that has given itself! "Maria Valtorta, *Lettere a Madre Teresa Maria 1*, op. cit., pp. 299-300.

[630] Albo Centoni, *Una vita con Maria Valtorta. Testimonianze di Marta Diciotti*, op. cit., p. 117.

Maria was more precise: "I'm in great pain. I have terrible suffocation sensations especially at night... I say that like St. Thérèse: I cannot breathe the air of the Earth. When shall I have the air of Heaven? It is probably the lung, barely alive, which is dying... On my back, the bruises have reappeared like years ago. It looks like someone whipped me... Some fanatics could say: 'She shows clear signs of flogging'. No. They are simply broken capillary vessels in the grip of the excruciating pain. But the lashings are on the soul: the divine ones, and they are so sweet in their soreness, and the human ones are on the heart, and they hurt so much!..."[631] These are not contradictions, but two explanations given by Maria Valtorta of a single event, told at different levels. She gave Mother Teresa Maria a medical explanation, as if she had some doubts about what had happened to her, trying to minimise, out of humility, what had happened to her. To do this, she talked of the less important medical aspect; to Marta she defined, instead, the deep and paramystic aspect using different words.

Another mystical gift – which, however, was not a constant one as it is only mentioned in 1944 – is this: "...*in seeing people, not as what they appear to be, but as what they really are within.* [...] seeing *someone* with the face of a demon, so ugly as to be repellant. [...] I exclude Paola [Giuseppe Belfanti's daughter]. But that phenomenon remains *just the same*. I almost never see my cousin, and if I see him, it is for a few minutes a day [...] so much for him. A very *vivid and clear sensation*. The most distinct and difficult to overcome. Regarding the others, whether or not they are in the house, it endures. But no one else is in that pitiful state"[632]. This gift is called 'cardiognosis'[633] and indicates the *knowledge of the human heart*. Nothing psychological or preternatural (that is, demonic), but a gift from God to whoever He wants, when He wants and how He wants. According to St. John of the Cross, this is typical of the purified person, but always as a gift and never as

---

[631] Maria Valtorta, *Lettere a Madre Teresa Maria 2*, op. cit., p. 107.
[632] Maria Valtorta, *Notebooks 1944*, op. cit., dated 14 August, pp. 526-8.
[633] Cf. Luigi Borriello – Raffaele Di Muro (editor), *Dizionario dei Fenomeni mistici cristiani* [Dictionary of Mystical Christian Phenomena], Ancora, Milano 2014, p. 32; cf. John of the Cross, *Salita al Monte Carmelo* [Ascent to Mount Carmel], Libreria Editrice Vaticana, Roma 2004, II, 26,13-4.

a natural ability - a rational study or a technique which can be acquired by means of human strength or will.

Foresight

Maria Valtorta also never lacked powers of foresight. She talked about it herself: "Since 1931, I have been experiencing the fourth type very intensely, by which I *knew* that terrible things would soon be taking place, doing harm to poor mankind, and also the third type quite intensely in special predicaments, along with the first type as well. I remember having seen in a figurative form, the occupation of Belgium, Holland [the Netherlands], Norway and Russia's entry into the war. It was through a symbol in the form of swarms of black airplanes, *completely* black with monstrous shapes which fanned out from a point, Berlin or Moscow, and reaching the established destinations with a point of each stick comprising of a fan. [...] Later, in November 1941, came the notification that within a month, the enemies would be in Benghasi. *Three days later, the English offensive began, and by the end of the month, they were in Benghazi.* In March 1942, the same voice in dreams told me: 'The *defensive line is no longer at Palermo, but further up because Libya has been lost'.* And unfortunately, with regards to the future of us city-dwellers, I have already received two or three not very clear notifications. [...] Before the heavy bombings of civilians began in the autumn, I saw them in my dream, and I told Marta"[634].

"When the war had not yet broken out in Ethiopia - the night of 23-24 May 1935, I saw with marvellous clarity the entrance of our troops – specifically, the foreign and indigenous Carabineers riding in trucks - in Addis Ababa, whose *tuculs* were burning. [...] A year later, on 9 May 1936, our troops and the Carabineers in trucks, victoriously entered and conquered Addis Ababa, which, was burning. On account of that dream, so evident and accompanied by *that concrete sign* during the nine months of the Ethiopian War, I never doubted its outcome. *I knew it would be won and quickly.* The same applied with the Spanish War, all of whose foul and heroic deeds I saw. I would prefer to speak directly about this to you. I have told

---

[634] Maria Valtorta, *Autobiography*, op. cit., pp. 322-3.

you this just to make you understand what it is about"[635]. On 24 July 1943, foresight had come for the first time in an unusual way, but it came back often later in *The Gospel*. Maria described what she saw without completely appreciating the magnitude of the content: "I don't like those who cry out, 'Death to them!' after having cried, 'Hosanna!' [...] It is inconsistency, dishonesty and cowardice to be pitiless towards the defeated - whatever their defeat may be"[636]. In this passage, I have brought forward the fall of Fascism by a few hours, although the news was made public in Italy, and therefore to Maria, only on 26 July. In the dictation of 28 July, she insisted: "For a fallen idol, do not raise up many little idols, all adorned with the same satanic signs of lust, haughtiness, deceit, overbearance and the like"[637]; and she added turning to the people: "... *the mass should be such as to impose on its Leaders a conduct worthy of my reward. For always remember this, the Leaders commit Sins, but it is the mass, which by its lesser sins, that bring the Leaders to the great Sin*"[638]. Foresight always hounded her without Maria being able to control it in any way: it would arrive whenever it wanted. Finally, we must mention the ecstasies. "I have taken you to 'shared love' *which is the perfection of the love involving fusion*, that I spoke to you about in autumn"[639]. Ecstasy and love for fusion should not be confused with the visions or the dictations she had. Ecstasy means 'exiting the human body, body and soul, exiting the borders of the self, and becoming a stranger from oneself'[640]. When Maria Valtorta saw or heard a vision, she could be interrupted and then restart from where she had left off; this applied to both the conversations-dictations and with the visions[641]. However, she had

---

[635] ibid.
[636] Maria Valtorta, *Notebooks 1943*, op. cit., dated 24 July, p. 193.
[637] ibid., dated 28 July, pp. 199-200.
[638] ibid., p. 200.
[639] cf. Maria Valtorta, *Notebooks 1944*, op. cit., dated 13 February, p. 153.
[640] Luigi Borriello – Raffaele Di Muro (editor), *Dizionario dei Fenomeni mistici cristiani*, op. cit., p. 54.
[641] Already in 1944, Maria knew many differences: "Father [Migliorini], I have striven to state what I experience. But it is futile. Among all the ecstasies which God can give me, it will always be the one involving his suffering that leads my soul to my seventh heaven. I find that to die of love

some surprising aspects, "for my ecstasy is wonderful in this respect: it allows me to reflect, analyze, consider what I am experiencing, and to remember it afterwards; I do not know if it happens this way with other ecstatics"[642]. In 1946, Maria explained to Mother Teresa Maria what happened to her during an ecstasy following a discussion she had had with Father Mariano, who had told her what Father Migliorini had been saying about her at the priory: "I am not in ecstasy as it usually happens. It is true. But if the Lord, so as to keep his servant's secret, leaves my subconscious free, *rather* relatively free, so much so that external things sound to me as being very far away *and with such an effort that makes me cry out of pain,* I can stop seeing what I am seeing in order to answer those who talk to me. If the Lord leaves my subconscious a little bit free out of pity for me, who has always asked to suffer for Jesus without showing extraordinary exterior signs, the ecstasy, the joy, is within me, and it is my face that reveals that because Marta, my cousins, and whoever sees me while I am writing, say it is *transfigured.* Even my lodgers say the same, even if they are evacuees who are *totally in the dark, those who do not attend Church, and the clergy.* They perceive the supernatural in me, sometimes just by looking at the expression on my face. If there is no ecstasy in its external form, there is a suspension of my physical pain, a physical strength that miraculously comes back every time, the joy that lingers on, the spiritual improvement. What else do they want? Is this not an ecstasy and the result of ecstasy? Maybe it is the 20th-century ecstasy! That's it! Can God not assume other forms of manifestation than the classic ones?"[643]. This raises an important question. Does God, in terms of mystics, always use the same rules automatically? The answer is obviously no because He is free to act as He pleases, and man replies with the freedom, qualities and limits received at conception. Maria Valtorta experimented with various forms of union with God. The one described here is one of them. It may be unusual, as it was for her, too, but she also experimented with other forms, the ones better known and acknowledged by theologians. For

---

while looking at my suffering Jesus, is the most beautiful death" (Maria Valtorta, *Notebooks 1944*, op. cit., dated 7 March, p. 215).

[642] Maria Valtorta, *Notebooks 1945-1950*, op. cit., dated 16 March 1947, p. 375.

[643] Maria Valtorta, *Lettere a Madre Teresa Maria 1*, op. cit., p. 75.

instance: "And Mary came to me: alive, real, just like in Lourdes.... One of the most intense and most complete ecstasies I have had. The world was utterly obliterated around me. Mary *alone* with Maria alone.... I received much more than seeing a statue passing by... I returned to – what shall I call it? – an awareness of what the world is, I would say, after about an hour, I believe, for when She came, there was still daylight and when She left me, there was deep darkness. And I found that my face was moist with tears"[644]. All the protagonists of mystical and paramystical experiences are a little special[645], and in this, Maria Valtorta was no exception.

What is typical about Maria Valtorta?

To understand the peculiarity of Maria Valtorta's mission, let us compare it with that of another immolated victim soul: Marthe Robin[646]. This is how Jean Guitton[647] summarily described her life: "Born in 1902 in a small French village between the Rhone and the Alps, Marthe Robin died in 1981 at the age of 79, in her father's home which she never left. For fifty years, this simple and humble woman never ate nor drank, and every Friday she suffered the agony of the Passion and carried the Stigmata. Blind [photophobic] and completely paralyzed, she founded through her assistants, over fifty prayer centres, the *Charity Homes* scattered all over the world"[648]. This, very briefly, is her story, but what needs underlining here is the reply to Jean Guitton in a book which is fundamental for understanding her in depth. He asked her: "I tried to talk to her about the 'phenomena' linked to mysticism: visions, ecstasies, levitations, mind-reading, etc. I tried to insist on the phenomenon of the 'gold ring', when a mystic believes they can see a gold ring on their ring

---

[644] Maria Valtorta, *Notebooks 1945-1950*, op. cit., dated 8 September, 1947, p. 454.

[645] Famous for example is the case of the Blessed Mary of Jesus Crucified, Mirjam Baouardy, and her levitation above trees. Cf. Amédée Brunot, *La Piccola Araba* [The Little Arab], Edizioni OCD, Roma 2004, p. 53.

[646] cf. Jean Jacques Antier, *Marthe Robin. Il viaggio immobile*, op. cit.

[647] Jean Guitton, *Ritratto di Marthe Robin* [Portrait of Marthe Robin], Paoline Editoriale libri, Milano 2001.

[648] ibid., p. 4.

finger. Her response: 'Yes, I know these things. They are superficial. We must get over them without making too much fuss. You mention the gold ring. I saw it on my finger, I think, a dozen times. But let me tell you that, as much as it is good to have it, it is even better not to have it. What you call a mystical life can be within you as it is within me. It consists in trying to be one with Jesus'"[649]. This clarification is important: "To be one with Jesus"; she did not say *only* "to imitate Jesus", she went well beyond that. It was certainly the fundamental desire of St. Francis of Assisi; it is like saying "to be Jesus". It is the same distinction that Luisa Piccarreta made between "Thy will be done" and the "Divine will"[650], which she spread. She also put herself on another level: not "*to do* the will of the Father", but "*to be* the *will* of the Father".

Undoubtedly, Marthe seems to have gone deep down in her union with God, where everything else simply disappeared. As late as 1956. Maria Valtorta did not seem to have overcome certain obstacles. So the impression is that Marthe Robin achieved radicality and a totality, unknown to Maria Valtorta. Perhaps. But after that date, Maria was so totally absorbed in God that she was constantly absent from this world. It is impossible to compile a leaderboard of such spiritual heights. Who of the two has gone higher or deeper inside the divine alcove of the *seventh mansion* – as St. Teresa of Avila would say? It is a pointless question: it is in the mystery of God, and it must be respected as such! Along with Msgr. Carinci, we can only kneel[651] in amazed adoration of the Glory of God who manifested Himself in these creatures, so perfectly corresponding to Him. One can say that they are both immolations, albeit in two different vocations; perhaps because a single person would not have been able to express both things. Marthe had to express the union with God, so absolute and

---

[649] ibid., p.75.

[650] Luisa Piccarreta, *Libro di cielo. Il regno della mia divina volontà in mezzo alle creature* [The Book of Heaven. The Kingdom of My divine will in the midst of creatures], Gamba Edizioni, Bergamo 2013.

[651] "Entering the room [of Maria Valtorta] and falling to your knees at the foot of the bed" (Albo Centoni, *Ricordi di donne che conobbero Maria Valtorta*, op. cit., p. 159).

deep in her, like the apex[652] of the soul in God, and conceivable only in Heaven; but at the same time she had to show in the *Charity Homes* – founded by her together with her spiritual director, Father George Finet[653] – a place of love for life among men, in imitation of the Trinitarian life and of the one that she was already living with God.

Maria Valtorta, on the other hand, had to act as the medium to take men – who are willing – to Jesus Christ in the fullness of His life on earth and therefore, to the fullness of faith in Him, to make them fall enthusiastically in love with Him by means of her descriptions, accompanying them day by day – page by page, step by step – beside Jesus, along the path in this world; showing everyone (back in those times, but with the cultural characteristics of our own times) His life, His hardships, misunderstandings, humiliations, etc. Once in love, He will lead them to an imitation without boundaries, until He will enter with them inside the deep mystery of God-Trinity.

Marthe suggested the destination; Maria indicated the path and the steps to get there. This seems to be the difference in their vocation. Certainly, it would have been easy for Maria Valtorta to compare what she was writing with what she sometimes saw, but in doing that, she would have run the same risk as St. Thomas Aquinas, and she would have stopped writing altogether[654].

---

[652] L. Borriello – E. Caruana – M. R. Del Genio – N. Suffi (editor), *Dizionario di Mistica*, op. cit., entry: *anima* [soul], p. 104.

[653] Bernard Peyrus, *Vita di Marthe Robin* [Life of Marthe Robin], Effetà Editrice, Cantalupa (TO) 2009, p. 200ff.

[654] "After an hour [that he was in ecstasy], his companion approached the teacher and, shaking him vigorously by the cloak, finally managed to wake him from sleep, so to speak, of contemplation. Then, sighing, Thomas confided to him: 'Reginald, my son, I tell you in secret, but I forbid you to repeat it to anyone as long as I am alive. My writing has come to an end, in fact, things have been revealed to me that in comparison to what I have written and taught, seems to me to be very little (*Palea est*: is straw) like straw. For this reason, I trust in my God that, just as the end of my writing has come, the end of my life will also come soon'" (Guglielmo di Tocco, *Storia di San Tommaso 47* [The story of St. Thomas (Aquinas) 47], quoted in: *https://www.amicidomenicani.it/mi-dice-qualcosa-in-piu-sui-motivi-per-i-quali-tommaso-mai-completo-la-somma-teologica//*, consulted 22 October 2018).

Saints understand each other: Msgr. Carinci

Msgr. Alfonso Carinci was born in Rome on 9 November 1862 and died in Rome on 6 December 1963, aged 101. To understand who, he was, what his background was and how important he was within the Roman Curia, we must keep in mind that he had been first a student, and then the rector of the Almo Collegio Capranica[655], a real breeding ground of prelates of the Curia in various fields. As a child, he had served as an altar boy in St. Peter's Basilica, and once ordained, he became Pope Leo XIII's Master of Ceremonies. For many years, he was the Secretary of the Sacred Congregation of Rites – which today is known as the Congregation for the Causes of Saints. When the Second Vatican Council began in 1963, he was 101 and was acclaimed as the oldest bishop in the world. He died in the odor of sanctity, and he was remembered by Pope St. Paul VI with the title of 'decorum of the Roman Clergy'[656]. It has been written that "During his lifetime, he had made a valid contribution as Secretary of the Sacred Congregation of Rites, for the canonization of 64 Saints and the beatification of about 500 Blessed"[657]. It must be stressed that all this was accomplished before the election as Pope of St. John Paul II, who broadened, if possible, the verification of holiness. During his long Pontificate, he proclaimed 1,338 Blessed and 482

---

[655] The institute which, in the last centuries, formed many future leading leaders of the Church; it was based on training excellence, very accentuated spirituality, and linked with the Pontifical Gregorian University. A host of bishops, cardinals, and popes – including Pius XII, who reigned at the time – were formed here.

[656] Thus recalled Saint Paul VI: "In memory of his noble long life spent with absolute dedication to the service of the Church, we love to point out this worthy prelate, always animated by a true priestly spirit, with zeal, piety, disinterestedness and humility. As a bright example of Roman clergy, he who built it admired its virtue, was moved, and he mourns their disappearance. And gathered in prayer, he supports his chosen soul. While we invoke the Lord for the eternal prize for this good and faithful servant, we impart with a comforting heart in mourning and propitiatory of heavenly graces our apostolic blessing" (cited in: *https://www.luiginovarese.org/scritti/morte-monsignor-carinci/*, consulted 22 October 2018).

[657] ibid.

Saints[658]. We must not conclude, therefore, that Msgr. Carinci did not work hard. In 400 years, the Holy See proclaimed 300 Saints; and Msgr. Carinci, 64 in 30 years. So, *in his own small way*, he did a lot, and he also tried to proclaim the maximum possible number of Saints. So, we admit that thanks to this very characteristic of his, and to his experience as Rector of the Almo Collegio Capranica, Msgr. Carinci must have developed a certain *sixth sense* regarding spotting at once a person's holiness. Verifications, comparisons, analysis, close examinations, criticisms, and very meticulous research led him to judge very well what was holy or fake in a person's life; what was humble or proud; transparent or vain. For Maria Valtorta, there could not be a better judge and true friend[659]; so to speak. His testimony in her favor would be enough to declare the holiness, honesty, and humility of Maria Valtorta; and the same thing would be valid for her writings. It is in this light that the importance of the devotion of Msgr. Carinci for her, stands out. He had understood perfectly!

We do not have reliable data on Msgr. Carinci's attitude towards other people who died in the odor of sanctity, but the testimony of Marta Diciotti was clear: "He came to see Maria several times and he also celebrated Holy Mass in her bedroom. [...] He left a long statement on the Work and on Maria Valtorta, both of which were very favorable"[660]. To celebrate Holy Mass in Valtorta's house is a great sign of esteem, affection and judgment towards Maria Valtorta. The same thing is clear from the letters between them which have

---

[658] cf. *https://www.focus.it/cultura/storia/la-fabbrica-dei-santi*, consulted 21 October 2018.

[659] Marta Diciotti could only testify to this: "Monsignor Alfonso Carinci, for example, the archbishop in charge of the Congregation of Rites who was a great expert on the subject, as he was a special officer in the causes of beatification, had no doubts about the Work and Maria Valtorta, whom he regarded with great veneration and affection: 'Leave it, let the author do it. Trust in Him. The Master will resolve everything, you'll see. Nobody can do it better than He can.' This was, in fact, what he said to comfort her, to give her peace. Or, at least, this was the sentiment, even if the words were probably different" (Albo Centoni, *Una vita con Maria Valtorta. Testimonianze di Marta Diciotti*, op. cit., p. 359).

[660] ibid., pp. 361-2.

been published⁶⁶¹. And again, Marta Diciotti has reported his words: "Monsignor Carinci wrote: 'Everything considered, it seems impossible that a woman with a very mediocre theological knowledge was able to write *suo marte*⁶⁶² such sublime things with such precision'. And making a distinction, he set aside the descriptive part within the Work, which he attributed to the writing ability of Maria Valtorta from all the rest which he, without any doubt whatsoever, regarded as pure and simple '*dictation*'. In so doing, he took her side and openly declared his full faith in her"⁶⁶³; "Thinking of him after all these years, I find it was quite a huge deal, and an unusual one, that this man, a confidant of popes (a of Pius XII, and loved and esteemed by John XXIII and Paul VI), was on such friendly terms with Maria and an admirer of the Writings, that he made his feelings known in various ways: from his attitude in his letters, to Holy Masses in her bedroom, to his coming back to Viareggio again and again to see the invalid and to even prostrate himself, as witnessed by Maria Teresa Mencarini, who saw him"⁶⁶⁴. Undoubtedly, the word 'to prostrate oneself' dominates this short description. With the faith and knowledge that distinguished him, he knew the meaning of that gesture perfectly, which was, in a way, *extreme*. There are many things that we are also told while looking at that elderly Monsignor of the Curia prostrate at the foot of Maria Valtorta's bed. A neighbor, Maria Teresa Mencarini, was present at the scene, which she found very moving: "I can still see the tall and aristocratic figure of this venerable prelate... come into the room and fall on his knees at the foot of the bed of the poor invalid. I see him again engrossed in prayer and cry, yes, weeping out of deep emotion [...]. Maria [...] looked a little confused, embarrassed, as if she was receiving undeserved recognition. [...] It was an unexpected thing - kneeling at the foot of that bed, between its end and the radio-stand on the left, and bowing his head out of deep devotion with tears falling. The tears of that elderly Monsignor

---

[661] cf. Maria Valtorta, *Lettere a Mons. Carinci*, op. cit., pp. 19, 24.

[662] Latin for "with his own strength" (cf. Luigi Castiglione Scevola Mariotti, *IL Vocabolario della lingua latina* [The Dictionary of the Latin language], Loescher Editore, Torino 1966, p. 882, entry: *Mars*).

[663] Albo Centoni, *Una vita con Maria Valtorta. Testimonianze di Marta Diciotti*, op. cit., p. 371.

[664] ibid., p. 398.

deeply affected me and it has remained unforgettable"[665]. Msgr. Carinci was therefore convinced of her function and sanctity, and he accepted the presence of God as real by means of the gift made through her. When he arrived at the house of Maria Valtorta, Msgr. Carinci was already so convinced that he celebrated Holy Mass in Maria's little bedroom. It was 11 April 1948. We could deduce that the intermediary had been Father Berti. It is indeed possible that he had spoken very highly of her to Msgr. Carinci and that he had handed over to him some of the manuscripts typed up by Father Migliorini. One of the earliest mentions of the interest towards Msgr. Carinci can be found in a letter to Mother Teresa Maria dated 19 September 1946[666]: the tone of the letter shows that she already knew at least his name and importance. After their first meeting, they started to exchange letters[667]: long letters from her, and short notes albeit important ones, from him. She always asked for the *imprimatur* of the writings and Msgr. Carinci could only point out that there were various problems: "It is wise to examine any book in all its parts before publication, and even more so in this case, as it is about a very delicate matter, with new and original allegations which can give rise to discussion, which could, at the least, result in a more or less long suspension, causing setbacks for the administration because of the possible, more or less daring comments, etc."[668] However, Msgr. Carinci stuck his neck out, making it clear that he believed in the sanctity of Maria Valtorta and in her writings, and drawing a clear distinction between what she was the author of and what came from Heaven. The editor of the letters wrote: "In the margin of the page, at the beginning of the letter dated 20.01.1949, Msgr. Carinci writes: During the audience of 28 January, I read this letter to the H.F. [Holy Father, Pope Pius XII] which greatly impressed Him, and of which he praised the spirit of humility and obedience. As for the publication of the Work, he said that it was handled by the H.O. [Congregation of the Holy Office] and I had the impression that the judgement probably given by the H.O. + A. Carinci would not be very

---

[665] Albo Centoni, *Ricordi di donne che conobbero Maria Valtorta*, op. cit., p. 159.
[666] Maria Valtorta, *Lettere a Madre Teresa Maria 1*, op. cit., p. 260.
[667] The first letter is dated 9 January 1949 (cf. Maria Valtorta, *Lettere a Mons. Carinci*, op. cit., p. 19).
[668] ibid., p. 26.

favorable"[669]. So Msgr. Carinci had bravely spoken to Pope Pius XII, who had well received Maria Valtorta's writings. The insurmountable obstacle turned out to be, instead, the Sacred Congregation for the Doctrine of the Faith. With the death of Pope Pius XII, Cardinal Prefect Ottaviani took matters into his own hands and placed *The Poem of the Man-God* on the Index of Forbidden Books. Yet, we must take a small step back in time. Just before Msgr. Carinci went to see Maria Valtorta, something important had happened: Father Berti, through Msgr. Norese, a Bishop, had managed to get on Pius XII's desk ten tissue-paper folders of the writings by Maria Valtorta[670]. The Pope was seen reading them, so they gathered up their courage and asked for a papal audience to plead Maria's case. There were three of them: Father Migliorini, Father Berti and their Prior, Father Cecchin. The result was the sentence so often repeated: "Publish it as it is. Whoever reads it will understand"[671]. But this was not an imperative statement, only a confidential one. In fact later, Cardinal Ottaviani was able to disregard it, and what concerns the approval of the writings became more and more complicated. In the meantime, Maria Valtorta gave Msgr. Carinci terrible news: "On 14 June 1948 [the Holy Spirit] told me not to write His comments on the Letters of St. Paul anymore because it was useless, given the opposition to His other Words. So I stopped writing them, *not receiving them*, leaving them truncated at the 4th verse of the 8th Chapter to the Romans"[672]. She then resumed at the beginning of 1950, 18 months later, to confirm that it was not a whim, but she was obeying God's will[673].

The last note by Msgr. Carinci is dated 23 December 1955: it is a Christmas card. During these six years, Maria Valtorta had gone on pushing for the approval of the writings with Msgr. Carinci braking,

---

[669] ibid., p. 28.

[670] cf. Emilio Pisani, *Pro e contro Maria Valtorta*, op. cit., p. 63.

[671] ibid. Unfortunately, there is no recording of that day. Perhaps it is found in Father Berti's unpublished archive.

[672] Maria Valtorta, *Lettere a Mons. Carinci,* op. cit., pp. 31-2. In fact, there is a gap between 14 June 1948, in which Rom 8:4 is commented, and 6 January 1950, when the comment continues. These dictations ended on 16 November 1950 (cf. Maria Valtorta, *Lessons on the Epistle of St. Paul to the Romans,* op. cit., pp. 182, 196).

[673] ibid., p. 191.

not by his own will, but because he knew very well the human obstacles that needed to be overcome. The refrain that he often repeated was: "He is the Teacher. He is the Author. So, leave all the problems to Him, let Him solve them. Nobody could do it better than He. And you know this very well"[674]. As a matter of fact, although he was certain of the gifts granted by God to Maria Valtorta, so much so as to prostrate himself at the foot of her bed, he had no choice but to trust in divine Providence, in the hope that all obstacles would go away. Msgr. Carinci, an expert in men, saints, but also in fakes and in spiritual frauds, had become convinced of the authenticity of what this bedridden woman had been writing for years. So he went on fighting for Maria Valtorta's writings, but he was *defeated*, to the point of seeing those works placed on the Index of Forbidden Books which had convinced him as many heretic, misleading and anti-Catholic texts.

Èroma Antonini[675], one of the family

Although Maria Valtorta declared herself a 'recluse', a few people were brave enough to surround her with affection and little bits of help (even financial, during the years of extreme poverty). Nothing compared to the incredible number of people – we are talking of

---

[674] Albo Centoni, *Una vita con Maria Valtorta. Testimonianze di Marta Diciotti*, op. cit., p. 377.

[675] Èroma Antonini (1909-1995) was unmarried and lived with her sister, Anna Maria Antonini (1916-2010); the latter was married (1938-2011) to Guido Mencarini († 1983). Guido and Anna Maria had five children: Maria Teresa (1939), Livia – Livietta (1941), Giuliano (1943), Maria Cristina (1947) and Martino (1958). They lived in via Antonio Fratti (two doors away from Maria Valtorta, whom they knew as their neighbor) from 1945 to 1962; then they moved 200 meters further away. The whole family, but in particular Èroma and Anna Maria, helped Maria Valtorta free of charge for many years; Maria Cristina and Livietta recounted, in private conversations, that to arrange her sick-bed, Guido would take her in his arms, while his wife, daughters and Marta Diciotti made the bed; Maria Cristina as an infant sometimes wet Maria Valtorta's bed, and it happened that she would fall asleep in her arms.

100,000[676] – who entered the gloomy bedroom of Marthe Robin, but hers was a different path. However, besides Marta Diciotti, other people helped Maria Valtorta, starting with her neighbors.

Èroma Antonini, together with her sister Anna Maria – who married into the Mencarini family– and her nieces and nephews, was practically one of the family. The Mencarinis helped Maria and she helped them where she could. Èroma was a friend, she confided in her, and she acted a little as Marias's nurse, giving her injections whenever needed, for instance. Anna Maria was good at touching her without hurting her too much. They only realised who this invalid was, whom they served as a friend, when Maria Valtorta received the dictation of the Holy Hour on 14 June 1944. As we know, Father Migliorini made several copies of it, which he distributed for the purpose of comforting people in that tragic time of war and evacuation. In the early months of 1945, a young man evacuated to Viareggio, who was helping in a myriad of different ways and was also serving in the parish church. He got hold of these papers; he showed them to Èroma so that, if she wanted, she could distribute them. The following day, delighted, thinking that Maria would very much like the text, she showed them to her in the hope that she could make a few copies, given that she was very fast at writing. And that is how Èroma found out who Maria Valtorta really was: "She looked at them, then she called for Marta, and she expressed her disappointment, her sorrow, in these words: 'There, the water has come back to its spring, to its source…' and she would not give them back to me"[677]. In the end, Maria gave the text back, but with the request that it would not be disclosed, despite admitting: "I wrote this"[678]. So, they were part of the family, and they also happened to be present during an apparition without realizing it. Marta Diciotti, amused, said: "Yes, Èroma came and she said: 'Let me pass, I just need to tell Maria something'. And she went in all lively, engrossed as she was in her present problem. But… we were flabbergasted at Maria's warning… I did not know myself that the Virgin Mary was

---

[676] Cf. *https://www.martherobin.com/it/sa-vie/un-rayonnement-immense/*, consulted 12 January 2019.

[677] Albo Centoni, *Ricordi di donne che conobbero Maria Valtorta*, op. cit., pp. 108-9.

[678] ibid., p. 109.

there. […] Yes, Maria let Èroma talk, she patiently listened and only then, she sweetly asked her to moderate herself out of respect for the presence of the Virgin. 'Oh, God!' replied Èroma, 'If only I had known! Why did you not tell me straightaway?'"[679]. Èroma also said something interesting regarding scents. Maria Valtorta told her of the stench she perceived in the vision of the resurrection of Lazarus which lingered on in her nose for a long time: "a horrible stench of decomposition, just like that of a rotting dead body"[680]. Èroma also personally witnessed extraordinary whiffs of scents[681]: similar to carnations on St. Anne's day; violets and lilies when St. Maria Goretti was canonized[682]; similar to cinnamon, nutmeg, cloves – actually, Jamaican pepper – for the beatification of Antonio Maria Pucci[683], the *little curate* of Viareggio.

Anna Maria Antonini

Anna Maria Mencarini lived next door to Maria Valtorta for 16 years [684] and what she appreciated the most was the discretion of the whole family. Maria loved the Mencarini family, and she knew she could ask them for some company even at difficult times; for example, when she received a visit from Professor Pende[685]: "Maria told us: 'Please, do not leave me on my own'. I went to let Prof. Pende in. While in there, Maria Teresa was with her to whom she had said: 'Sit here, by my side, do not leave me alone because I would like someone here'. And so Teresa did not move"[686]. On that occasion,

---

[679] ibid., p. 112.

[680] Maria Valtorta was completely engrossed in visions: she saw, observed, listened, and perceived smells, heat, etc.

[681] Anna Maria also testified to this (cf. ibid., p. 124).

[682] They listened to the beatification ceremony of Saint Maria Goretti on the radio. Eroma remembered precisely what Maria Valtorta said: "Yes, the Lord sent this perfume to me" (ibid., p. 113).

[683] ibid.

[684] ibid., p. 118.

[685] Prof. Pende was an advocate of racism and a spiritist.

[686] Albo Centoni, *Ricordi di donne che conobbero Maria Valtorta*, op. cit., p. 123.

Maria wanted to make sure that she was not misunderstood and that she well understood what she was told.

She certainly received a lot, but she also gave a lot: Anna Maria recalled that she gave her daughters lessons as they did their homework on Maria's bed, sometimes even while she had visions and dictations[687]! Another example of *giving* is this episode which describes Maria Valtorta's intercession: "I am writing when Èroma comes to let off steam about her brother-in-law's eccentricities… You know, don't you? The man who was exemplary in every way: hard-working, serious, a good father and a good Christian. Perhaps because of a nervous breakdown caused by the war, he had been acting like a maniac for a couple of years. He was convinced that his wife, Èroma's sister, was cheating on him with *her own brother*. Imagine that! He imagined evidence of her cheating everywhere. And he was tortured to the point of beating those poor women… You should have heard how the three little ones cried! It broke one's heart to listen to that… His wife, who is a real angel, lost her health in not reacting. The man knew about me because he was told by Dora [Barsottelli]… but he never came despite showing deference towards me much greater than that shown by many others. On the evening of 2 January 1947 at 11pm, Jesus tells me: 'Let the Mencarini babygirl be named Maria-Cristina so that Christ will always be among them' and explains: 'She is born on the first Friday of the month and the first Friday of the year, on the Eighth of my Name. She is sacred to me'. I write, but as it was late, I did not send Marta to Èroma. I think I will do it tomorrow. On the following day, the first Friday of the month and of the year, at 6am while Father Mariano was here with Holy Communion, Èroma comes to the window and says: 'Pray, because Anna is ill'. Anna had been in labor since 2am the day before but she was by now exhausted and things were turning for the worse. I say: 'Yes' and nothing more because I had the host in my mouth. I dedicated the Eucharist to Anna and the unborn child. Half an hour later, Anna gives birth safely to a baby girl. I send Marta with the piece of paper on which I had written: 'The baby girl must be named Maria-Cristina so that Jesus is with you'. Nothing else. But on

---

[687] cf. ibid., p. 124. Anna Maria also testified to it in private interviews with me.

Saturday, seeing Èroma was sad because her brother-in-law was ranting about how the baby looked like his brother-in-law (!?!?) I tell her: 'Look, Èroma, it was Jesus who said she should be given that name'. Èroma goes back in and says: 'She must be named Maria-Cristina' and Guido Mencarini, glaring, goes to the Town Hall to register the birth of the baby girl. His wife stays at home, crying... Èroma is furious... Father Pietro arrives. Èroma, fuming with rage, brings him in to me and leaves... Ding dong... the door bell rings. Marta goes to the door. It is Èroma's brother-in-law with a letter for me. He hands it over and leaves. Marta opens it for me and gives it to me. I read it. It says: 'Dear Miss. Please excuse me for writing, even if I do not have the honor of knowing you, but I feel I know you well through a shared faith: the Christian faith. I am pleased to announce the birth of my fourth child, Maria Cristina. She will be christened on the day of the first Easter of the year, the day of Our Lord's recognition. You, Miss, will certainly know that our family had a sad past, which upset the peace and the good because of my wrong views about my wife's brother. I wish to put an end to this past, so I ask you, Miss Maria, to intervene in this reconciliation, by adding grace and value to the acknowledgment that I owe my wife, after all the suffering and offence I subjected her to. Miss Maria, I will find in your prayer and in forgiveness, the peace and good that is a grace of God. Yours faithfully, Guido Mencarini. P.S. I would like Maria Cristina to have my brother-in-law Alberto as the godfather and his fiancée as the godmother'. I assure you that in front of such definite proof, it is Jesus who speaks to me and makes miracles through His Word. I was in such frenzy that I made the bed shake. I thanked Jesus for that family that He has pacified and for giving me the proof that it is really He who comes to me"[688]. This episode, on one hand, shows the miracles which took place for Anna Maria, her husband Guido and little Maria Cristina thanks to the intercession of Maria Valtorta, and on the other, it also shows her great confidence in Mother Maria Teresa, who alone, was able to understand, console, comfort and help Maria Valtorta. Besides, that *frenzy that made the bed shake* shows how she was involved, active and yet perfectly normal.

---

[688] Maria Valtorta, *Lettere a Madre Teresa Maria 2*, op. cit., pp. 14-5.

The parish priest

We do not know much about Msgr. Rocchiccioli. We know that he was 'an exorcist and a saintly priest'[689]; that he was the confessor of Maria Valtorta for a period – although she preferred Father Migliorini as a spiritual director, maybe because of his experience and because he was a Friar rather than a diocesan priest. And we know that he believed in what was happening to Maria Valtorta. He was the Parish Priest of San Paolino in Viareggio, the parish church of Maria Valtorta from 1933 - 1949. Maria had a premonition of his death a few days before it took place, so she sent Èroma to look for him until she found him: "I saw the Monsignor. But he looked so ill that I suggested he take a taxi to go back to the church. But he declined, saying: 'It is not far, I will walk there slowly'"[690]. We do not know what they said to each other but in any case: "the following morning, or [...] a few days later, Msgr. Rocchiccioli was found dead in his own bed"[691]. As we have already written, he had a few disagreements with her mother Iside and he said to Maria who must have had a few qualms regarding her mother: "Just do what you like! You are your own mistress, and it is not right that you let her vex you in this way'. I also remember that he told her that she was free to fiddle the expense book, so that she could have some money at her disposal, money which was also hers, after all. Yes, Signora Iside kept her broke! 'See where and how you can do it because you need to have something too'"[692]. He looked for a nursing nun who would, as an act of charity, go and give injections to the 'sick lady' of Via

---

[689] Albo Centoni, *Ricordi di donne che conobbero Maria Valtorta*, op. cit., p. 115.

[690] ibid., p. 117.

[691] ibid.

[692] Albo Centoni, *Ricordi di donne che conobbero Maria Valtorta*, op. cit., p. 213. This is the memory of Marta Diciotti. Maria Valtorta's painful situation is evident here: she did not work because of her precarious physical conditions, but even more so because her mother, Iside used her as an unpaid servant. Evidently, she would leave her without money, and she had to get by as much as she could with the money of the family of which she was an integral part: Msgr. Rocchiccioli gave her impeccable advice.

Fratti"[693] and he found Sister Antonia Lucchini. The greatest courage he showed, however, was with his bishop Msgr. Torrini. On that occasion, Msgr. Rocchiccioli was brave, and we must give him credit for it. Very few of the clergy and the friars followed him, each for their own reasons. The courage and the testimony of the Monsignor remained. The fears of the Bishop of Lucca were clear. The note that was out of tune, so to speak, was that he could have gathered much more information, but he refused to do it because of the already-mentioned prejudices. Msgr. Rocchiccioli was left alone, and despite not being able to act as a *trumpet* in the case of Maria Valtorta, he remained loyal and fearless[694] till his death.

The politician

An important figure in the Italian landscape for the first half of the 20th century, Camillo Corsànego welcomed Maria Valtorta and her writings like a Godsend. His curriculum is remarkable[695]. He was born in Genoa on 20 March 1891, and he studied until he became a Professor of Comparative Criminal Law at the Pontifical Lateran University. Then he also became Promoter of Justice (Prosecuting Attorney) in the State Tribunal of the Vatican City. An active Catholic layman, he was a friend and collaborator of Don Sturzo at first, and then of Alcide De Gasperi. He was the President of the Italian Catholic Youth from 1922 - 1928. Opposed by the ruling Fascism, he waited for it to end. At the end of World War II, he took part in the Constituent Assembly and he was also a member of the Italian Parliament for many years. He was a Roman councilor and his political presence as an active Catholic basically ended with his own death on 9 October 1963. He was married and fathered six children. We do not exactly know when he discovered Maria Valtorta's writings; he was probably contacted by Father Berti, who in the early

---

[693] ibid., p. 17. Thus recalled Sister Antonia Lucchini.

[694] Msgr. Torrini could have threatened Msgr. Rocchiccioli with a transfer to the upper Garfagnana, which would have been a considerable consequent inconvenience for him and for his sister with whom he lived. Thank God he didn't go that far, even though in those times – before the Second Vatican Council – it was a solution used many times.

[695] cf. Emilio Pisani, *Pro e contro Maria Valtorta*, op. cit., p. 76.

1950s was busy looking for acknowledgments by people who had been pointed out to him as being in favor of Maria Valtorta. We can imagine that he had read the typed dossiers of the works by Valtorta – at the time still unpublished – and that his enthusiasm came from that. So, he met her in person and that is why he thought of giving her a radio when he saw the poverty and solitude in which she lived, a radio which is still in her house-museum in Viareggio. His figure stands out in the photograph of her funeral procession[696] and he made sure of helping the editor Pisani with the publication of the first edition of *The Poem of the Man-God*. The writings and the figure of Maria Valtorta must have dazzled him and, brave as he was, he never held back when it was necessary to support the *Work* and the *person*. His acknowledgment, which could not be scientific *in the strict sense*, was however without reticence; he used all his experience and his knowledge to support it. For a university professor, in the past as it is today, it must not have been easy to write about a sick and recluse psychic: "In my long life, I have read many apologetic, hagiographic, theological, and criticisms of biblical works; but I have never found a combination of science, art, piety, and of adherence to the traditional teachings of the Church as in the Work on the Gospels by Miss Maria Valtorta"[697]. He then added the weight of all his studies, his readings and researches, claiming: "Following a careful and repeated reading of those many pages, I must, in all conscience, declare that with regard to who wrote them, only two theories are possible: a) either the authoress is a genius comparable to Manzoni or to Shakespeare and has a perfect theological knowledge of the Scriptures and of the Holy Places, and in any case superior to any living creature in Italy today; or b) 'digitus Dei est hic'![698]. The authoritative statement by Camillo Corsànego makes the Indexing of 1959 by the Holy Office even more mysterious, as it took place before the texts were carefully read and analyzed[699]. The 1950s were

---

[696] ibid., p. 77.

[697] ibid., p. 75; also in Albo Centoni, *Una vita con Maria Valtorta. Testimonianze di Marta Diciotti*, op. cit., p. 371.

[698] ibid., p. 371; also in Emilio Pisani, *Pro e contro Maria Valtorta*, op. cit., p. 76-7.

[699] "The consultant of the Holy Office, Msgr. Ugo Lattanzi, Professor of theology and Dean of the Pontifical Lateran University, left written that

years of a contraposition between the Catholic world and the Communist Party. The latter, a conscious bearer of atheism to fulfil its goal, did not waste time in using even slander to bring down those who were considered its enemies[700], the Catholic Church *in primis*. Then as is today, it was therefore essential for an active Catholic layman to agree with the Church. In fact, in the document, Corsànego added: "Obedient as I am, and as I, with the grace of God, intend to remain all my life to the supreme and infallible Magisterium of the Church, I will never dare to take its place. However, as a humble believer, I declare that I think that the publication of this Work will help bring many souls to God and will have an apologetic resonance in the modern world and will act as a leavening of Christian life, only comparable with the effects of the private revelation of St. Margaret Mary Alacoque"[701]. To Maria Valtorta, he was a friend, a supporter, an advocate. He was never afraid, and he stuck his neck out for her till his death.

An old and dear friendship

Arturo Bottai was very esteemed by Marta Diciotti who died at the age of 97 in 1964. Therefore, he was born in 1867 making him 30 years older than Maria. "He was a retired railway officer, a distinguished-looking fellow, who resembled [Guglielmo]

---

he did not consider it absolutely possible that the woman who is the author could have written so much material, *a running pen*, without having suffered the influence of a preternatural power" (Albo Centoni, *Una vita con Maria Valtorta. Testimonianze di Marta Diciotti*, op. cit., p. 371. There are doubts as to what the theologian meant by using the word "preternatural". In fact, this term is used to indicate the angelic spirits who surpass our human nature. Therefore they are superior to men; but they are still created. Therefore they are not equal to God. The angels, however, are divided into good and bad (the demons). To which was Msgr. Lattanzi referring?

[700] Plutarch's "slander without fear: something always remains attached" (*De dignitate et augmentis scientiarum*,8,2,34 [Of the dignity and growth of science] has become Voltaire's "slander that something remains" and has been widely used by the revolutionaries of yesterday and today.

[701] Albo Centoni, *Una vita con Maria Valtorta. Testimonianze di Marta Diciotti*, op. cit., p. 37; also in Emilio Pisani, *Pro e contro Maria Valtorta*, op. cit., p. 76.

Marconi[702], and he had a kind disposition"[703]. To describe the affability of Mr. Bottai in his relationship with Maria Valtorta, just look at the photo taken in 1948: Maria is in profile and Bottai is facing the camera with the French window (now just a window) overlooking Via Fratti behind him; they both look smiling and serene. Bottai and Maria had known each other since she was a child when they both spent time on the beach in Viareggio with his daughters. In fact, "Maria went to the beach with the three daughters of that distinguished-looking gentleman whom she learnt to hold in esteem from back then. He also had a son"[704]. According to Marta, he was "a great Christian"[705]. His usual confessor in Pisa was Father Sostegno of the Friar Servants of Mary who was probably the one who mentioned Maria Valtorta. And Arturo was intrigued by the fact that the child whom he had met by the sea and who had played with his daughters, had received such great spiritual gifts. He made some enquiries and went to see her. Then he did it on a regular basis until his age would allow it. When he went to Maria "He would always come with his little tray of pastries (which she would then pass on to me because she did not like creams as they made her sick) and he would sit beside her with such a fatherly tenderness that warmed the heart"[706]. When he arrived at Valtorta's home, Marta announced him to Maria: 'Mr. Bottai is here', I said. 'Oh, good, come in! Take a seat, Mr. Bottai'. He was a serious person and he could smile pleasantly, but the rediscovery of Maria Valtorta changed his life forever. Marta Diciotti told of these episodes. "Mr. Bottai [...] said in a warning tone: 'Ladies, do not gossip!' to the female group of sunbathers under the beach umbrella. In fact, his wife Pia who was blind as a bat, or at least very short-sighted, had put on her glasses and, with other lady-friends, she would move her eyes around starting the chorus: 'Who is she?', 'Where does she come from?', 'What does she do?', 'Where

---

[702] Guglielmo Marconi (Bologna, April 25, 1874 – Rome, July 20, 1937), known for being the inventor of the radio.

[703] Albo Centoni, *Una vita con Maria Valtorta. Testimonianze di Marta Diciotti*, op. cit., p. 315.

[704] Albo Centoni, *Ricordi di donne che conobbero Maria Valtorta*, op. cit., p. 256.

[705] Albo Centoni, *Una vita con Maria Valtorta. Testimonianze di Marta Diciotti*, op. cit., p. 319.

[706] ibid., p. 408.

do they come from?', 'Yes, right!', 'Well, imagine that!'. In short, as the proverb said: 'Whoever walks past here and does not stumble, will go as far as France'. And Mr. Bottai, kind and fatherly said: 'Come on, ladies, no gossiping!'"[707]. He was able to play things down even regarding the writings: "He was hoping for an imprimatur for the publication, as it also transpires from a postcard to Mr. Bottai dated 22 March 1950, in which she writes: 'I waited in the hope of being able to tell you something. But I see that things are dragging on and so I am writing to you. I really feel like Madame Butterfly: *One fine day we shall see...* but that day never comes, and *I am weary of the long wait*...'"[708]. And he could also be very serious: he had put into practice an ingenious idea in its own way. He felt that it was necessary to clarify at the very source what was happening to Maria Valtorta, so he typed up some questions and asked her to reply in writing. So today we have the Bottai-Valtorta questionnaire, of which – although it has not been published yet – I have a copy, which I was given by Dr. Emilio Pisani himself. The questions and answers are very interesting. Despite not being an *expert*, Arturo Bottai touched on very important issues. They consist of nine typed pages with numbered questions, each followed by the answer of Maria Valtorta in italics. Bottai wrote at the top "Collected from Miss Valtorta in Viareggio on 28/10/1948". To the first question: "Have there been many apparitions up till now?" Maria Valtorta replied: "About 720 evangelical ones, about 100 different ones, but in writing them, I do not know how many I described out of joy and help I received". It was 1948: the visions of *The Gospel* had ended, but the dictations-comments of *Lessons of the Epistle of St. Paul to the Romans* went on for six months, together with a few visions and many dictations. The second question asked: "In which year did you have your first vision?" And she replied: "The first one? Back in June (11/6/1916) then from time to time, or rarely, up till 1941. They became more frequent from 1941 onwards. From April 1943, my eyes and voice rejoiced in the supernatural almost daily". Maria Valtorta was not very precise because while she says it "became more frequent from 1941 onwards" there seems to be no trace of this in the *Autobiography*;

---

[707] Albo Centoni, *Ricordi di donne che conobbero Maria Valtorta*, op. cit., p. 256.
[708] ibid., p. 259.

she probably preferred to keep silent. Also, it is very likely that it was these "eyes and voice" that prompted her to find a spiritual director: Father Migliorini came into her life in 1942. The number of apparitions which she declares, "720+100" is also approximate. *The Gospel* has 652 chapters, but the visions have been broken up sometimes, and you must also add those present in the various *Notebooks* to these. So, they are an estimate, but not real numbers.

To the ninth question, Bottai asked: "How could you endure such strain given your health problems?" Maria Valtorta gave a somewhat longer reply: "I do not even know myself. A miracle. Sometimes I wrote for over six consecutive hours. Sometimes with a high fever. I must add that... while Jesus dictated or because I saw and heard evangelical events at the same time, I stopped feeling my physical pain, or the fatigue in writing. If I write a letter, even a short one, I get so tired that I feel sick: the blood goes to my head, my spine aches, my spinal nerves ache, my heart struggles, my vision gets blurred, and if I went on writing, I would have a heart attack. Whereas if I write or wrote from dictation by Jesus, or I see and I write what I see - some facts that Jesus shows me, *I do not get tired*, and I can write for up to 5, 6 or more hours". This part of the ninth question answers a very important question, useful in understanding what was happening to Maria Valtorta. Abnormality was when the supernatural intervened; normality was painful, with limited strength, about to get tired and to make her heart play up. On the contrary, the supernatural was strength, prolonged stamina, without any heart or other organ failure, and painless. There is also another important detail: it was not Maria who decided when, for how long, and what she would see and hear. She only decided how to write it. There was never any form of automatic writing, or an altered state of consciousness: it was always the supernatural intervention that stirred things up.

The thirteenth question asked: "Did your physical pains increase or decrease following the extraordinary events of which you were the witness and the protagonist?" The answer was: "My pains increased naturally, *regardless* of the supernatural fact. If anything, it was the hatred of people, jealous of the gift I was granted, that with their actions made my physical state worse. The Work did not make it any better or any worse. It was joy for the soul, but for the flesh *nothing*". The questions go on to different themes: ecclesiastical authorities, approval, and there are also a few clarifications on some expressions found in the writings. In the last point, in the second clarification, there is this sentence: "I prefer to disappoint those who expect to see in me an ecstatic person, rather than lifting the veil, in front of strangers, on my mystical relationship with my Lord who supports me and interrupts the action when strangers arrive, or waits for them to leave before making me at one with Himself". She was always very lucid, and the Lord acted like a real lover who wanted to act discreetly: a beautiful image, deeply honest and real. Arturo Bottai in his ingenious simplicity gave us a glimpse of what was happening to his daughters' former playmate.

The creative artist

Prof. Lorenzo Ferri (1902-1975)[709] was a scholar of the Turin Shroud: this was his real passion[710], so much so that he wanted to reconstruct the man of the Shroud, not theoretically, but with a real clay sculpture. In the meantime, he worked as an artist making sculptures all over the world, but always studying, investigating and trying to reconstruct what that linen in Turin showed him[711]. The work itself, as beautiful and ingenious as it was, was necessary for him to survive[712]. He personally met Maria Valtorta in 1949. It was

---

[709] All his personal information is taken from: Leonardo Ferri (editor), *L'uomo della Sindone nella ricostruzione dello scultore Lorenzo Ferri. Quarantacinque anni di studi dal 1930 al 1975* [The man of the Shroud in the reconstruction of the sculptor, Lorenzo Ferri. Forty-five years of studies from 1930 to 1975], Edizioni Kappa, Roma 2007.

[710] Prof. Ferri had been driven to study the Shroud by a very strong desire to know the features of the face and the shape of the body of Jesus, to be able to recreate them in clay, on a sheet or on canvas, since he was a painter and a sculptor. Father Berti recounted more than once that this was the reason that brought Ferri closer to Maria Valtorta, who had visions of Christ and his earthly affairs (cf. Albo Centoni, *Una vita con Maria Valtorta. Testimonianze di Marta Diciotti*, op. cit., p. 288).

[711] cf. ibid., p. 201.

[712] The proof is that he continued to work on it without ever stopping until the end of "his life, which unfortunately ended on 25 February 1975 following a heart attack" (Leonardo Ferri (editor), *L'uomo della Sindone nella ricostruzione dello scultore Lorenzo Ferri. Quarantacinque anni di studi dal 1930 al*

maybe Father Berti who talked to him about her some time before, when Pius XII organized a public exhibition of the project to build the portal of the Holy Door in St. Peter's. On *Palm Sunday* in 1950, he and his brother went to Maria Valtorta's house. At first the meeting was not a promising one, but then it got better: "Between Maria, who was always very careful, and a very critical and sharp observer, and the professor, who seemed to be hard to convince and to be trusted, there was a quick, almost immediate and unusual understanding"[713]. As a matter of fact, he felt Maria Valtorta seemed "to be lucid, pragmatic and sharp - the exact opposite of an exalted woman"[714]. He showed her the reconstructions of the Shroud face, but she told him that in her visions she saw it differently[715]. "The artist, a skeptical man who could barely control his own impulsiveness, and Valtorta, with her imperious, frank, attitude"[716], studied each other. It could have all ended here, but Ferri, generously, had a brilliant idea: "He asks her to describe what she sees, and he will try and sketch it"[717]. There started a long, fruitful and creative collaboration, where Ferri was less skeptical than he thought himself to be. "He sat with a sketchbook in his hand, with his back to her so that she could follow his quick sketching and give her own suggestions"[718]. And Marta Diciotti said that one day when he "had the necessary tools, he sat beside her bed and immediately sketched the profile of Jesus. It was easier to do it that way. It is placed in the

---

1975, op. cit., p. 74). The book, edited by his son Leonardo, does not explicitly report this, but everything leads us to understand that he worked until the end of his life on the Man of the Shroud.

[713] Albo Centoni, *Una vita con Maria Valtorta. Testimonianze di Marta Diciotti*, op. cit., p. 288.

[714] Pietro Ferri, preface to *Ferri and Valtorta*, Centro Editoriale Valtortiano, Isola del Liri (FR) 2006, p. 13. This book collects all the charcoal drawings that Lorenzo Ferri made under Maria Valtorta's instruction in her home.

[715] cf. ibid.

[716] ibid., "It is evident that My father, despite all his pragmatism, his common sense and healthy skepticism, was a utopian, a visionary" (Leonardo Ferri, editor, *L'uomo della Sindone nella ricostruzione dello scultore Lorenzo Ferri. Quarantacinque anni di studi dal 1930 al 1975*, op. cit., p. 75).

[717] *Ferri and Valtorta*, op. cit., p. 13.

[718] ibid.,

other room at the foot of my bed (but this is not the original, just a photograph). He did it almost at once, without much difficulty. Maria was guiding him; one could say that she was directing his hand [...] 'No, professor, not like that... but this and that way..."[719]. Or: "'This is right. This is not. Correct it this way..."[720]. Or again: "'Longer... higher... wider..."[721]. So, he discovered a beautiful truth: "With time, the professor's hand became more and more agile and quicker under the guidance of Maria until it flew over the page, creating during the collaboration, much more work than what he usually did in his normal daily activity, far away from her"[722]. Out of that first work, the Professor sketched with a sanguine pencil on paper, a huge number of drawings, sketches, studies and drafts of Jesus, Mary, the Apostles, and of the many episodes of *The Gospel*. There are no paintings, except those dedicated to Maria herself; but he also created two high-reliefs of the faces of Jesus and Mary, one in wax and the other in ceramic. Maria Valtorta was always fussy about Ferri's drawings: "The [Last] Supper that you sent me is fine as far as the setting is concerned, but the faces!... Why have you not done the faces like you did them here with me in 1950? Even the Resurrection of Lazarus is only half good, so naked whereas he was all bandaged up... That face of Jesus is beautiful, suave, expressive, perfect, just like I remember Him in the (rare) moments when he was happy and praying serenely"[723].

For Lorenzo Ferri and Maria Valtorta, the summer of 1952 was the most intense as far as the drawings were concerned. It was then that he made with a sanguine pencil on paper, the faces of the Apostles, Mary Magdalene and other characters. In Rome, he met Father Migliorini and, almost as a reward for his work, he made a magnificent and very detailed bronze bust of him[724]. Maria Valtorta

---

[719] Albo Centoni, *Una vita con Maria Valtorta. Testimonianze di Marta Diciotti*, op. cit., p. 295.
[720] ibid., p. 288.
[721] ibid.
[722] ibid.
[723] *Ferri and Valtorta*, op. cit., p. 14. This is a letter from Maria Valtorta to Prof. Lorenzo Ferri from 21 June 1953.
[724] Albo Centoni, *Una vita con Maria Valtorta. Testimonianze di Marta Diciotti*, op. cit., p. 295.

was not a woman who could be dominated, and not even Ferri could: it was she who was aware of who she was and what task she had been given and carried out. As Marta said: "One day, I remember Maria was resolute and said: 'Professor, follow my instructions because it is me who sees everything. You do not see anything'. She probably saw, at least on that occasion, and she remembered what she had already seen and described in writing. That is why she spoke with such authority and confidence. 'And you, Marta, and you, Signora Vittoria, please go back to the kitchen, or else you will burn something. Professor, do not waste time, follow me because things are as I say, as I see them'... So, I am not surprised that he was never on a first name basis with her, unlike with everyone else. Well! It was an altogether different situation here: the person who was in front of him was very uncommon"[725].

Among the many things that he did for Maria Valtorta, there was also this: "In July 1952 he was here with us on holiday [...] with his family. Towards the end of the month, before leaving on 31 July, he brought Maria the photograph of the Holy Shroud"[726]. It was not a small photographic format, but a life-sized photo; 441cm by 111cm. "He took a stepladder and unrolled it in front of her eyes, letting the front side down along the large wardrobe mirror and resting the back side of the figure, still rolled up, on the top and on outer shelf of the cabinet that was, and still is, right at the foot of the bed, exactly in front of her. The figure was coming down, covering the wardrobe mirror, down, down, to the floor"[727]. And in front of that photographic reproduction on the cloth, at the time rather expensive and very rare, Maria stayed up all night in prayer. Marta Diciotti recalled that "Maria prayed all night, as she told me herself, because I... who lay by her side in the little bed beside hers, as I always did, at some point fell asleep. As I woke up the following morning, I found her still there, so I realized she must have prayed all night. Yet, I wanted to make sure, and she answered my questions very simply: 'Yes, it is true. I did it... because who knows? Maybe this will never happen to me again'"[728]. This detail is also little known: "In the

---

[725] ibid., p. 291.
[726] ibid., p. 199.
[727] ibid.
[728] ibid., p. 200.

bottom part of Maria's wardrobe there is, among other things, a drawing on paper of a dead Christ, in full figure, in full-size, a sort of reproduction of the Holy Shroud, in which the wounds are painted in red with an amazing effect. That large rolled-up sheet was another gift from him to her"[729]. Marta Diciotti herself was very grateful to Ferri, so much so that a whole chapter in her memoirs is dedicated to him. Ferri was very important to Maria. Now thanks to his drawings – although they are made in charcoal and not in color – he is important to all the readers of the writings, to whom he somehow gives a glimpse of what Maria saw, letting us into the world that Maria Valtorta lived from within a little bit more.

The tribulations of canonical approval

If the *Autobiography* describes the life of Maria Valtorta in a rather detailed way up to the beginning of 1943, making her known in a linear way, what happened afterwards, is a mixture of various events and of their historical consequences in an almost inextricable whole. The main themes can be outlined in this way: Maria Valtorta and her mystical life; Maria Valtorta and her physical life (illnesses); Maria Valtorta and the Order of the Servants of Mary; Maria Valtorta and the drafting of the texts; Maria Valtorta and the *imprimatur* of the texts; Maria Valtorta and the publication of the texts. Even the problem of the tomb of St. Peter is part of the mix. The *Autobiography* that she wrote is diachronic[730]: it follows time as it happens. From 1943 onwards, it would certainly be possible to do the same thing, but the need for clarity about so many interwoven events, makes us anticipate things that will happen later, following therefore a synchronic scheme[731]. So, for a better understanding, we will look for parallel events rather than for a sequence of interwoven events.

Right from the beginning of the visions, Maria Valtorta received the request from Heaven that all her writings should obtain the official approval of the Church, the *imprimatur*. Therefore, a sort of

---

[729] *Ma sperando che tu possa comprenderti*.p. 294.

[730] In the sense that the unfolding of events is described according to time.

[731] Seen as if they were happening at the same time, as if one could see events that happened at different times all together at the same time.

clash began between Maria Valtorta and her supporters on one side, and on the other, the ecclesial authorities (the Congregation of the Doctrine of the Faith) in charge of scrutiny and judgment – to accept or to refuse and condemn – the writings that were proposed. The process lasted at least 15 years, from 1945 to 1960. The first stage ended with *The Poem of the Man-God* being placed on the Index. But the process is still ongoing today in the hope that something similar to what happened to Blessed Antonio Rosmini Serbati could happen also with Valtorta's writings, who was condemned and re-condemned[732] at first, and then he was cleared and added to the list of the Blessed and considered a forerunner-precursor of the Second Vatican Council[733]. It must be clarified that the indexing among the forbidden books only affects the writings and not the person Maria Valtorta, since no criticism has ever been directed at her by the Holy Roman Church.

Still as a premise, it must be remembered again that 57 years since the death of Maria Valtorta (12 October 1961), not all her writings have yet been published[734]. All this has an important consequence:

---

[732] The placement on the Index of Forbidden Books of the text *Le cinque piaghe della Chiesa* [The Five Wounds of the Church] dates to 1849; the "Post Obitum" decree, with the sentencing of 40 propositions, dates to 1888; His rehabilitation took place in 2001 and beatification in 2007. Cf. http://www.rosmini.it/Objects/Pagina.asp?ID=14, consulted 30 October 2018.

[733] For example, cf. http://www.noisiamochiesa.org/Archivio_NSC/attual/Antonio.Rosmini.NSC.htm, consulted 10 November 2018.

[734] They are certainly missing: the part of Father Migliorini's archive which is in the possession of the Order of the Servants of Mary, but it is not said that the ones kept by the CEV are also completely included in the correspondence already published; the entire archive of Father Berti: the one in the possession of the Order of the Servants of Mary, the personal one now in the possession of the grandson of his secretary and the one owned by the CEV; the Albo Centoni archive, both the personal one (probably owned by the Albo Centoni Foundation) and the one held by the CEV; all diagnoses, medical prescriptions, therapies, etc. are in the possession of the CEV; all the economic accounts, little pieces of paper and various cards, are probably in the possession of the CEV; all the various letters from famous and non-famous people who contacted Maria Valtorta and to which she replied, are now held by the CEV; secret letters and notes that came from Heaven: dictations and visions, are owned by the CEV.

until all her story is published – or at least made available to all – it will not be possible to write it in its complete form either. If at first sight, this may seem a trivial issue, even a pointless one, it is simply because people are not aware of the punctiliousness with which the Church examines the life of the person who dies in the odor of sanctity and has a bishop who tries to make them a saint. Ten thousand pages would not be enough to strongly emphasize this concept. To this *void* can be added – through nobody's fault – those words and those facts that nobody recorded in written form.

In fact, we should also keep in mind the oral conversations which took place between Maria Valtorta and all the people who, for various reasons, crossed her path: Father Migliorini and Father Berti in particular, but not only. These dialogues have obviously been lost forever – and we must accept that. However, a few of them can be deduced from the effects they had on events.

One last preamble to keep in mind. Divine Providence acted little by little: not everything was said at once and not everything was said explicitly. Whoever thinks that Heaven had already given all the guidelines in the first or second dictation on the conduct to be adopted – how to do something, what to say and not say, etc. – have never reflected on the freedom that Divine Providence gave to Maria Valtorta and to every man; a freedom respected to the point of the risk of losing everything Divine Providence wanted. The tower of Babel and the Great Flood show how God is respectful of human freedom; the only limit is man's self-destruction, which God does not allow.

Vanity is a very common sin. Many people are seduced by the pleasure of their appearance. Those who work in the cinema or television industry know about the onslaught of questionable actors/actresses, or those that desire to appear on screen – albeit fleetingly, to express their views on this or that issue. This is a lure that attracts everyone, the simple and the educated. Many fall for it, many get angry if it does not happen, and many send others in their place purely out of reluctance or fear. This temptation can affect everyone, but it becomes disruptive to those who have received some supernatural gifts from God. The sisters of the venerable Mary of

Agreda (1602-1665), showing much naivety for some time[735], showed her to visitors just while she was manifesting her mystical gifts: they made her "a spectacle of herself"[736]. In the end, thank God, Mary of Agreda asked for the intervention of her confessor, Fr. Giovanni de Torrecilla, and the vanity of her sisters ended. Maria Valtorta never fell into such a trap. In the dictation dated 24 September 1944, there are two important statements. In the first one, she underlines the hardship of being a medium at the Lord's disposal: "If only you knew, O men, all of you, what slavery it is to be instruments of God! Holy, but complete slavery! The slavery of a galley slave at the oar: sleeplessness, hunger, sufferings, weariness, the desire to think of something else, to read things which are not the words of ultramundane sources, to say and hear ordinary words, the desire to be at least for one day, ordinary creatures and lead an ordinary life. These are all things which the inexorable lash of God's will keeps them from having and turning into reality. And upon all of this, the resentment of men pours its salt and its acid, as if the master of the galley were to make salt and vinegar fall upon the wounds caused by the whiplashes"[737]. At the end of this dictation, Jesus added for the first time: "You are not Maria and must not be known as Maria… Your persona is annulled… No one should know you as a writer of my thought, apart from two or three privileged persons…"[738]. What had previously been an obvious human caution necessary for the mission, became an explicit command from Heaven at that point which everyone had to obey. Only on this date – one year and five months after the first conversation – did the request come for total concealment, which may have been already said, but not written; as

---

[735] It happened in 1623 in Burgos, in the convent of the Order of the Immaculate Conception. cf. *https://madreagreda.weebly.com/biography.html*, consulted 30 October 2018. The venerable Mary of Agreda wrote: Mary of Jesus of Agreda, *Mistica Città di Dio* [Mystical City of God], Edizione Porziuncola, Assisi 2000, 2 vols.

[736] It seems that the sisters and the superior of the time tried to transform her into a circus act. However, she rightly complained of this treatment until the Provincial of the Franciscan order intervened to prevent this spectacle.

[737] Maria Valtorta, *Notebooks 1944*, op. cit., dated 24 September, p. 568.

[738] ibid., dated 24 September, p. 573.

it now became essential for it to be a command known to everybody. Then from that moment on, it was said to, and an order for, everybody. This attitude is a pattern in all the works by Maria Valtorta: *The Gospel* itself often has omissions due to, among other reasons, the concealment of Maria Valtorta. "Silence", "concealment" and "solitude" in mystical life can be synonyms, and in Maria Valtorta, they became so because her path was one of *immolation*. The term may be frightening, but if one thinks about it, it was experienced by many. We could give several examples: above all, that of the soldiers of any army during both world wars; coming out of the trenches while on the other side, the machine-guns were ready to shoot; being in a submarine hit by depth charges; consciously risking one's life behind enemy lines as a member of the secret services; being willing to die rather than betray one's own country, even as a captive. Yet, in mystics and in Maria Valtorta, there is a difference: every concealment, every immolation is made in the faith of Christ, for eternal life in which one firmly believes, and in view of the eternal salvation of souls to which one aspires in becoming more and more at one with Christ, offering oneself as a victim soul, in the belief that God will accept all this[739].

Still, the approval is necessary

In the texts by Maria Valtorta – and especially in *The Gospel* – there is a very special request which was the source of many problems. On 7 April 1946 on the eve of the punitive move to Rome of her spiritual director Father Migliorini, Maria wrote: "My afflictions derive entirely from observing every day that the Words which God has spoken to me are *in the hands of everyone*, disseminated, altered, and used with no approval at all... *What, great, great pain* this disobedience to the very clear orders of Jesus brings me...! Only God can measure the breadth and depth of the torment induced *by the acts of disobedience*

---

[739] cf. L. Borriello – E. Caruana – M.R. Del Genio – N. Suffi (editor), *Dizionario di Mistica*, op. cit., entries: *Immolazione* [Immolation], *Offerta di sé* [Self-offering], *Corredenzione* [Co-redemption]. cf. also L. Borriello – E. Caruana – M. R. Del Genio – R. Di Muro, *Nuovo dizionario di mistica*, op. cit., entry: *Immolazione* [Immolation].

by others[740]. The determinant clause "without any consent" was always stressed until her death. One could legitimately wonder why this request was only made after one year and not before. One could answer that there was probably some oral conversations which we do not know about. Anyway, the determination with which Maria Valtorta obeyed, and the harshness which hit Father Migliorini, make us think the following was the right solution. Right at that time, Heaven sent clear guidelines on how to act: it was 2 June 1946, Father Migliorini was by now in Rome for good, and Maria Valtorta had to write: "*Seek approval*"[741]. The situation was clear and it remained so throughout all the troubles until 6 January 1949 when a change occurred due to human causes: "If it is finally decreed with sacriligious stubbornness that *My* work is to be condemned, just as they condemned Joan of Arc's 'heavenly voices' as the voices of delerium and Satanism [...], I will permit the Work to be published like any human piece of writing [...] but [...] justice must impose new terms. Human ones. So it is with all supernatural things - one tries to make them human"[742]. But that was not enough; Jesus also added these clarifications: "(I) that the Work, 'Words of Eternal Life' [which

---

[740] Maria Valtorta, *Notebooks 1945-1950*, op. cit., 7 April 1946, p. 229. The dictation from 15 February: "In the face of my intimate reflection on why the Lord was now spurring me – rather than merely allowing me - to receive people and not conceal who I am – and this aspect frightens me because I fear diabolical deceit. He responded to me as follows: "Obey and do not be afraid. [...] in ninety percent of the cases, the true 'voices' remain secret and secluded. Enough. That's enough for you. May at least the uncertain be able to compare and choose. And each will choose according to his merits, for the real seekers of God will go in one direction, and the impure seekers of God, in another. [...] And this is not inconsistency in my conduct, but lofty, farsighted justice. And also awareness and knowledge of time. The river mouth is drawing near... Let the river nourished by Me, be known before it is lost in the supernatural sea" (ibid., dated 15 February 1946, pp. 204-5). The two dictations are not in contradiction, first because Jesus does not tell her to advertise herself, but one thing concerns her writings and another her person; here he talks about her person. The refusal by Msgr. Torrini to visit her would have closed the door on this.

[741] Maria Valtorta, *Notebooks 1945-1950*, op. cit., dated 2 June 1946, p. 269.

[742] Maria Valtorta, *The Little Notebooks*, op. cit., p. 179.

after two changes will be published under the title: *The Gospel as Revealed to Me*] was received through Divine Will and written under Divine dictation by Maria Valtorta, who is therefore *the only instrument used by God in writing the Work*. (II) If mankind *does not accept the supernatural nature of the Work and consequently, denies its true Author but the writer Maria Valtorta, the Work must be dealt with legally and financed as a human work, and also the person who insists she is the author*. Therefore she, like any person who writes a work, is the owner and proprietor of her Work, and automatically becomes the sole arbiter of the destiny of her work. She can sell it to a Publisher or she can become a part of the Publishing Company, accepting an annuity from the proceeds of her work for herself and for her heir. [...] If you agree to these three things, the Work will remain with you: (I) a legal declaration that Maria is the one who received the Work of supernatural origin. This declaration is *necessary for the present moment and the future*; (II) the legal sale or well-founded joint participation in the profit of the editions; (III) the pseudonym of the spokesperson is placed at the top of the Work. If this is not the case, *Maria is free to sell it to a Publisher,* according to what is customary in these cases, *placing a legal ban on anyone using all or part of the work*. If you refuse any such clause, you will lose every human right, just as others have made sure the work has lost the only qualification which its origin entitled it to"[743]. Unfortunately, a human refusal took place, and with the completion of the *Lessons on the Epistle of St Paul to the Romans*, every light for mankind through Maria Valtorta came to an end. The Servants of Mary ended up rejecting the inheritance and refused to take Holy Communion to Maria; they ordered Father Migliorini to stay put and forbade Father Berti to go to Valtorta's house. But to circumvent the ban, he went as far as dressing up as an odd-looking plumber[744], which made those who knew him, smile.

A fifth gospel?

One of the very first debates – which caused great confusion, but only to those who did not know theology – was whether the visions that Maria Valtorta had were a fifth gospel, a new and complete, or

---

[743] ibid., pp. 181-3.
[744] Emilio Pisani, *Pro e contro Maria Valtorta*, op. cit., p. 51.

more complete fifth gospel. To convert it into a formula, the debate was: St. Matthew, St. Mark, St. Luke, St. John... and Maria Valtorta? This was the impression that many people had and wanted. Even Emilio Pisani, about 60 years later, published this memory: "One day, at lunch, I heard 'Miss' Valtorta being mentioned again, and without a word, I stood up, I went into the drawing room which was next to the dining room, and I opened the cabinet with colored-glass panels where my father had put the famous typed dossiers. I took one out, I opened it at random, I looked at a page (I looked at it, rather than read it) and understood. Rather than a discovery, however, it was like the awakening of a slumbering knowledge, just like when you bump into a person you have already met, briefly and then forgotten. And looking back, later, I could not rule out that as a child, in a once-in-a-lifetime moment of grace, in the depths of my consciousness, I felt, almost in its infancy, the desire and the need, if not the existence of a Gospel rewritten in a more complete way. In short, my fate was sealed"[745]. Yes, it was a wonderful, personal, supernatural experience even though what is striking is the penultimate sentence, that 'Gospel rewritten in a more complete way' which reminds us of a fifth gospel that should be canonical[746]. And yet in a dictation dated 17 October 1944 where Jesus replied to the objections and ideas of Giuseppe Belfanti, which back then was still imbued with the theories of Pietro Ubaldi. He said: "And now we come to the so-called fifth gospel. There are four Gospels. Now I am explaining them in order to bring to light others which are lost or downplayed. But I am not creating *another* Gospel. There are four, and four there will remain. Understood in detail or left in their broad outlines, four and no more"[747]. But the debate went on and even today there is someone,

---

[745] ibid., p. 21.

[746] On the same wavelength, the CEV published: Emilio Pisani, *Quello che i Vangeli non dicono. Le private rivelazioni a Maria Valtorta* [What the Gospels do not say. The private revelations of Maria Valtorta], Centro Editoriale Valtortiano, Isola del Liri (FR) 2015.

[747] Maria Valtorta, *The Little Notebooks* op. cit., p. 42. Numbers 66 and 67 of the Catechism of the Catholic Church provide the interpretative key to the entire Valtortian work. To reiterate that it is not the 5th gospel is obviously obvious!

from time to time, who tries to support such an idea (of a fifth gospel), even in misleading and indirect ways.

Writing and transcribing

From the start, Father Migliorini asked Maria to write what was happening in her heart and he decided to type up the manuscripts. From what we know, nobody requested that of him - it was his own decision; and what's more, there is no record of when he started. Maria had already written the *Autobiography* and, earlier still, the novel, *The Heart of a Woman*, which was later burnt[748]. It was likely after he advised/ordered Maria Valtorta to write that he realized that it would be advantageous if the texts were easy to read by everyone and therefore, typed up. When Father Migliorini was sent to Rome, the problem arose as to who would continue this task. There were no alternatives due to poverty and the discretion that needed to be preserved. So that is how the weight of the task fell on the shoulders of the heroic Marta Diciotti[749]: after April 1946, it was she – and she

---

[748] All that is known of the content of *The Heart of a Woman* is briefly described by Prof. Luciano Raffaele, who evidently was able to leaf through it before it was burnt: "A novel, of autobiographical intonation, written in the early years of infirmity and titled *The Heart of a Woman*, which illustrates some events in the life of the author, above all her unhappy and hopeless love, which nevertheless offered her the means to make her suffer and rejoice deeply in a typically human feeling that would enrich her sensitive soul with emotional advantages which were also found in her main 'writings'. Contrary to what is found in the other works, the handwriting in this novel, which covers about a thousand pages recorded, is irregular, has frequent erasure marks and corrections. The content, moreover, for some is evidently reminiscent and a subsidy of the inspirational books, which were provided to her by Marta! (Luciano Raffaele, preface to Maria Valtorta, *The Poem of the Man-God*, op. cit., 1961², p XX). [Not in the English edition.]

[749] "Think about it: writing under dictation for 2 or 3 hours as the first operation of the day. Second: correcting what I wrote because there are words that are illegible because of haste. Third: dictating to Marta while she types it, and therefore speaking loud and strong for at least six hours. Fourth: correcting what Marta wrote..." (Maria Valtorta, *Lettere a Madre Teresa Maria 1*, op. cit., p. 93).

alone – who typed up the notebooks written by hand by Maria Valtorta.

From the start of the paramystic events – personal conversations, dictations and visions – and thanks to his continuous transcription work, Father Migliorini had come to know in detail the words and visions that Maria received. He knew their supernatural value and the comforting extent for everyone. That the writer had to remain anonymous was obvious to Heaven, but not to the world. With a World War raging and the masses in the pangs of agony, it was easy to look for consolation from anyone with a little compassion. And that was what Father Migliorini did. Not for economic reasons, or for any other human value, but only for the wish to console, which is totally understandable, despite the fact that in this case, it was out of place. The wording on the remembrance card for the thirtieth day after the death of Antonia Del Bo[750], was enough to let out the secret

---

[750] "[…] On the death of this lady who had offered her life to God for the salvation of Italy and the world […] This poor woman, despite her great sacrifice, had a very troubled death that baffled those present, among which, some thought that she was damned. It really seems […] as if she damned herself […]. Her parents, her husband, her relatives were very affected by her death. They were shaken and very worried about the fate of the soul of the poor deceased. So they asked Father Migliorini to turn to the 'spokesperson', asking him to give them a ray of hope… And they said to him, 'Father, see if you can ask the spokesperson anything about this strange thing, about this tragic end that has deeply disturbed us. We need to understand and put our hearts at peace a little…". Father Migliorini reported it to Maria, who replied: 'Yes, Father, if by chance I receive the light, I will be happy to give it.' This of course took place in secret because these people did not know that the spokesperson was Maria. And they insisted: 'Father, if you enlighten us …'. Father Migliorini gave Holy Communion to Maria and went away. But immediately, as soon as he was gone… and had arrived near the corner of Via XX Settembre, I went after him quickly to call him back because Maria had said to me: 'Go now, call Father Migliorini back and tell him that I have something to tell him.' So, I left the house as I was, I called Father, and Father came. He found Maria writing continuously… writing the answer that the Lord, or in short, the dictating voice, had given to Maria about this deceased lady. And the answer was as follows: 'Since she was taken by mercy, she offered herself as a flower on the altar, a communion wafer for national misfortunes. She knew

on Maria Valtorta; Heaven's plan went up in smoke. The evacuation of most of the inhabitants of Viareggio slowed down the distribution of the card, but by Christmas 1944 following the return, "the Spokesperson" was known to everyone. And the troubles started for "the spokesperson, [...] more and more exposed to the curiosity, at times gross, and to the reproach, if not even to the shame of the so-called experts who perhaps did not bother to read or to meditate before judging. On the contrary, they made sure to avoid reading it"[751].

Then came the mass distribution of the messages and ideas of Dora Barsottelli. In the end, Sister Maria Gabriella – aka Emma Federici – was also there wishing to find a new congregation for illegitimate girls, which she was unable to do[752]. These events were

---

the night of Christ in Gethsemane and the bitterness of the ninth hour on the cross. But even before the resurrection of Jesus-Life, He had revealed what is the bliss of the elect, and with the anticipated possession of Love, she exhaled the spirit sanctified by His heroism by looking at Mary, the star of his eternal morning'. In particular, I will say that Mrs. Antonia Dal Bo Terrazzi was born in Como on 29 November 1907, and died in Viareggio on 4 January 1944, with the Barbantine sisters. The quoted writing above is from eight days later, on 12 January. On the thirtieth anniversary of her death, this funeral remembrance card was made to be distributed to friends, relatives, just about everywhere. In it, in addition to the text in question, the following was added: 'Dictated by the Celestial Voice to his spokesperson in Viareggio on 12 January 1944. Fr. R. Migliorini spiritual director of the spokesperson'. But wouldn't the text have been enough? What was the need for this addition that compromised everything?" (Albo Centoni, *Una vita con Maria Valtorta. Testimonianze di Marta Diciotti*, op. cit., pp. 141-2).

[751] ibid., p. 142.

[752] Cf. Maria Valtorta, *Notebooks 1945-1950*, op. cit., 10 January 1945, p. 20, Footnote 4 at the bottom of the page.

accompanied by very serious allegations[753] against Father Migliorini which led to his famous relocation to Rome[754].

His departure was sudden, although there had been several signs. On 17 March 1946, he went to say goodbye to her at 9am, an unusual time. Maria Valtorta could not help but write to Mother Teresa Maria: "I still do not know what prompted this order which deprives me, at the end of my life, of the Priest who knows me as a soul and as a medium"[755]. She felt extremely bitter, to the point of lamenting: "So there should be no surprise that a Marina Rossi[756] who ruined my innocent Parish Priest, is left alone, as well as Dora, while poor Maria who only ever said 'yes, yes, yes' to God and was always a Catholic who never brought on scandal, is tormented. Well!"[757] The only consolation she got was through the Lord: "In the sea of bitterness which engulfs me from all sides, there comes the sweetness of honey to me which God had promised through my angel"[758]. Father Migliorini moved to Rome bringing with him some of the notebooks. Maria Valtorta soon realized this and immediately set about to retrieve them. That Heaven did not want the notebooks to be scattered here and there is so obvious that we would be surprised if it wasn't. The order she received was strong: *"The manuscripts must*

---

[753] Maria Valtorta, *Lettere a Madre Teresa Maria 1*, op. cit., p. 274. "For months, she sees so much… condescension, indulgence and more in Fr. M. […] and his company, that he has failed her in some way and therefore, it is convenient for him to become corrosive" (cf. ibid., p. 117). But on 13 May, there had been a disagreement with Maria Valtorta over Mother Gabriella.

[754] Three years later, Maria Valtorta wrote: "F.M. [Father Migliorini] was under investigation by the H.O. [Holy Office] for three years due to M. Gabriella and Dora Barsottelli from Pieve di Camaiore being directed by him against the advice of God … (I had always prayed that F.M. never appeared to be close to the Work because I knew his dubious situation with the H.O. and the Congregation of Rites…)" (Maria Valtorta, *Lettere a Madre Teresa Maria 2*, op. cit., p. 193).

[755] Maria Valtorta, *Lettere a Madre Teresa Maria 1*, op. cit., p. 84.

[756] cf. ibid., p. 313. A turbid story of a poor slanderer of the Parish Priest, who was helped by the bishop out of Christian charity, but then the gesture turned against him.

[757] ibid., p. 85.

[758] ibid.

return here, to in the house of my spokesperson"[759]. The race started on 13 May. Maria had written to Father Migliorini[760] that her cousin Paola will come to collect the notebooks. It became fast-paced until Paola was able to send her a telegram on 29 August saying that she had retrieved everything[761]. Even the use of the telegraph shows how urgent it had been for Maria Valtorta, and how frightened she had been. The loss of the writings would have been irreparable.

Broadening the mind

As soon as Father Berti gained Maria Valtorta's confidence, he realized that to be successful, the Work of Valtorta would have to broaden its horizons and emerge from the shoals of Viareggio which had led it to a dead end. The confusion and misunderstandings caused by Father Migliorini and his own Order could have been overcome only by doing things with a broader mind and on a wider scale worldwide. But Maria Valtorta could not move, so he had to act. On top of that in 1946, dictations and visions were far from over; it is very probable that many people expected a comment of the whole Bible, and that therefore, Maria would still have a huge number of notebooks to write. As a matter of fact, she had had some visions of martyrs and of other moments of the early Church, and in the various published *Notebooks*, there are comments to several passages of the Old Testament.

The order to keep the writer and the distribution of the writings secret, albeit true, had to be interpreted with reasoning: the writer had to remain anonymous to everyone, except for a microscopic number of people, as selected and as influential as possible. This was

---

[759] Maria Valtorta, *Notebooks 1945-1950*, op. cit., dated 12 July 1946, p. 275.

[760] "Rev. Father, please hand over to the bearer of this note, all the notebooks I have written. For reasons of understandable prudence, I will explain to you separately the reason for this decision. For the moment, please understand my silence. The manuscripts will be treasured by me and preserved for use on my death. With thanks and much obliged. M. V." (Maria Valtorta, *Lettere a Madre Teresa Maria 1*, op. cit., p. 116).

[761] "On 29 [August 1946] my cousin Paola left suddenly for Milan, and when passing though Rome, she went to San Marcello and withdrew all the notebooks. At least that is what she telegraphed to me" (ibid., p. 246).

in order that the knowledge of the people who would express a positive, authoritative judgement could help obtain the canonical approval, the printing – which the more Maria Valtorta wrote, the more expensive it became – and the scientific-theological support necessary to present it, not as a novel but as the real narration of the life of Christ. We must bear in mind that the sanctity and the psychological normality of Maria Valtorta were the tools but not the goal of Father Berti's action. If these were the guidelines which Father Berti followed, we cannot fail to also see from what happened later, the mistakes, the hitches, the delays, the misunderstandings, the narrow-mindedness, and the impossibility (fortunately!) to convince Maria Valtorta herself, of a psychic-scientific-spiritist point of view. Here are the three-action guidelines: to find respected scientific validations; to look for important figures who would declare the deep theological value of the writings; and to publish the complete works. Father Berti took care of the above-mentioned goals. The spiritual direction of the writer was given to someone more local than he; and yet another person would do the typing. It must be stressed, however, that these were action guidelines, a rough outline, just like when you watch the armies in a battle: then, as in a battle, there are small personal or group clashes or tactical manoeuvres, all subordinate to the overall strategy. So it is with this outline that the small variations can be many, but the guidelines remain the same.

The spiritist deviation

Yet, right from the start, the imprudence[762] of the otherwise excellent Father Berti came to the fore: there came the contact with

---

[762] "I cannot fail to notice another notable inconsistency of the spiritual direction. Instead of resorting to the most obvious and sure means to test the authenticity of the Valtortian 'dictates'; that is, to ask for authorization to practice an exorcism, what came instead was ... a practitioner of radiesthesia, who would also claim to adduce it as proof that Valtorta was not... possessed! [...] It seems to me, however, that there exists an undue confusion of skills here" (Fabrizio Braccini, *Il caso di Maria Valtorta* [The case of Maria Valtorta], in "Rivista di Ascetica e Mistica", Edizioni Nardini, Firenze, n. 3-4 / 1979; cit. in Emilio Pisani, *Pro e contro Maria Valtorta*, op. cit., pp. 247-53).

some radiesthesists, top spiritists of various types such as Prof. Nicola Pende and Prof. Luciano Raffaele. Even if no other names are mentioned, it can be deduced that probably, among Father Berti's circle, there were other similar characters. What Father Berti lacked was the insight typical of Jean Aulignier and Jean-François Lavère, some tens of years later, that the Valtorta writings are also a mine of scientific data[763]. The impression is that this was not part of his mindset; he did not realize that without the background and support of Galilean science, everything would be useless for 20th-century people. A 16th-century essay, however wonderful, written by the Venerable Mary of Agreda, today sounds less convincing. The personal revelations of the Blessed Anne Catherine Emmerich, who dictated in German dialect to the fairytale writer Clemens Brentano, are outstandingly beautiful, yet they leave our contemporaries in doubt. Nowadays, to convince a person who grew up with rationalism – at times blind, absolute and to the point of brutal nihilism, it is perhaps one reason to use the only language they know – real facts – proven by Galilean science. And the life of Jesus Christ written by Maria Valtorta is like that. Being impossible to access Father Berti's personal writings and letters, we cannot go any further. We know from the facts that what followed was awful and that it is still hampering the whole Valtorta Work. What did Cardinal Alfredo

---

[763] Prof. Braccini affirmed: "We always thought that it was that sort of regurgitation that aroused resentment at the success of a non-scientific Work, which displaced scholars (theologians and exegetes) illuminated by science" (ibid., p. 253). Professor Braccini was justified in 1979 to write this. Today, neither he nor anyone else, could write the same things because science has proven otherwise; and it is precisely because the Valtortian writings are a continuous interweaving of science and grace that they can be taken into consideration today. Without the presence of continuous verifiable data, the writings could be considered only pious thoughts of a woman in agony.

Ottaviani[764], Cardinal Pietro Parente[765] and Professor Father Ricciotti[766] think, when they had in front of them a text – the first of nine – with a long preface by a spiritist of the calibre of Professor Luciano Raffaele? It must have looked worthless, spiritist trash, full of dreams, of fantasies and reveries, of nonsense, of false ideas, of historical, philosophical, geographical mistakes, etc., etc. The result: at first the garbage dump and then the Index. It must also be noted that in the post-war period, Cardinal Ottaviani, Secretary of the former Holy Office[767], had to deal with 295 would-be[768] psychics, among whom was St. Faustina Kowalska who he also condemned in the same year 1959, when he placed *the Poem of the Man-God* on the Index. Father Berti's huge, fundamental mistake of looking for psychic validations capable of convincing where it was not possible, could not have resulted in anything different.

The final separation from the Order of the Servants of Mary came when, on the advice of the Bishop of Lucca, the Friar Servants should have let the diocesan priests be the ones to take Holy Communion

---

[764] From 1953 to 1968, he was the Secretary of the Holy Office. To understand the character of Cardinal Ottaviani, it should be noted that, together with Cardinal Bacci in 1969, he signed the "Breve esame critico del *Novus Ordo Missæ*" [A short critical essay on the Novus Ordo Mass], in fact, a completely harsh criticism of the new rite of the Holy Mass universally used today. The paper gave, and gives, arguments to Lefevrians and sedevacantists (cf. *http://www.unavox.it/doc14.htm*, consulted 30 October 2018).

[765] Emilio Pisani defines him "the Enemy" (cf. Emilio Pisani, *Lettera a Claudia* [Letter to Claudia], Centro Editoriale Valtortiano, Isola del Liri (FR) 2014, pp. 105-13). An entire chapter is dedicated to Cardinal Pietro Parente. Regardless of the bookish and economic issues related there, the point of view of Cardinal Parente was, and is, perfectly acceptable, given the absolute and adequate lack of archaeological and scientific comparisons in those years. Was it ever conceivable that without at least archaeological evidence, he would accept *The Poem of the Man-God*? Certainly, the ending of this chapter is totally acceptable: "the enemy of Maria Valtorta is only one: the human pride of man": it is totally true, all around.

[766] A notable biblicist, he wrote *La vita di Gesù Cristo* [The Life of Jesus Christ], republished many times and always with great success.

[767] Today it is called the Congregation for the Doctrine of the Faith.

[768] cf. Karl Rahner, *Visioni e Profezie* [Visions and Prophecies], Vita e Pensiero, Milano 1955, p. 10.

to Maria Valtorta. In fact, the whole 'Valtorta case' was a continuous divisive point among the members of the Order. Heaven reproached them harshly, and the dictation dated 30 March 1949 is an example of that: "I leave man free to act but ready to help if he turns to goodness. And I also left them (the Servites) free to act. And to keep their accusations and those of the whole Order against you – as fickle, insincere, demented, exploitative, impulsive and more – from taking the appearance of truth, I deemed it necessary to let them descend *right to the bottom*. In that way, the gold has been separated from the tinsel, and the truth about you and about them is clear. And no one who is just will be able to think that you have betrayed them and the Order because you are mentally, morally and spiritually ill, as is being said; but the just will say that you had to act to defend God, the Church, your soul, and the Work along with it, now that their descent into an abyss, which would be illicit for anyone because of the actions being carried out from there, has provided the measure of *their* morality"[769]. In the end, with a certain contradiction, the Order of the Servants of Mary, after having refused any inheritance (consisting in a few things besides the notebooks and the letters) decided to ask for – or at least to accept – that the remains of Maria Valtorta, after the exhumation of 1971, be placed in a small chapel of the cloister of the Basilica of the Most Holy Annunciation in Florence, the Mother Church of the Servants of Mary. The Voice from Heaven that spoke to Maria, several times complained with them, about them, and about their attitude towards her.

The real burial place of St. Peter

Meanwhile, a new problem was slowly arising. During the maintenance works commissioned by Pius XII at the tomb of his predecessor, Pius XI, a sort of sarcophagus which seemed to contain the remains of St. Peter was discovered. To make sure, the Pope had official investigations on what was the original tomb carried out from 1940. The excavations continued without a break until 1949. The following year, a Holy Year, and the year of the dogmatic definition of the Assumption of the Virgin into Heaven body and soul, Pius

---

[769] Maria Valtorta, *Notebooks 1945-1950*, op. cit., dated 30 March 1949, p. 509.

XII was able to proclaim on the Vatican radio: "The tomb of the Prince of the Apostle has been uncovered"[770]. There was great emotion all over the world. But not for Maria Valtorta! The story, to be clear, had started a couple of years before. On 11 July 1948, Father Berti wrote[771] to Maria Valtorta: "the priest from the Secretary of State begged me to ask you to ask an Angel, or I don't know who, **WHERE THE BODY OF ST. PETER IS**. Many excavations have been carried out in St. Peter's in Rome but so far, they haven't found anything... Of course, this isn't good. I'm expecting an answer. Of course, it would certainly be good for the Work which speaks a lot about St. Peter (I remember having read a sermon by St. Peter during a Mass). Thanking you in advance. Too early? I would never have asked... It is not me asking..."[772]. Besides, the request made to have a clever and legitimate possibility of speaking in favor of Valtorta's Work to the prelates of the Holy See, one might wonder – perhaps with a touch of malice – whether the Secretariat of State knew of Maria Valtorta back then, and so well as to give her credit and make such an unusual and interesting request. On his part, Father Berti well knew that it was not wise to drag Maria into it as she had to remain hidden, and that is why he almost sounds apologetic. Maria's first reply was clear: "Leave those poor bones in peace! We will see them whole again when the world comes to an end!"[773] Then the story continued with Maria Valtorta's visions. The painter, Lorenzo Ferri sketched images[774] of St. Peter as "old, (75-80 years old) and bent from old age as if from a life of hard work. He is bald with very pale sunken cheeks and a small thin, white beard"[775]. On 26 August 1948, Maria had a vision of the aerial view of Rome and of St. Peter himself,

---

[770] cf. *https://digilander.libero.it/gog magog/TombaPietro/Ossasanpietro2.htm*, consulted 22 November 2018.

[771] Emilio Pisani, *Pro e contro Maria Valtorta*, op. cit., p. *3. Finally, here we have something written by Father Berti. There must be many letters and writings from Father Berti. In the small section concerning the tomb of Saint Peter, we have published some fragments from it.

[772] Maria Valtorta, *The Little Notebooks*, op. cit., dated 11 July 1948, p. 250 (These are the pages in the last section called Saint Peter's Tomb).

[773] ibid., p. 251.

[774] ibid., sketch on p. 252.

[775] ibid., p. 255.

grey with age. A few days later, on 18 September, she saw the burial plot where St. Peter's body lay. Her Guardian Angel Azariah (her inner voice) told her that "This is the catacomb crypt of the martyrs Titus and Marcellianus, the first to be placed here. He lies near them"[776]. "Later, the Lord tells me not to talk about this for now, or better still in His exact words, *not to communicate it* in writing but to say the word when He tells me"[777]. On 26 August, Azariah again informed her that "When night came, the Christians removed the body from there and took it to the place where Peter had preached the Lord, the Ostrianum"[778]. Father Berti – addressing Maria Valtorta as "My dearest Sister" – after telling her of the pleasure on the part of Father Bea (a future Cardinal), asked her the precise spot where St. Peter is allegedly buried. Maria Valtorta tried to give technical directions and added: "Even at the cost of disappointing those who hope for more more than I can give, perhaps by mistakenly attributing to me supernatural powers which I absolutely do not have, I do not allow myself to add or remove even a comma or insignificant detail of what I see and hear, and which is all I can give because it is given to me"[779]. Jesus intervened with a vision- dictation on 3 October: after explaining the reason for the change of names topographically. To a precise question by her, Jesus replied... by leaving[780]. Again, on 26 October Jesus reaffirmed that "My Simon Peter did not find peace in his body, not even after his death. His spirit found peace [...]. Let them not insist further. Let them never insist. I know whether to tell and when, with justice"[781]. On 21 November, Jesus again, repeated: "No, I tell you. <u>No. After his martyrdom, Peter was not buried anywhere except where he was martyred, preaching</u>"[782] . Almost a year later, on 29 September 1949, Msgr. Carinci, probably asked by someone, joined the number of those requesting an answer: "They tell me that you know where the body of St. Peter lies. As they are now preparing a report on the

---

[776] ibid., p. 258.
[777] ibid.
[778] ibid., p. 256.
[779] ibid., p. 267.
[780] ibid., p. 269.
[781] ibid., p. 271.
[782] ibid., p. 278.

excavations carried out in the Vatican Grottoes beneath the central Altar, I would request you to inform the Holy Father of what you know: I would willingly present what you write to him, which would cast light on this subject which is so important to all of Christianity"[783]. Right away, on 1 October, Maria Valtorta replied: "I had an order from Our Lord to talk about this only to Fr. Berti, and that he should keep silent for as long as God wanted. However, I was not to hand over the Quinternion booklet, or else something bad would happen to me. Indeed, regarding the last place – I did not see others, after that – Our Lord made me promise to keep it secret for a specified time. I disobeyed by handing over the Quinternion booklet. I was told His Holiness greatly desired it in order to put an end to costly excavations and disputes with the Protestants etc. etc. As Jesus said, something bad did happen to me"[784]. Several months went by and on 28 June 1953, St. Peter himself intervened: "If the world doesn't change, especially in Italy, then the time will never come when the remains of the 'Rock on which Christ built His Church' will be pulled from their current darkness to the light of worship, from obscurity because I am hidden away, to the veneration of the faithful"[785]. Unfortunately, the world has not changed, Maria Valtorta has died, and according to Maria Valtorta herself, the tomb is not where it seems to be today. However, the place she mentioned is still too vague to initiate very expensive excavations. For now, besides the novel by Antonio Socci[786] on this subject and with this data, we wait for Heaven to speak.

Looking for attestations

Therefore, Father Berti contacted various figures: not all were interested in Maria Valtorta, but a good number wrote authoritative statements. So, it seems appropriate to do a run-down of these names, including some of those already mentioned.

---

[783] ibid., p. 282.

[784] ibid., pp.282-3. A "Quinternion" consists of five sheets folded in two and inserted one into the other.

[785] ibid., p. 285.

[786] Antonio Socci, *I giorni della tempesta* [The days of the storm], Rizzoli Libri, Milano 2012.

Prof. Nicola Pende (21 April 1880 – 8 June 1970) was introduced by Dr. Emilio Pisani as follows: "a full professor (later, emeritus) of the University of Rome and Senator of the Kingdom. He was the most renowned physician in Italy, and he was world-famous in the fields of Endocrinology and Functional Pathology. The Sacred Congregation of the Rites (which dealt with the causes of saints) included him among its Experts for the scientific analysis of the alleged miraculous healings[787]. However, we must add two important things, that he was a scientific racist and a spiritist[788]: which is why he never accepted the case of Maria Valtorta as having supernatural implications[789].

Camillo Corsànego (20 March 1891 – 9 October 1963) specialized in Legal Sciences and he was important thanks to his ecclesiastical and political links. But he could not say much about the historical-geographical-archaeological elements because they were not his specialty.

The biblical knowledge and capacity of Cardinal Augustin Bea (28 May 1881 – 16 November 1968) – from 1930 to 1949 Rector of the Pontifical Biblical Institute and confessor of Pope Pius XII – are undeniable. He read the *Poem* when it was still a bunch of typed sheets of paper and he gave a good attestation on 23 January 1952 with the letterhead of the Pontifical Biblical Institute. Yet he did not seem to

---

[787] Emilio Pisani, *Pro e contro Maria Valtorta*, op. cit., p. 85.

[788] cf. Paolo Cortesi, *Medium e Gerarchi* [Mediums and Hierarchs] in "Query" n. 30, year 8 pp. 64-6, Padova 2017. This is the magazine put out by CICAP. The article is also found here: *https://www.cicap.org/n/icle.php?id=278483*, consulted 3 November 2018.

[789] "However, he could not accept the supernatural origin of the Work, for which he sought in vain a scientific explanation" (Emilio Pisani, *Pro e contro Maria Valtorta*, op. cit., p. 86). Emilio Pisani is wrong at the root of the matter; what Prof. Pende was looking for in Maria Valtorta was proof that mediumship was a real fact, subject to rules to be discovered. Scientists and the Church have never accepted the facts brought by the spiritists, as mediumship has nothing to do with science. Then the fact that there have been some scientists who have believed in mediumship – like Cesare Lombroso, for example – is the classic *exception that confirms the rule*. Maria Valtorta always maintained that everything that is mediumism is demonism! So Prof. Pende was not looking for a "scientific explanation", but a "mediumistic explanation", and obviously he did not find it.

fully understand the greatness of what he was holding in his hands: he stressed the remarkable archaeological and topographical precision, but he also said that the Work "should be properly shortened, purged and corrected"[790]. He then requested that it be published simply, without the Authoress' name, as a 'Life of Jesus, narrated and illustrated for Catholic people'"[791]. In 1952, it was difficult to take a more compromising position, even though the basic misunderstanding is clear. That is, it is a nice, fictionalized fabrication and nothing more. Cardinal Bea failed to see its profound importance, even though he thought that it could do great good to many families.

Cardinal Giuseppe Siri (20 May 1906 – 2 May 1989) wrote a short statement with no commitment for the *imprimatur* with a note saying that he had paid attention to what he had read. "The characters speak in the literary style of our times, not of those times. At least, that is what I think"[792]. It is certainly a very punctual and precise comment, but one that does not consider the context, that it is a personal revelation suitable to the people of today, and therefore, it disregards the real times in which those events took place. That it must excite the people of today and it must not be a work of linguistic archaeology[793] was not Maria Valtorta's mission. Card. Giuseppe Siri was probably contacted for his theological and ecclesiastical importance and consequently, for his possible influence on the Holy See.

The painter, sculptor and sindonologist, Prof. Lorenzo Ferri (1902-1975) also submitted this important testimonial: "I personally met Miss Valtorta and I saw that she was a simple, energetic, intelligent and sincere woman. As I was drawing her portrait, I felt a *great sense of peace* [...]; I have never worked with such spontaneous

---

[790] Emilio Pisani, *Pro e contro Maria Valtorta*, op. cit., p. 66.

[791] ibid.

[792] ibid., p. 95.

[793] Term used by Pope Pius XII against certain types of liturgical abuse, but perfectly usable also here. cf. *Mediator Dei* [Mediator of God], p. 1277 in: *Tutte le encicliche dei sommi Pontefici* [All the encyclicals of the Supreme Pontiffs], Editore Dall'Oglio, Milano 1986. However, to many readers, the language of Jesus and of the many characters seems like a very Aramaic translation.

happiness"[794]. He then pointed out that she gave him "an *amazing confirmation of the image of the Holy Shroud, for example, the sprained left shoulder of Christ*"[795]. The part played by Ferri is wonderful: his effort in trying to reproduce what Maria Valtorta saw, allowed the readers to get even closer to the world as seen by her, to visually narrate the rationality of what she wrote and underline its total lack of inconsistencies.

In this context, we must also mention again that Msgr. Carinci, as an influential witness, got very busy. Msgr. Carinci knew everything about the people involved and the (human) intrigue within the Holy See. Maria Valtorta wrote long and very detailed letters to him, but he only replied with short notes. His had the stealthy gait of a cat, which silently but efficiently, moves around the house: that's how it will catch a mouse! This attitude is obviously not described *apertis verbis* (clearly), but can be found in every line: light, slow, silent[796], "flat on the ground", almost crawling to make no noise, but then striking. It was almost a refrain in every note: "So, be quiet and, I add, be glad. Keep on writing calmly, under the usual dictation until the Speaker or the legitimate ecclesiastical authority forbids you to write any more"[797]. He then spoke more openly, but always "sinuously", with Pius XII[798]. He did not obtain much, but he could do nothing more. Cardinal Ottaviani – nicknamed "God's policeman"[799] – did not allow any interference with his own tasks, so he had to be cautious. We could almost see him: convinced of the gift of Maria Valtorta[800] yet always *tactical* to get results. But at the Vatican, it was not enough to be a great man or even a holy man:

---

[794] Emilio Pisani, *Pro e contro Maria Valtorta*, op. cit., p. 80.

[795] ibid., pp. 78-9.

[796] "The Holy Father, to whom I showed the previous letter, was very happy and satisfied with the spirit of humility and obedience" (Maria Valtorta, *Lettere a Mons. Carinci,* op. cit., p. 47).

[797] ibid., p. 26.

[798] cf. ibid., p. 26.

[799] Cf. http://www.data.unibg.it/dati/corsi/84065/79833-Sin%20e%20Ottaviani.pdf, consulted 3 November 2018.

[800] "From this, I note that the Lord has really granted you a great mental balance. His conduct is commendable and just" (Maria Valtorta, *Lettere a Mons. Carinci*, op. cit., p. 63).

there were not enough "political" forces on his side. And we can only imagine his disappointment at the 1961 preface by Prof. Luciano Raffaele, which, on the contrary, must have made someone on the opposing side, smirk.

Before going on, it is important to point out that all those contacts in favor of Maria Valtorta were off target. There was no theologian who could critically examine the Valtorta theology[801]. Father Allegra spoke in favor, but according to what he knew. Not even he investigated the Valtorta case in depth, but like everyone else, he also remained on the surface. Obviously, as an *expert*, he did not take long to realize that all that he had translated into Chinese was in front of him, in Maria Valtorta, but he did not mention in detail why things were that way. Regarding the *imprimatur,* as Cardinal Siri stated: "it is not my business", so Blessed Father Allegra seemed to take for granted the things that everyone else did not know at all. In reality, it must be said that back then, there was no archaeologist, geographer, linguist, astronomer, etc. and neither an exegete nor a theologian who, with the aid of the science, would examine the writings in depth. Only after 2012 did some academic scholars go public and, armed with scientific method (scientific, not psychic), they critically examined the whole work, eliminating any doubts and taking it to

---

[801] Two people gradually became aware of this need in the following years. Father Roschini, who published a very refined treatise on Mariology (cf. Gabriele Maria Roschini, *La Madonna negli scritti di Maria Valtorta* [Our Lady in the writings of Maria Valtorta], Centro Editoriale Valtortiano, Isola del Liri (FR) 1973). The other is Father Berti himself: despite the right insights and attempts at theological insights, the personal judgment of Dr. Emilio Pisani on the efforts of Father Berti is not one of the most flattering: "Father Berti exaggerated again in the apparatus of the footnotes to the other minor works, forcing me to restrain him. He was not used to being contradicted and began to stiffen and close himself off. Since he could no longer count on the full bond of his true collaborator, who above all had been an executor, *he took the initiative to draw up memorials, draw up lists of facts and names that had populated the Valtortian events, and hold presentations in small conferences* [our italics]. In his growing physical debilitation, he had been helped by some good people who attended to and assisted him, involuntarily contributing to his isolation with a somewhat fanatical devotion" (Emilio Pisani, *Pro e contro Maria Valtorta*, op. cit., p. 51).

another level – a deeper one – the study and the judgment on both the person and the writings of Maria Valtorta.

An interweaving has been mentioned because the line of action that Father Berti had put in motion was varied. While he looked for support within the circle of important and famous people, he also moved within the Vatican to get the necessary *imprimatur* that Maria Valtorta continued to demand under pressure from the real Author of her writings. On the other hand, the problem which arose straight away was about how to publish the writings. The secrecy of the authoress had been thrown out of the window, thanks to the awkward actions of Father Migliorini; so, they had to find out how to pave the way, looking for and finding a publishing house that would and could publish a 4,500-page work. On top of that, there was also the problem of the necessary investment. In the 1940s and 1950s, there was no digital printing – with this technology it is possible to print ten volumes, already properly formatted, at a much lower cost. Nowadays, it is possible to print just one volume without having to invest an impossible amount of money due to the number of copies and storage. At the time of Maria Valtorta, the publication of a book required the precise amount of copies to be known, large enough to contain the cost. The relatively small investment of today would have been a real editorial enterprise in 1950. So the problem was not one alone: they had to find a publisher, calculate the minimum number of copies, make an estimate of the costs, find the right format for the thickness of the volumes, deal with the distribution and relative costs, and finally, find a way to make them known, in other words, how to publicize them. Without losing heart, Father Berti started to prepare the groundwork. First, he thought of founding a new publishing house which was willing to do the job and had the necessary means. The idea came from the need not to depend on anyone, and to be free to edit, distribute and set the price. But there were two problems: the approval and the printing of the text. They were closely linked. The second problem depended on the first one, and the second one could not start without the *imprimatur*.

It must be said once again that there is no documentation detailed enough of the events and the people involved. Based on the various published letters, we can notice Maria Valtorta's steely, lucid, sharp, hard, and persevering determination to accomplish both things[802]. The years between 1947 and 1949, in fact, were marked by the anxiety of seeing all her indescribable hard work go up in smoke because it had been huge. To her glory, it is indeed appropriate to relate a short passage that she wrote to her spiritual and human confidante Mother Teresa Maria: "Let us begin with something that Jesus told me. A pearl, a guideline, a light. As He gave it to me, He told me that it is useful to every soul as it has no defined limit. Here it is: 'What is the measure to reach in order to be holy according to what God expects from a soul? *To give in proportion to what one has received*', and to me, he says: 'I gave you everything. So give me *everything*'. All right. I thought I had already given everything, but clearly, this is not so. I think… what else can I give? My own roof, the house that is so dear to me that I would rightfully like to leave to Marta? My eyesight, my intellect, and the satisfaction of seeing my work approved? So be it! May God take what He wants that is *exclusively mine*. I ask His justice that I can leave the house to Marta, as she, in turn, has given *everything* to me"[803]. This passage is also the plausible reply to the immolation that Jesus had prophetically announced to her a month earlier: "How I will miss these songs afterwards, when *the Gospel* is finished! What a longing for the perfect song of Jesus - and for His looks when He speaks to the crowds or his friends!" He appeared to me, saying: 'Why do you say this? Can you think I would deprive you of that because you finished the work? I will always come. And *for you alone*. And it will be even sweeter because it will be entirely for you. My little John, faithful spokesman, I will not take anything away from you which you have merited: to see Me and hear Me. But, on the contrary, I will take you higher up, into the pure spheres of pure contemplation, enveloped in the mystical veils which will form a tent for our love. You *shall only be Mary (Magdalene). Now* you are having to

---

[802] Marta Diciotti testified that: "[Maria Valtorta was] strained in the effort to save the Writings, to obtain an ecclesiastical approval, and terrified by the idea of incurring disciplinary sanctions, which excluded her from the Holy Mother Church and took away the help and the comfort of the Sacraments from her" (Albo Centoni, *Una vita con Maria Valtorta. Testimonianze di Marta Diciotti*, op. cit., pp. 160-1).

[803] Maria Valtorta, *Lettere a Madre Teresa Maria 2,* op. cit., pp. 90-1, letter dated 18 April 1947.

be Marta too because you have to work actively to be the spokesman. From now on you shall only contemplate and everything will be beautiful. Be happy. Very. I love you greatly. And you love Me greatly. Our two loves...! Heaven is already welcoming you! The lovely season is coming, O my hidden turtle-dove. And I will come to you in the midst of the living fragrance of the vines and the orchards, and I will *make you forget the world in my love...*"[804]. Maria Valtorta was ready to renounce everything had Jesus asked her, and so it was: her immolation was total, complete, unreserved. Prof. Braccini[805] repeated a sentence by Father Berti, making it his: "[Maria Valtorta], besides obedience to God, [asks] also for obedience... to herself"[806], escaping the huge effort that she had to sustain all by herself, in order to keep the writings safe from any contamination, cover-up, from those who wanted to confiscate them and to keep them subjected to the laws of the Church.

Pius XII receives

We do not know exactly when the need for the approval of the Church or of a Bishop arose, but it is certain that this anxiety afflicted, with endless worry, at least the last 16 years of Maria Valtorta's life. The earliest recorded warning is in a letter to Mother Teresa Maria: "Get well soon! [...] so that I will be soon able to say: 'Sister, the Lord's Word can be read because it has been approved'"[807]. The following day she repeated herself, showing fear and determination at the same time: "I pray for them more than for

---

[804] Maria Valtorta, *Notebooks 1945-1950,* op. cit., dated 16 March 1947, pp. 376-7. Marta Diciotti testified that: "The acceptance of her supreme holocaust took place, yes, but not immediately ... For me, the precise sign that she no longer had control of her mental faculties was that she did not recognize the Writings in that first large volume of the Poem that arrived at this house in June 1956. Nine years had passed since the time of her offering" (Albo Centoni, *Una vita con Maria Valtorta. Testimonianze di Marta Diciotti,* op. cit., pp. 160-1).

[805] Emilio Pisani, *Pro e contro Maria Valtorta,* op. cit., p. 250.

[806] ibid., p. 264.

[807] Maria Valtorta, *Lettere a Madre Teresa Maria 1,* op. cit., p. 80, letter dated 14 March 1946.

myself. For myself, I only ask that, if I should be condemned, that I never doubt my voices and, just like Joan of Arc whom I invoke a lot, I can always say: 'My voices have not deceived me. They came from Heaven!' Satan would use doubt to make me lose faith in God, creating fears of ultra-terrestrial punishments. The second thing that I ask for myself is that in case of an approval, I become even more humble, so that the satisfaction for the acknowledgement does not produce fumes of pride, even more damaging than doubt and despondency. I think I'm asking for the right things"[808]. So, her fear was only pride, vain-glory and self-congratulation; this is a good sign of a living sainthood. Every influential person that she met was only viewed for the advantages they could bring to the writings, as it could be used to convert many. Heaven itself intervened with determination, with the dictation dated 2 June 1946: *"Seek approval which defends and ensures the Work. Seek it at once and do not desist until you find it"*[809]. This command was her guideline and she never deviated or gave up. Meanwhile, Father Migliorini thought of contacting someone important in the Church. Maria Valtorta received a letter from him, which she also showed Mother Teresa Maria, in which he wrote: "When Cardinal of Palermo comes to Rome (Ruffini? asks Maria), who is very well-disposed towards the Order and known to Fr. Berti, we will be able to give him a copy of the Pre-gospel along with one of the notebooks so that we can have his comment in writing on the various points of view that we will express. If the Armenian Cardinal is in Rome, he is also in our favor, and we will use him (and who is this? I ask). And then there are two bishops in Rome, for sure. When we have a favorable judgment from these influential people in writing, then we will be able to decide on how to proceed. After these attestations, an imprimatur will not be unlikely, at least from the Cardinal of Palermo. All this will be done if it is approved…etc., etc."[810]. The dictations and visions continued, but on 6 January 1948, a new course was heralded: "I have done everything to convince them but it is as was written: 'We played the flute for you, but you did not dance; we sang a dirge, but you did not

---

[808] ibid., p. 81.
[809] Maria Valtorta, *Notebooks 1945-1950*, op. cit., dated 2 June 1946, p. 269.
[810] Maria Valtorta, *Lettere a Madre Teresa Maria 1*, op. cit., p. 180.

mourn'. But these are not pages for them. Indeed, I order you to remove them from here and make them into a separate notebook to be given in the manner and to the persons I indicated to you. They have received what was needed to obtain the approval for Jesus' Work. *The rest is a treasure which one must merit in order to possess it*"[811]. Father Berti, who had not yet been told of this, rightly continued to work towards obtaining an audience with the Pope, until he was successful: "It was 26 February 1948 when Pius XII received Fr. Romualdo M. Migliorini and Fr. Corrado M. Berti, accompanied by their Prior, Fr. Andrea M. Cecchin. It should have been up to Fr. Migliorini to present the petition, but the emotion forced him to give the floor to his young and self-confident confrère. The Pope seemed to have familiarized himself with the Work and gave blunt advice: 'Publish it as is'. He was shown the text of a preface which spoke of supernatural phenomenon, but He disapproved of it and added: 'Whoever reads it will understand'. His most authoritative opinion was however an unofficial and personal one"[812]. Unfortunately, this is all that is known. It is said, verbally[813] that Pope Pacelli was approached on a staircase in the Vatican palace, where the short dialogue mentioned above took place. Pius XII was probably in favor, but his deep knowledge of the Curia told him to tread carefully and with respect for the various roles: that is why he could not do anything more. Unfortunately, no written report was made by the three participants.

Maria Valtorta, however, kept asking for an *imprimatur* for what she had already written. And the *imprimatur* arrived! An editorial note informs that: "Barneschi Costantino M. Attilio, of the Order of the Servants of Mary […]. In 1948, when he was Titular Bishop of Tagaste and Apostolic Vicar of Swaziland, he gave the imprimatur to the Work of Maria Valtorta, which the newly-formed publishing house 'Words of Life' should have published in Italy on behalf of

---

[811] Maria Valtorta, *Notebooks 1945-1950*, op. cit., dated 6 January 1948, p. 477.

[812] Emilio Pisani, *Pro e contro Maria Valtorta*, op. cit., p. 63.

[813] In the ten Valtortian conferences organized by *the Maria Valtorta Foundation*, many words were said on this topic. This testimony was given verbally, in public, by an authoritative connoisseur of Valtortian history.

that Apostolic Vicariate"[814]. But it was too easy. Maria Valtorta said: "As is already known, on 25 October [1948] the Holy Father, acting through the official channels, had advised a more certain approval to safeguard the writings from future threats. So, having contacted His Excellency, the Bishop of Sora, he checked and said he would be willing to approve it. But on 29 November [1948] as the presses were about to start, the Holy Office summoned the Solicitor General of the Order of the Servants of Mary and ordered him to tell Fr B. And Fr M. [Fathers Berti and Migliorini] not to concern themselves with the Work any longer unless they wanted to be hit by the decrees of the Holy Office for having illegally obtained (?) the approval of Monsignor Barneschi, contrary to the rules of Canon Law because such a Monsignor is not the Bishop of the publishing house, or of the Author, and especially because: 'He is the Bishop of the Zulus'. (Do Zulus not have a soul? And just because an Italian Bishop is in Africa, is he less of a Bishop than one who resides in Italy?) Father Berti rushed to Fr Bea and to Monsignors Carinci and Fontevecchia, as well as to other Monsignors and other Jesuit Fathers, and they replied unanimously: 'Proceed anyway. They cannot do anything to you'[815]. Maria Valtorta, obviously, could not help but feel upset and dizzy at this decision, even though, with the lucidity that always characterized her, she was even able to joke about it. There would be many attempts made with the Bishops of Como, Varese and Vicenza, but they were unsuccessful. As Msgr. Carinci entered the scene, new attempts were made by him too. On 9 January 1949, Maria Valtorta wrote: "The presence of Your Excellency gave me great comfort and I felt that with the benevolent intervention of Your Excellency, the hope of seeing the will of the Lord (the Work's approval) soon accomplished is growing"[816]. And after pointing out the approval of one of the many books on Fatima, she added: "On 11 April, I asked you for one thing only: the approval of the Work thanks to the

---

[814] Maria Valtorta, *Lettere a Madre Teresa Maria 2*, op. cit., p. 346. The text also contains the cover pages complete with an imprimatur (cf. ibid., pp. 166-7).

[815] ibid., letter dated 16 December 1948, p. 165.

[816] Maria Valtorta, *Lettere a Mons. Carinci*, op. cit., p. 19.

supreme intervention of the Holy Father. I now ask you the same thing"[817].

America too

On 6 April 1949, writing to Mother Teresa Maria as her strictest confidante – and above all, very discreet and totally trusting her – Maria informed her of an initiative of Father Berti[818]: the plan was of publishing the Work in Italy through a new publishing house without attracting much attention, then go to Cardinal Francis Joseph Spellman (1889-1967)[819] who was clearly perceived as being in favour and capable of prevailing in the Vatican, and then bring the *imprimatur* back to Italy and start a new publication and sale. Here, Maria Valtorta's self-control, honesty and lucid determination, stood out. Yes, she was seriously affected by her illness, but she had a clear head and was able to immediately understand bullying, deception, cunning and fraud. Among the many people involved, there arose endless arguments, fake news and more. Maria Valtorta could not help but intervene: "The truth is this: the Holy Father, through Msgrs. Montini and Tardini, let Fr. Gargiani know (the Attorney-General of the Order of the Servants of Mary), that he is to go to the Bishop of Aquino in order to obtain a second and *more* valid approval, and to publish and hold conferences in publishing houses and halls *which do not belong to the Vatican City*, in order to avoid any damage to the writings caused by hostile prelates"[820]. The debate became heated and, in an undated letter, she was not afraid of putting everyone under scrutiny, starting with Father Migliorini: "In the awful letter dated the 29th, Fr. Migliorini accuses me of acting 'as a mistress who promises her maid a gold brooch and then she does not give it to her and expects the maid to be more grateful as a result of the promise

---

[817] ibid., p. 24.

[818] cf. Maria Valtorta, *Lettere a Madre Teresa Maria 2*, op. cit., p. 194.

[819] The Cardinal of New York from 1939 to 1967. An interesting fact: he was the one who bought Pope Paul VI's headpiece when it was put on sale; now the headpiece is kept in the Basilica of the Immaculate Conception in Washington (Cf. *https://www.viaggiandoconluca.it/la-basilica-dellimmacolata-concezione-di-washington*, consulted 3 November 2018).

[820] Maria Valtorta, *Lettere a Madre Teresa Maria 2*, op. cit., p. 160.

alone... '. I would be the mistress who 'promised to give and then I never gave'. Bottom line: I should have handed over the Work, let Father Migliorini and Father Berti do whatever they wanted with it, resulting in their suspension *a divinis*, causing the Order to be in trouble with the Holy Office, and I, the innocent one, excommunicated because the H. O. would never admit that I did not know anything, and the Work placed on the Index..."[821]. So, despite being bedridden with no means of communication apart from an exhausting and laborious correspondence; certain that she had done her duty as a sick and martyred woman in pouring rivers of ink; certain also that she had written to the best of her ability without ever giving up or asking for a *day off*; instead of leaving everything to its human fate, enduring immolation and leaving to others the worry of the *imprimatur* and of the publication; here she is, fighting two terrible battles, emulating her beloved St. Joan of Arc, always alert so that the holy Word she received could be accepted by the Church and spread to everyone by means of the press!

But the story was not over yet. Since Heaven had stopped the dictations[822] following the clear refusal of those who could have (really) understood and also given the many transcription mistakes, on 22 April 1949 Maria Valtorta wrote to Msgr. Carinci: "With mercy and goodwill from both sides: to those who examine it, I/we can clarify what seems obscure and get rid of what could constitute an insurmountable obstacle to get the approval. And I say this because right from the earliest dictations of Our Lord, which started on *23 April 1943, Good Friday*, there is mention of these future difficulties

---

[821] ibid., p. 249.

[822] cf. ibid., p. 32. "Even more clearly on 14 June 1948, when He told me not to write His explanations on the Pauline Epistle anymore because it was useless, given the opposition that was made to his other words" (Maria Valtorta, *Lettere a Mons. Carinci*, op. cit., pp. 31-2). Here, there is a small editorial puzzle: the date quoted is certainly the one in which the first part of the lessons ceases, but there is no trace of what Maria Valtorta says. The note of the same date refers to the 26th dictation of the Lessons on Paul's epistle to the Romans, but these editorial notes are so simplified as to become incomprehensible (cf. Maria Valtorta, *Lessons on the Epistle of St. Paul to the Romans*, op. cit., footnotes of pp. 177-8). [Not in the English edition]

and how to deal with them"[823]. Maria Valtorta's approach was not intransigent (either this or nothing); she looked for possible compromises over the form, while remaining firm over the content.

The publisher

Having put aside the idea of founding a publishing house, Father Berti looked everywhere for a publishing house willing to print Maria Valtorta's work. Father Gabriele Roschini suggested a publishing house known in the Vatican because, among other things, it printed "a voluminous six-monthly periodical titled Archivium Historicum Societatis Jesu"[824], on behalf of the Historical Institute of the Jesuit Order. After various ups and downs, the publishing house was by then in the hands of Michele Pisani, who, contacted by Father Berti, was persuaded of the goodness of the project. On 6 October, Pisani and Berti went to Viareggio to Maria Valtorta, and signed a contract for the publication. At this point, a new task began: they took the papers typed by Father Migliorini and Marta Diciotti which Maria Valtorta had corrected from memory and grammatically [...], taking for granted that the transcription was precise. It is highly probable that haste was fatal in making this choice despite knowing that the manuscripts had resulted in two versions of typed sheets, plus a third version, instead of starting from scratch. This is something that was only done after 1960 where they took the typed version not corrected by Maria Valtorta, justifying their choice as follows: "During the process of proofreading, whenever we found some sentences that we felt we should eliminate because they were not clear in terms of ideas or form, the method was always the same: immediate elimination or arbitrary correction. The same method was also adopted, not right from the start of the Work, but quite soon. Even with regards to punctuation, T2 [second typed copy] very flawed. This was introducing a very dissimilar system from the one regularly adopted by the writer in her manuscript"[825]. Convinced of the importance and the value of the text, as shown in their hard work, it was only the rush

---

[823] Maria Valtorta, *Lettere a Mons. Carinci*, op. cit., p. 56.
[824] Emilio Pisani, *Pro e contro Maria Valtorta*, op. cit., p. 170.
[825] Maria Valtorta, *The Poem of the Man-God*, op. cit., vol. 1 p. XLI. [Not in the English edition].

A meteor: Luciana

In the letters of Maria Valtorta to Mother Teresa Maria, there came like a meteor, a certain Luciana[826]. In two undated letters to which Mother Teresa Maria replied on 5 August 1950, and which can therefore be dated back to July, Maria described in detail one of the interventions between Pope Pius XII and the Monsignors of the Vatican Curia. Who was she talking about? There have been several theories. The most plausible concerns Luigina Sinapi (8 September 1916 – 17 April 1978)[827], but this is far from certain. Sinapi was a mystic with several paramystic gifts, among which is a photograph (!) of the face of Holy Mary. Close to some saints, including St. Philip Neri and St. Pio of Pietrelcina, she is also remembered as having foretold the apparitions of the Holy Virgin at Tre Fontane (27 April 1947) in Rome to psychic Bruno Cornacchiola. Guided by Pius XII and St. Pio of Pietrelcina, she died in the odor of sanctity. On 22 May 2009, the beatification cause ended and, for the time being, she is a Servant of God. Maria Valtorta claimed that "these are all reports *checked and confirmed* by people such as Honorable Corsànego, who came to see me on Saturday, *1 April*, and by Prof. Ferri who came on *2 April*. [...] You must know that in Rome, there is a soul guided along extraordinary paths, a woman under thirty, who is often called by the Holy Father for her supernatural guidance. [...] She was, at the beginning of her mission, decried as a *'hysteric'*, *'demonic'* etc. She was exorcised, they tried to put her in an asylum at first, and then in a monastery. But they had to give up and let her be"[828]. To be honest, the information related by Maria Valtorta sounds more like rumors and gossip blown out of proportion, than real facts. "Towards the end of the month of January, O. L. J. C. ordered her to go to the H. O., to reproach those... gentlemen for the harm they were doing to

---

[826] Maria Valtorta, *Lettere a Madre Teresa Maria 2*, op. cit., p. 279ff.

[827] cf. Speziale Vincenzo, *Serva di Dio Luigina Sinapi* [Luigina Sinapi: Servant of God], Edizioni Segno, Tavagnacco (UD) 2016.

[828] Maria Valtorta, *Lettere a Madre Teresa Maria 2*, op. cit., p. 279ff.

people by forbidding the publication of the Work... Imagine what happened! They attacked her, enraged, saying that '*she must not deal with it* because they knew what they were doing, and if they forbade its publication, it was because the Work was the creation of a demoniac etc.'. And since this Luciana said: "Now I'm going to the Holy Father to tell him how you are acting'. They warned her: 'Woe betide you if you speak to him about this! We forbid you'. And Luciana: 'God wants me to speak, and I will'. They hit her and they did exorcisms until she said 'Do them to yourselves because the Devil is inside you, not me'. Then... they tried to rape her (do you understand?), saying: 'We'll soon cure you of the visions! As soon as your uterus is tired and satisfied, you will be fine again!' [...] Luciana came back a few days later with a complaint in which she states that 'Msgr. Carinci, the Hon. Corsànego, the Hon. Tredici, Msgr. Lattanzi, Fr Roschini etc., have read and judged etc., etc. Therefore they ask His Holiness to intervene etc., etc.'. The Holy Father put it in his Breviary, assuring them that He had always been in favor of the publication and *wants it*. [...] Luciana again went to the Holy Father to repeat that the Work, by direct communication of Jesus, *comes from God* and He wants it to be published. This is with regards to the Work"[829]. On 5 August, Mother Teresa Maria replied: "What you wrote does not surprise me because, as usual, we come to the painful uncovering of deception. Even as Luciana is concerned... it is obvious that Satan is trying hard to encircle us with enemies in order to prevent us from succeeding"[830]. Luciana did not appear in any other letters. Perhaps Maria Valtorta herself understood that – even though it was told by influential people – what had happened had been exaggerated. The anxiety for an *imprimatur* and the need to publish must have played a nasty trick on everybody. The most unbelievable rumors, suspicion of betrayals and the fear of persecution reached her.

Maria Valtorta and the clergy

If there is an aspect in the life of Maria Valtorta that needs to be told with caution, it is her relationship with the clergy and not with

---

[829] ibid.
[830] Maria Valtorta, *Lettere a Madre Teresa Maria 2*, op. cit., p. 305f.

the Church. Maria Valtorta was a 'Catholic by nature', meaning that no aspect of the doctrine of the Church was too constricting or dubious. It was obvious for her to be a Catholic, to think like the Church to the very core of her being, to identify with it, to never be any different apart from a few aspects of the doctrine left free to debate[831]. On the contrary, it was quite the opposite: it was she who clarified the Catholic doctrine! It is like saying that if you believe what she believed, then you are a Catholic; if you act differently, then correct yourself. If anyone is looking for further evidence of this, they must only remember her relationship with her cousin Giuseppe Belfanti. She did not look for compromises or half measures, but she acted so that he could rediscover the fullness of the Catholic faith. In the end, and with the help of Jesus, she brought him back to Catholicism. So, the thoughts and actions of Maria Valtorta can be perfectly identified with those of the Church. The Church is hierarchical because this is how its founder, Jesus Christ, wanted it. Therefore, it has a hierarchy of persons leading it: the Pope, bishops, priests, deacons; and then there are the mixed figures: the religious and finally, the laity, with these two groups: the religious men and women who are not priests. Potentially, Maria Valtorta was in harmony with everyone. She respected the vocation of everyone, although she had her favorites; she loved the Carmelites to the point that she felt like one of them. Her best friend and spiritual confidante was Mother Teresa Maria, superior of the Carmelite Convent of Camaiore (Lucca).

On this basis, it seems difficult then to explain the harsh reproaches against some of the people who belonged to the ecclesiastical hierarchy. In fact, her invective[832] was never against the

---

[831] An example for all: did the Holy Virgin die or not die before being taken to heaven? Maria Valtorta never had doubts about Mary's Assumption into heaven: it is the doctrine of the Church. About her death, however, she followed her own path, because on this fact, not even the definition of Pius XII of 1950 takes a definitive position.

[832] I add a personal memory. In 1974, Msgr. Aldo Forzoni, bishop of the diocese of Massa Carrara – Pontremoli, told me that a seminarian together with a few others, many years earlier went to find Maria Valtorta still fully present. He recounted that it left an impression on him how she

hierarchy per se, but how it acted; the hypocrisy, the falsehood, the spiritual mediocrity ingrained in the system. This is what she and Heaven that appeared to her, condemned. So confusing the issue and putting her among the destroyers of the Church, is a deeply unjust and wrong thing to do.

It is possible for someone to be moved by the invective found in various books against the spiritual mediocrity of the clergy and the religious orders. But there is a problem that to be perfectly understood requires an in-depth analysis. We must wonder whether the medium used any revelation - canonical or personal – which is neutral or whether it influences the message; whether the medium, a psychic or a prophet, is able to modify/adapt/specify the message. It is a very complex question, but there are some clear examples.

The canonical gospels are different, so much so that in some cases, they allowed the enemies of Christianity to show these apparent contradictions as alleged proof of the falsehood of Christianity itself[833]. The motives are various, but one: the evangelist-man - a different evangelist with a different style and sensitivity, but the message is the same. The method and the style changes: how different the gospels of St. Mark and of St. John are! But they both bring the Gospel.

We can therefore say that Maria Valtorta was chosen by the Lord because she had that somewhat strong temper which He used to say, in a certain way that was suited to her, what He wanted to tell everyone. The message of Lourdes by means of St. Bernadette is to tell people of the need for perfect humility and courage in sharing one another's burden. The message of Fatima is just a stern follow-up on Lourdes, with two keywords: prayer and repentance. We can therefore say that Maria Valtorta was chosen by God to also remind the clergy and the religious orders of the need for an intense, fervent, and enthusiastic spiritual life, even to the point – if God wants it or allows it – of martyrdom. The message of Jesus to mankind passes through her, who willingly lived a life consecrated to the Lord, to the

---

spoke firmly to priests and bishops, and that in the end she apologized for this excess of zeal.

[833] For example, cf. Aulo Cornelio Celso, *Contro i cristiani – Il discorso di verità* [Against Christians – The Speech on Truth], BUR Biblioteca Universale Rizzoli, Milano 2016.

point of a slow martyrdom of illnesses and infirmity, all with the burden of joyful severity of which it is abundant. No wonder then, that this blessed invective must be considered as a merciful warning to all, starting with the clergy in all its ranks. It is true, anyway, that this blessed sternness can be wrongly manipulated: it has happened and it still happens, and it does not take a mind imbued with 'conspiracy theories' or 'apocalyptic scare-mongering', but sometimes just 'blessed pride' is enough, or someone looking to find out who the next antichrist is or will be, or when the New Jerusalem will descend from Heaven.

As a matter of fact, even the harshest sentences written by Maria Valtorta must be read in her total love for the Church and the souls; to open the door of Divine Mercy to them. Outside this context, misunderstanding is inevitable. If we want to use an evangelical image, she can be compared to the person who at the sight of the 'prodigal son' starving among the pigs, takes him by the scruff of the neck in the hope that he will react and, coming back to his senses, will run into the arms of the Father who is waiting for him. It is objectionable, but after all, Maria Valtorta is a means, just like that of Heaven that manifested itself to her and to the world. Those who look for ways of measuring the sins in others and not in themselves first, are on the right path to misunderstand the Valtorta message. The conversion of mankind starts with the readers themselves and not with those who do not know. To sneer looking at mediocrity in others and not in oneself is the opposite of what Maria Valtorta has written.

It is understandable, then, that these are harsh words for everybody, but they are words that come from divine love for men, that does not let them self-destroy through their behavior. The message that comes to us through Maria Valtorta is one of mercy. The Holy Virgin in Guadalupe asked for harmony among people, instead of racism and extreme nationalism. At Lourdes she asked for conversion and humility. At Fatima she asked for penitence and love for all. All three messages are present in the writings by Maria Valtorta. The first conversation, the first dictation, is nothing other than the merciful dominant theme of all Valtorta's work, which was followed by the great work of Love Incarnate who wants to save everyone, giving everyone the possibility.

This is how the long 'symphony' began on 23 April 1943: "The first time to purify the Earth, my Father sent a lavacre of water. The second, he sent a lavacre of blood - and what Blood! [...] Men preferred hell to Heaven and their dominator - Lucifer - tortures them to spur them to curse Us so as to render them his sons and daughters completely. I would come a second time to die, to save them from an even more atrocious death... But my Father does not allow it... My Love would permit it; Justice does not. He knows that it would be useless"[834]. It was 1943 and the second Great War was claiming a huge number of victims. (In the end, it would be 50 million); *gulags* (Russian camps) and *lagers* (German concentration camps) were triumphing: the hell *evoked* by men had arrived on earth and mankind was suffering its consequences.

Certainly, harsh words followed, even accusations, but all were directed to the eternal salvation of everyone and without ever falling into repetition, always urging people to change. It was never an ideological accusation aimed at destroying the existing to substitute it with some dreams, which then, in practice, turned out to be nightmares, even though on reflection, that is what they were even in dreams.

There are many harsh words, and not all are against the hierarchy. The point of view from which Maria Valtorta was writing, was always God's and the need that all men must live with God, save their soul and "earn Heaven". As an example, let's remember the words received by Maria Valtorta on a great and valuable scientist, the Nobel prize-winner *Madame* Marie Curie. Success in the world, even if it is well deserved, does not ensure the salvation of the soul: "They are humanly perfect creatures. In them, everything has reached perfection, *except their spirit, which has regressed more* and more until *becoming an embryonic spirit.* They have perfect genius, perfect seriousness, perfect honesty and perfect humility. But everything is humanly perfect. *Their virtue is* a flame *which gives no warmth. It is a cold fire. It has no value for Me. I prefer an imperfect Spirituality to a perfect humanity.* [...] *They are beings full of knowledge, but lacking the thread leading to exact knowledge of all that is.* They are inventors of what is new, *but deniers of what is eternal.* Discoverers of secret forces, *but indifferent to the*

---

[834] Maria Valtorta, *Notebooks 1943*, op. cit., dated 23 April, pp. 19-20.

Force of the forces: God. They do not seek Him - indeed, they deliberately deny Him. At the very least, they neglect Him. [...] In this specific case, the woman did not harm, but, rather, benefitted her brothers and sisters. That is indeed great. But reflect on the impetus she would have impressed upon her school [...] if she had joined a deep religiosity in the appeal of her *self*. Also believe, soul of mine, that in the hour of judgment, certain insignificant illiterate creatures will stand forth as greater than some luminaries of science. *The former, set aflame by love, will be living stars in my heaven.* The others, though I will not condemn them on account of the good they have done in human terms, will simply be hazy in my Paradise. They will be the ones saved by my Mercy, without any merit on their part, but saved more on account of the prayers of those who benefitted by them, than on their own account."[835]. Maria Valtorta reminded us that only by looking at the world from the divine point of view, can one see the true spiritual state of a person.

Mystical absence?

Towards 1956, something unexpected occurred in Maria Valtorta[836]. Her illnesses got worse and they remained critically stable, but a sort of almost 'total absence from the present' arrived. Marta Diciotti, in this situation, could have abandoned her to her fate as a long-term patient, but she did not do that. Indeed, the remaining five years were marked by an endless watching over her, taking care of her continuously with infinite love, day after day, and night after night. Maria Valtorta was not present anymore; she seemed to be vegetating, repeating a few words from time to time: "The sun is so bright, so bright, here!"[837] or writing the same sentence over and over: "Jesus, I trust in you"[838]. Marta Diciotti, the meticulous and kind

---

[835] Maria Valtorta, *Notebooks 1943*, op. cit., dated 24 August, pp. 269-70.

[836] Albo Centoni, *Una vita con Maria Valtorta. Testimonianze di Marta Diciotti*, op. cit., p. 46. "Gradually starting in 1956, she drifted away, gradually withdrawing into psychic isolation" (ibid., p. 149).

[837] ibid., p. 157.

[838] "There was a first period in which she, on her own initiative, filled sheets of paper and pictures with the words 'Jesus, I trust in you', writing it countless times and making the calculation (she who was terrible at

witness, recalled: "And now, to look at her so passive... so indifferent to everything that was happening around her... I felt a very bitter pain and I could not get used to the idea of seeing her turn slowly into a wreck, more and more lifeless, more and more silent"[839]. At this point, however, we cannot forget the total gift of herself that Maria Valtorta made in 1947, when Jesus promised her: "I will make you forget the world in my love."[840]. Now that happened: "The first big volume of *The Poem of the Man-God* arrived here exactly on the morning of 27 June 1956. To what I have already said, I need to add some detail which I was reminded of by the letter in question: and that is, that I let her kiss that book and that I obviously kissed it too. And Maria kissed it, doing as I said, like a robot, without a word"[841]. And yet, Maria Valtorta was not totally absent, as there are two events which were a *litmus test* that made her real mental state more evident, even during that period of serious *failure*. The first has already been mentioned and it was when she sent the spiritist Dr. Luciano Raffaele[842] out of her bedroom: his very presence caused a huge reaction in Maria Valtorta, and made her radical anti-spiritism very evident, almost like a warning to everybody. She was absent, but only to a point. That is why we can very well assume that her condition was not caused by a new illness, but rather by a supernatural intervention which put Maria Valtorta into a paramystic state[843]. The second episode confirms this interpretation. It was 5 January 1960 and the radio was talking about the placement of the *Poem* on the

---

numbers and mathematical calculations!) of the attached indulgences. Later, however, she remained inactive, despite having the ability to sign her name or write under dictation" (Emilio Pisani, *Pro e contro Maria Valtorta*, op. cit., p. 40). cf. also Albo Centoni, *Una vita con Maria Valtorta. Testimonianze di Marta Diciotti*, op. cit., image n. 16.

[839] ibid., p. 156.

[840] Maria Valtorta, *Notebooks 1945-1950*, op. cit., 14 March 1947, p. 374.

[841] Albo Centoni, *Una vita con Maria Valtorta. Testimonianze di Marta Diciotti*, op. cit., p. 161.

[842] cf. Albo Centoni, *Ricordi di donne che conobbero Maria Valtorta*, op. cit., p. 278.

[843] This was the case, for example, for Marthe Robin, Alexandrina Da Costa, Luisa Piccarreta and Saint Pio of Pietrelcina with his stigmata: all mystics of the twentieth century with paramystic manifestations.

Index. Marta Diciotti says: "The terrible words *announcing* that *The Poem of the Man-God* by an anonymous writer in four volumes, published by Pisani of Isola del Liri, had been placed on the Index, were ringing in my ears. So? Was it all a trick? Was it a deceit which had pitifully crumbled in front of reality? I just could not think that night. In a fury, I went into Maria's bedroom who was lying there, as usual, half-leaning on the pillows. I grabbed her by the arm and shook her, like you shake the fruit off a tree, and said: 'See? They placed your writings on the Index!' She turned, she looked at me... and she gave me such a look! [...] that I cannot put into words [...] but I had an indescribable feeling [...]: she gave me the impression that she already knew about it 1 before I did, and that her sorrow was immense. In fact, she very clearly replied: 'I knew it'. And she plunged back into silence, like that of a closed and sealed tomb. I felt annihilated by the huge pity taking over me. I stopped, horrified at the violence that had come over me a few moments earlier, and I was unable to utter a word"[844]. Maria Valtorta had given everything. Her immolation had been total. Now, Maria Valtorta was really at one with the Lord Jesus, sacrificed on the Cross and therefore Saviour of Mankind. Her long, immense hard work seemed to be cast to the winds and her enemies seemed to have won; the devil and his assistants seemed to have won. But these very two episodes show that even the devil is part of God's plan and that his brutal disharmony serves to build a new and more perfect harmony, worthy of the merciful and infinite Divine Musician. Not immediately, however: He always sets the timeframe – sometimes mysteriously.

The envisaged tragedy

So between 1956 and 1959 the four voluminous books were published, with the only setback of the title of the first volume. The name chosen for the work was *The Poem of Jesus*[845], but there was already a book with that title in circulation, so on the advice of Prof. Pende, it was changed to *The Poem of the Man-God*[846]. At first (in 1956),

---

[844] Albo Centoni, *Una vita con Maria Valtorta. Testimonianze di Marta Diciotti*, op. cit., pp. 75-6.

[845] ibid.

[846] In 1993, the title changed to the current *The Gospel as Revealed to Me*.

the text seemed to go unnoticed but then came 1959 and its placement on the Index by the Holy See. But we must also understand the discerning difficulty on the part of the supreme authority of the Church: the situation that the Holy See was facing, and especially Cardinal Ottaviani – Secretary of the Congregation of the Doctrine of the Faith. Msgr. Carinci pointed out to Maria Valtorta the following: "It is no surprise that a judgment is given so hastily, since the Holy Office receives hundreds of reports of revelations, sometimes contradictory messages, many (besides?) other improbable (sic) without foundation, contrary to the evangelical revelation to the meaning of the Church. I also receive such reports: Jesus wants this, the Madonna wants or desires that, i.e. that other verses are introduced in the Litany; and if we listened to these proposals, the Litany of Loreto would be as long as those of the Saints, and the latter would get much longer. Out of 100 cases, maybe only one could be taken into serious consideration..."[847]. Whoever counted them wrote that in those years, there were 295 psychics with messages at the same time. How can we forget that 1959 also saw the condemnation of St. Faustina Kowalska: "The Holy Office, on receipt of the 'Placet' (I like it) of Pius XII with decree of 28 November 1958[848] (followed by a notification in 1959, Ed.) concerning the 'alleged visions and revelations of Sister Faustina Kowalska', clarified and ordered that 'the distribution of the images and writings showing the cult of the Divine Mercy in the forms proposed by the same Sister Faustina must be banned' and 'the task of removing such images, in case they had already been exposed to the cult, must be deferred to the discretion of the bishops'"[849]. On 16 December 1959, the first two titles[850] of Maria Valtorta published

---

[847] Maria Valtorta, *Lettere a Mons. Carinci*, op. cit., p. 104, letter dated 27 December 1950.

[848] There is a possible clue in the dates: Pius XII died on 6 October 1958; the sentence is on 28 November of the same year. It can be assumed that, as soon as the Pope died who had been in favor of the Work, Cardinal. Ottaviani, who instead was opposed to all private revelations, promptly intervened to condemn them.

[849] *https://benedettoxviblog.wordpress.com/2018/10/09/perche-il-vaticano-vieto-la-diffsione-del-diario-di-santa-faustina*, consulted 3 November 2018.

[850] *The Poem of Jesus* and *The Poem of the Man-God*.

anonymously were placed on the Index of Forbidden Books. On 5 January 1960, the "Osservatore Romano" published the notification and an article explaining its motive; the article is the responsibility of the Vatican newspaper editor, listing in a column on the right-hand side of the first page the main accusations: "A badly fictionalized life of Jesus [...] a long and wordy life of Jesus [...] Some pages are written rather inappropriately [...] could easily fall into the hands of religious women and students in their universities [...] specialists in biblical studies will no doubt find many historical and geographical blunders, and the like [...] would have deserved a condemnation even if it were only considered a romance novel, if for nothing else, for reasons of irreverence"[851].

This step of the Holy See was a very serious one and seemed to clip the wings of Valtorta writings. Even today, when the Index of Forbidden Books has ceased to exist, as it was abolished on 4 February 1966, there is still someone who repeats the mistaken *mantra*: "Maria Valtorta was condemned". The sentence and the concept expressed are wrong in many ways. Firstly, only the first two editions (1956-59 and 1961) were placed on the Index of Forbidden Books, but the writer Maria Valtorta was never condemned. Strictly speaking, the other texts were never placed on the Index. However, it remains true, as stated by the Holy See, that "the Index remains morally challenging as it warns the Christian conscience, out of a need that arises from natural law, to beware of those writings, which can put the faith and morals in danger; but at the same time, it warns that it no longer has the power of an ecclesiastical law with its relative censures"[852]. The real reason why *The Poem of the Man-God* was placed on the Index is not explained in detail in the decree. The anonymous article assumes that there are "many historical and geographical blunders, and the like", but no doctrinal charge was advanced. On top of that, today we know that there are no mistakes: either historical, or geographical, or even archaeological.

---

[851] "L'Osservatore Romano", Wednesday 6 January 1960, p. 1.
[852] Sacred Congregation for the Doctrine of Faith, *Notificazione riguardante l'abolizione dell'Indice dei libri* [Notification concerning the abolition of the Index of Forbidden books], Rome, from the Palace of the Holy Office, 14 June 1966.

Decades have gone by since that 1960, but now, since 2012, it has been demonstrated that none of the accusations made by the article are substantial. So, Maria Valtorta was not wrong, as opposed to the hasty judgment made by the anonymous columnist of the "Osservatore Romano". Consequently, not only are there no charges whatsoever, but it is by now a known fact that whoever reads Valtorta's texts gets closer and closer to the Church in a vital and not-devotional way. The unity between Maria Valtorta's Christ and the Catholic Church is so tight that, by welcoming the former in the joy of the new evangelization of which the texts are carriers, one also enters or re-enters the Church[853]. The hope of Dr. Emilio Pisani is fully acceptable: "With time, its condemnation will lose the character of infamy and assume that of pride and glory, as it happened with Jesus' Cross"[854]. The scientific discoveries made on the texts, by proving the accuracy of the Valtorta writings, have opened the door to the glory of the resurrection to the Work by Maria Valtorta too.

Entrance into Heaven

Towards the end of August 1961, Marta Diciotti realized that Maria Valtorta was getting worse – after 26 years that she had spent bedridden and about six where she had been "absent". She had always refused hospitalization for fear that eugenic attitudes might

---

[853] Emilio Pisani, in the fifth reprint of *Pro e contro Maria Valtorta*, also added an answer to the anonymous columnist: "The presence of historical, geographical, and similar variations is given for certain, but it is not ascertained. If there were, scientific blunders, they might deserve the reprobation of specialists in biblical studies, not the condemnation of those in charge of protecting the faith and morals. For this reason, perhaps the censor spared himself to track them down" (Emilio Pisani, *Pro e contro Maria Valtorta*, Centro Editoriale Valtortiato, Isola del Liri (FR) 2007⁵, p. 103). While sharing the spirit of the expressions of Dr. Pisani, however, it must always be kept in mind that it was precisely the general intention with which Maria Valtorta wrote that forced the then body of the Holy Office to intervene: the keystone was and is the verification in the field, whether the writings are true or not. At the time no one did a check of this; only in 2012 it was finally proved, evidence in hand, that the writings are completely right!

[854] Emilio Pisani, *Pro e contro Maria Valtorta*, op. cit., p. 108.

urge the doctors not to treat her well or even to kill her, although, as the years of widespread racism (1936-1945) had ended, such dangers would not have been there. On the urgent advice of doctors, Maria Valtorta was therefore taken to the Hospital in Pisa, where she remained from the 16 - 29 September 1961. Marta Diciotti recalled: "The gradual and slow deterioration of Maria was marked by the fact that she was not asking for anything, she did not show any desire, any need: she wanted less and less. Indeed, she did not want and she would not have anything. And she was not nervous: not at all. [...] Sometimes she would go pale, pale, pale... And then she would recover. She did not show any impatience. Absolutely none. She never said anything improper: ever. She never said or did anything that would reveal anxiety or rebellion. No, not at all. She would lie there still. Still! Maria's bed was very har because under the mattress, there was a plank which was good for her backache. [...] Anna Maria [Mencarini] helped me do all those things that we had to do for her. She would react to certain movements, which we had to subject her to, wincing in pain or instinctively contracting, showing pain. That's true. But she did not say anything. [...] Even if it was not sunny outside, if it was horrible, if it rained, maybe heavily, sometimes as I entered the room, she would say: "How bright is the sun here!" Even crying [...] after having cried so much during her life [...] she did not cry any longer. She was annulled in every possible way. She lay there and looked at us"[855].

Then her last night came: "The night of 11 October 1961, Maria's last night. She would die the following day at 10.35 a.m., as was written and specified on various occasions. We were almost in the small hours because it was already past 11p.m. I was alone, because Anna Mencarini had left, who had been coming every night for years to give me a hand with settling the infirm for the night, as Maria had become more and more unresponsive"[856]. At this point, there was a typical (paranormal) premonition witnessed by Marta Diciotti who says: "In the darkness of the votive light that to this day, is always lit in her room beneath the suffering Christ whom she loved so much,

---

[855] Albo Centoni, *Una vita con Maria Valtorta. Testimonianze di Marta Diciotti*, op. cit., p. 182.

[856] cf. ibid., pp. 180-90.

and in the silence, I heard something come crashing down beside me[857], having broken of its own accord. I did not want to turn on the central lamp in case the light disturbed the infirm, so I was unable to see what had broken. But my gut told me immediately: 'Here we go, it is time! It is over!' It was like the presage of her death. To me, at least, it was so"[858]. And she went in further detail: "I do not know, perhaps it is a weakness of mine, but I think that whenever something was going to happen in that house, it was preceded by a sign: a windowpane or an object would break of its own accord, or something would happen. This happened many, many times, in cases of involuntary accidents not caused by something or someone. An incident like this which happened here, was seen in this house as an alarming foretelling sign of an imminent disaster: be it a broken windowpane, or any object whatsoever, or a loud crack in a glass, a vase exploding, or a similar event, you know, that happened like that, by itself, with no apparent cause"[859]. This type of phenomena is typically paranormal and not extraordinary. Unexplainable, yes, but it does often happen, and we cannot understand what the laws are that regulate it, if indeed there are any laws in this field[860].

Dr Emilio Pisani recalls her last moments: "She died in her house in Viareggio on 12 October 1961, as if obeying the word of the priest who was reciting the prayer for the dying: 'Go forth from this world',

---

[857] "Only later did I realize that the glass on the picture frame of the blessing of Pius XII, sent to Maria on the 7 April 1941 by Sister Giovannina Venturi, one of the nuns from her Bianconi College in Monza, had cracked vertically from top to bottom" (ibid., p. 25).

[858] ibid., p. 24.

[859] ibid.

[860] This is one of many cases: "The psychiatrist, J. C. Barker collaborated with the 'Evening Standard' newspaper in the task of recording and using the predictions of future events. Barker took this initiative following the landslide of a huge pile of coal debris which, in Aberfan, Wales, on 21 October 1966, buried an entire school building with 144 victims, mostly children. His investigations revealed that at least sixty people had in some way predicted the disaster. He therefore thought that an office for the collection of precognitions concerning facts of collective interest could have had an important task in predicting the effects of other future disasters" (Cf. AA.VV., *PARA Dizionario Enciclopedico*, op. cit., p. 769).

Christian soul"[861]. And so, Maria Valtorta ended her immolation in life because even after death, the misunderstanding and persecution continued without a break.

Her last five years were not a vague absence from this world caused by a mental illness. The mental illness alone would not explain those lucid moments during which certain events occurred: rationalist reductionism does not it explain all. The correct interpretation must be a different one, to hold together all the elements, including the two cases mentioned before[862]. Maria Valtorta lived in the highest mysticism; the explanation must also take this dimension into account. The "absence" of Maria Valtorta was her total identification with Christ Crucified; her experiencing total immolation in Him and like Him; she was now to be found only in Him. She wanted this herself, freely, as an absolute act of love with no human limits; Jesus did what she wanted. Maria Valtorta wanted, even *by bullying*, annihilation and fusion in Jesus the Redeemer! So, Maria Valtorta went beyond any paramystic manifestation; beyond any manifestation of the mystery: a dark, uncomfortable cell, accepted for over five years for the salvation of souls. If it was not so, we should see a psychiatrist, but one of these, Prof. Giovanni Geminiani, was brave enough to state, "whoever says that Maria Valtorta is mad, is mad!"[863] The Valtorta "case" does not belong, therefore, to the category of human pathologies, but to a lofty path of a Catholic mystic that is granted only to a very few people.

Right after Maria Valtorta's death, a plaster cast of her face was made, with difficulty and with the risk of harming the cast and the face[864]. And finally, there was the funeral: not a magnitude of people, but rather a humble affair, as humble and recluse as she had been in that small room where Heaven had entered. Now a few friends followed her on the way to her final resting place on earth. To somebody, that earth which slowly covered her, put an end to her story once and for all, but not to God.

---

[861] Emilio Pisani, *Pro e contro Maria Valtorta*, op. cit., p. 13.

[862] That is to say, the paranormal event Marta Diciotti described and her death that occurred exactly during the ritual prayers. The factual and symbolic intervention of Heaven explains the two facts together.

[863] The statement was made verbally, in an interview that was recorded.

[864] Emilio Pisani, *Pro e contro Maria Valtorta*, op. cit., p. 252.

Father Berti in search of a miracle

Exactly ten years went by, full of events centred around *The Poem of the Man-God*, and civil law ordered the exhumation. Father Berti, according to Prof. Pisani, was very excited: he would have loved an extraordinary sign. He was said to be out of his mind with the desire for a miracle over Maria Valtorta's corpse. Already on her deathbed, those present had noticed that her right hand was much whiter than the left, and they all agreed that it must be confirmation of the gift she had received and of her loyalty. Dr. Emilio Pisani added: "There was a profound reason, only half-declared. He was expecting a miraculous sign... He started early to draft programs, plan and organize meetings. He did not neglect to anticipate what he would do in case the body was found to be intact. But he would have been satisfied with much less (but it was instead, much more): finding only the right hand intact, the hand used for writing, the hand which, after the death and during the public display of the body, had preserved a bright color, as if alive, unlike the left hand, which was very pale"[865]. Besides this in writing, there are other reports passed down orally, like that of Father Valfredo Zamperini – back then among the Servants of Mary, a confrère of Father Berti, and then founder of the Missionaries of Mary in Massa. He can also be seen in a photo taken at the moment of the burial[866] and who said that thanks to this sign, Father Berti was hoping for something extraordinary. However, that day had a sad ending: only a few bones were left, to the great disappointment of Father Berti and of those who had hoped for a miracle. Obviously, that was not the miracle which God wanted to give men. As a matter of fact, a real study would have shown the heroism of the life of Maria Valtorta, and this would have been enough to grant her the honor of a cult and the acknowledgement of the Church. The use of scientific methods (rejecting medium powers) would have sufficed on the writings and on *The Poem of the Man-God*, and evidence of the facts would have shown the miracle. So, the miracle had to be found elsewhere, but maybe at that time, it could

---

[865] ibid., p. 258.

[866] "Bollettino Valtortiano", op. cit., n. 16 – March 1977, p. 62. Father Valfredo Zamperini is in front, facing the pit, and is positioned exactly in the corner of the funerary monument that is in the background.

not be seen and understood because there were no suitable "reading glasses"; or maybe that was not the time chosen by God.

Maria dressed in heavenly white

This is how Marta Diciotti described the episode of 8 June 1976 when she saw Maria Valtorta again at night: "It was 2:50a.m., when I needed to go to the toilet half-way down the stairs. [...] I washed my hands, I came out and instead of going back up to my room every time I need to get up at night, I went down to the ground floor, with no real need, perhaps absent-mindedly, I mean lost in thought because to be honest, I do not know and I cannot say that I took that wrong turn in a particular state of mind. I was totally calm. As soon as I reached the last two or three steps (I do not know precisely which of the two), I raised my eyes and in front of me, through the always-open door to her bedroom in the eastern corner of her room, I see Maria sitting on the stool by the dressing table, not looking in the mirror, but towards her bed. Yes, I see Maria there, all bright in her heavenly white robe with light blue reflections, with her wonderful, shiny, loose hair: I see Maria, there as she appears in my dreams. She is sitting by the dressing table on the stool that during her time was not there. [...] She is sitting and she is not looking at me, but in front of her, towards her bed. No, she does not look at me and she does not speak: she is simply there in her shiny, heavenly white robe, just like I see her in my dreams, like I have always seen her, except for once, when – at Isola del Liri, I think – she came to me in a dream in a lilac-like brightness. I look at her, enraptured and glad [...] yes, full of joy, even if she does not look at me, even if she does not say anything to me [...[But I am not sleeping, I am there, wide awake! I am not sleeping, and I am going down the stairs, not in my mind, but with my own two legs! I do not sleep, and I come from the toilet, where I even washed my hands a short while ago! Yes, I come from there, and here I go downstairs with no need, no reason at all, without a motive [...["Oh my God, Lord Jesus!..." I want to exclaim… "Oh Lord my God, Blessed Jesus!" and I instinctively cover my eyes with the left hand because I have the right on the handrail, which I hold on to tight… I could not say for how many seconds I remained there, standing still with my eyes covered: I know that in my heart there is a succession of invocations, exclamations expressing a turmoil of thoughts, of feelings [...] not fear... oh, no! It is not fear, but rather astonishment, enchanted wonder, joy, fullness, happiness and a total absence of merit on my part [...] When I decide to uncover them, and I look in front of me [...] the heavenly image has gone. All is normal, sweetly familiar as always"[867].

Today, the most obvious answer to this episode is probably that of a paranormal event aimed at Marta Diciotti. We should genuinely rule out the presence of one of those souls in Purgatory where God allows them to show themselves to ask for or give help, if nothing else, because the usual methodology is different. After all, it seems obvious to think that Maria Valtorta is in Heaven: her love for Jesus and for souls, for which she offered herself, is proof enough. Case histories in the paranormal are almost endless. The purpose can be to confirm to Marta Diciotti that there is an afterlife; to show her the glory attained by Maria Valtorta; or it can be an invitation for Marta to persevere.

All these theories are equally possible because they all lead us to see a gift from God in Maria Valtorta, from Trinity to present mankind.

Conclusion

Contrary to what it seems, the story of Maria Valtorta who voluntarily and freely immolated herself for the salvation of her brothers is by no means over. She not only intercedes from Heaven for mankind – according to the opinion of the writer – but her story continues in her writings and especially in what today is called *The Gospel as Revealed to Me*. To obtain it, her total and daily immolation was necessary; the annihilation of her body and soul. Not a dreamed imitation of Jesus, but His concrete copy up to the bloody death, including total failure. Maria Valtorta has relived her immolation day after day, repeating the offer of Jesus to the Father: annihilated in her body, annihilated in her human hopes, abandoned and betrayed (this word is serious, but we must use it because she had to sustain even this blow) by the very people who should have helped and served

---

[867] Albo Centoni, *Una vita con Maria Valtorta. Testimonianze di Marta Diciotti*, op. cit., pp. 511-2.

her[868]. She was enclosed in a body which made socializing impossible, and she was mystically alone, misunderstood, not understood, insulted and considered mad; and yet never tamed, never hopeless, never depressed or inward-looking. In one of her last images taken by a photographer, we can see her sitting up in her bed of sorrows, but with her back straight, as if visually stating her determination. In the end, Jesus said to the Father: "Into Your hands I commit my spirit"[869]. Even here, the imitation was total. She equally gave everything to Jesus, unreservedly, leaving it all to Him. Jesus was persecuted even after His death and resurrection, and the seals on his tomb and the guards at the tomb are proof of that. The same thing with her. The insult of her writings being placed on the Index did not shock her: "I already knew it" she said, at the time of the sentence. But now her writings are travelling around the world and many people are talking about them, although few, at least until recently, thave been told people what an incredible gift she gave us. Her writings have been brought to people in thirty languages. And this is just the beginning. Jesus said of Himself: "When I will have risen from the earth, I will attract everyone to me"[870] and so it was. I think it is appropriate to believe that through the welcomed, lived and suffered immolation, well beyond any human understanding, what will happen to the Viareggio mystic, 'little John', is what happened to her Lord, endlessly loved. And this is what we expect, what we hope for, what we pray for and what we talk and write about.

---

[868] This title, above all, belongs to Father Migliorini. The same can be said for the Order of the Servants of Mary, and Father Berti can be added to this group. To those who try to understand, however, the big question remains: where did her writings, her letters, her reports, her memos go?
[869] Lk 23:45.
[870] Jn 12:32.

Bibliography

"Bollettino Valtortiano. Semestrale di informazione e cultura valtortiana", Centro Editoriale Valtortiano, Isola del Liri (FR), nn. vari.

AA.VV., *PARA Dizionario Enciclopedico*, Armenia Editore, Milano 1986.

AA.VV., *Tutte le encicliche dei sommi Pontefici*, Editore dall'Oglio, Milano 1986.

Agreda (D') Maria, *Mistica Città di Dio*, Edizione Porziuncola, Assisi 2000, 2 voll.

Allegra Gabriele M., *Il primato di Cristo in San Paolo e Duns Scoto. Le mie conversazioni con Teilhard de Chardin*, Edizioni Porziuncola, Assisi 2011.

Allegri Renzo, *A tu per tu con Padre Pio*, Arnoldo Mondadori Editore, Milano 2000^{10}.

Antier Jean Jacques, *Marthe Robin. Il viaggio immobile*, San Paolo Edizioni, Milano 1994.

Benedetto Abate San, *La regola di san Benedetto*, Shalom Editrice, Camerata Picena 2016.

Bertozzi Federico, *Attaccarono i fogli: si doveva sfolà!*, Pezzini Editore, Viareggio (LU) 2014.

Blavatsky Eléna Petróvna, *La dottrina segreta*, Edizioni Teosofiche Italiane, Vicenza 2003.

Boismard Marie-Emile, *All'alba del giansenismo*, Piemme, Casale Monferrato (AL) 2000.

Borriello Luigi – Caruana Edmondo – Del Genio Maria Rosaria – Di Muro Raffaele, *Nuovo dizionario di mistica*, Libreria Editrice Vaticana, Città del Vaticano 2016.

Borriello Luigi – Caruana Edmondo – Del Genio Maria Rosaria – Suffi Nicolò (a cura di), *Dizionario di Mistica*, Libreria Editrice Vaticana, Città del Vaticano 1998.

Borriello Luigi – Di Muro Raffaele (a cura di), *Dizionario dei Fenomeni mistici cristiani*, Ancora, Milano 2014.

Brunot Amédée, *La Piccola Araba*, Edizioni OCD, Roma 2004.

Centoni Albo, *Ricordi di donne che conobbero Maria Valtorta*, Centro Editoriale Valtortiano, Isola del Liri (FR) 1998.

Centoni Albo, *Una vita con Maria Valtorta. Testimonianze di Marta Diciotti*, Centro Editoriale Valtortiano, Isola del Liri (FR) 1987.

Cigliana Simona, *Due secoli di fantasmi*, Edizioni Mediterranee, Roma 2018.

Concilio Ecumenico Vaticano II, Decreto sull'attività missionaria della chiesa *Ad Gentes*. In *Enchiridium Vaticanum*, Edizioni Dehoniane Bologna, Bologna 1981.

De Foucault Charles, *Carnets de Tamanrasset 1905-1916*, Nouvelle Cité, Paris 1986.

Esteban Rubén Pineda, *La Inmolación como la clave de comprensión y el nexo de unión entre teología y vida mística en las obras de María Valtorta*, Facultad de Teología del Norte de España sede de Burgos, Burgos 2010.

Emmerich Anna Caterina, *La passione di Gesù dalle visioni di Anna Caterina Emmerich*, Centro Editoriale Valtortiano, Isola del Liri (FR) 2005.

Emmerich Anna Caterina, *Le rivelazioni di Caterina Emmerick*, Cantagalli, Siena 1998.

Ferri and Valtorta, Centro Editoriale Valtortiano, Isola del Liri (FR) 2006.

Ferri Leonardo (a cura di), *L'uomo della Sindone nella ricostruzione dello scultore Lorenzo Ferri. Quarantacinque anni di studi dal 1930 al 1975*, Edizioni Kappa, Roma 2007.

Giordani Igino (introduzione e traduzione di), *San Giustino. Le apologie*, Città Nuova, Roma 1962.

Giovanni della Croce, *Tutte le opere*, Bompiani, Milano 2010.

Giovanni Paolo II, *Enciclica Redemptor Hominis*, 4 marzo 1979. In *Enchiridion delle Encicliche*, Edizioni Dehoniane Bologna, Bologna 1998.

Gramaglia Pier Angelo, *Maria Valtorta. Una moderna manipolazione dei Vangeli*, Edizioni Piemme, Casale Monferrato (AL) 1985.

Guitton Jean, *Ritratto di Marthe Robin*, Paoline Editoriale libri, Milano 2001.

Hildesheimer Françoise – Francini Marta Pieroni, *Il giansenismo*, Edizioni San Paolo, Milano 1994.

Iandolo Maurizio, *La direzione spirituale e l'esperienza mistica: il caso di santa Gemma Galgani e dei suoi direttori spirituali*, Facoltà Teologica dell'Italia Centrale, Firenze 2015.

Ignazio di Loyola, *Esercizi Spirituali*, Edizioni San Paolo, Cinisello Balsamo (MI) 1995.

Ignazio di Loyola, *Esercizi Spirituali. Ricerca sulle fonti* (a cura di padre Pietro Schiavone S.J.), Edizioni San Paolo, Cinisello Balsamo (Milano) 1995.

Il Bollettino Valtortiano. Dal n. 1 al n. 30, Centro Editoriale Valtortiano, Isola del Liri (FR) 1985.

Introvigne Massimo – Zoccatelli PierLuigi (sotto la direzione di), Centro Studi sulle Nuove Religioni, *Enciclopedia delle religioni in Italia*, Elledici, Torino 2013.

Introvigne Massimo, *Il cappello del mago. I nuovi movimenti magici, dallo spiritismo al satanismo*, SugarCo, Milano 1995.

Invernizzi Marco, *Il movimento cattolico in Italia dalla fondazione dell'opera dei congressi all'inizio della seconda guerra mondiale (1874-1939)*, Mimep-Docete, Cassano con Bornago (MI), 1995.

La Vecchia Maria Teresa, *Antropologia paranormale. Fenomeni fisici e psichici straordinari*, Pontificia Università Gregoriana, Roma 2002.

Lavère Jean-François, *L'enigma Valtorta*, Centro Editoriale Valtortiano, Isola del Liri (FR) 2012.

Lessi Valerio, *Margherita Maria Alacoque. La santa dal Sacro Cuore*, Paoline Editoriale Libri, Milano 2014.

Lugli Remo, *Gustavo Rol. Una vita di prodigi*, Edizioni Mediterranee, Roma 2008.

Melton Gordon, *The Encyclopedia of American Religions*, Oxford University Press, Oxford (EN) 2016^9.

Menendez Josefa, *Invito all'amore*, Editrice Shalom, Camerata Picena (AN) 2015.

Mohler Adam Johann, *Simbolica*, Jaca Book, Milano 1984.

Mondin Battista, *Storia della teologia. Volume 1*, Edizioni Studio Domenicano, Bologna 1996.

Monteleone Franco, *Storia della radio e della televisione in Italia. Un secolo di costume, società e politica*, Marsilio Editori, Venezia 2001.

Paparone Giuseppe, *La teologia mistica in Padre Garrigou-Lagrange*, in "Sacra Dottrina monografie", Edizioni Studio Domenicano, Bologna n. 3-4 – maggio-agosto 1999.

Petersdorff Egon von, *Demonologia*, Mondadori, Segrate (MI) 1990.
Pisani Emilio (a cura di), *Note all'opera di Maria Valtorta con indici tematico e biblico*, Centro Editoriale Valtortiano, Isola del Liri (FR) 2001.
Pisani Emilio, *Catalogo dei quaderni autografi di Maria Valtorta*, Centro Editoriale Valtortiano, Isola del Liri (FR) 2010.
Pisani Emilio, *Lettera a Claudia*, Centro Editoriale Valtortiano, Isola del Liri (FR) 2014.
Pisani Emilio, *Pro e contro Maria Valtorta*, Centro Editoriale Valtortiano, Isola del Liri (FR) 2017^6.
Rahner Karl, *Visioni e profezie*, Vita e Pensiero, Milano 1955.
Roschini Gabriele Maria, *La Madonna negli scritti di Maria Valtorta*, Centro Editoriale Valtortiano, Isola del Liri (FR) 1973.
Speziale Vincenzo, *Le profezie della Beata Madre Elena Aiello*, Edizioni Segno, Tavagnacco (UD) 2014.
Speziale Vincenzo, *Serva di Dio Luigina Sinapi*, Edizioni Segno, Tavagnacco (UD) 2016.
Teresa d'Avila, *Il Castello Interiore*, Figlie di San Paolo, Milano 2005.
Tolkien J. R. R., *Il Silmarillion*, Rusconi libri, Milano 1992^{10}.
Ubaldi Pietro, *La grande sintesi*, Ulrico Hoepli Editore, Milano 1939.
Ubaldi Pietro, *Le Noùri*, Ulrico Hoepli Editore, Milano 1937.
Valtorta Maria, *Autobiography*, Centro Editoriale Valtortiano, Isola del Liri (FR) 2009.
Valtorta Maria, *Autobiography*, Tipografia Editrice M. Pisani, Isola del Liri (FR) 1991.
Valtorta Maria, *Notebooks 1943*, Centro Editoriale Valtortiano, Isola del Liri (FR) 2001.
Valtorta Maria, *Notebooks 1944*, Centro Editoriale Valtortiano, Isola del Liri (FR) 2001.
Valtorta Maria, *Notebooks 1945-1950*, Centro Editoriale Valtortiano, Isola del Liri (FR) 2002.
Valtorta Maria, *The Book of Azariah*, Centro Editoriale Valtortiano, Isola del Liri (FR) 1993.
Valtorta Maria, *Il Poema dell'Uomo-Dio*, Tipografia Editrice M. Pisani, Isola del Liri (FR) 1961^2, 4 voll.
Valtorta Maria, *The Gospel As Revealed To Me*, Centro Editoriale Valtortiano, Isola del Liri (FR) 2015, 10 volumes.

Valtorta Maria, *Lettere a Madre Teresa Maria 1*, Centro Editoriale Valtortiano, Isola del Liri (FR) 2012.

Valtorta Maria, *Lettere a Madre Teresa Maria 2*, Centro Editoriale Valtortiano, Isola del Liri (FR) 2012.

Valtorta Maria, *Lettere a Mons. Carinci*, Centro Editoriale Valtortiano, Isola del Liri (FR) 2006.

Valtorta Maria, *Lettere a Padre Migliorini*, Centro Editoriale Valtortiano, Isola del Liri (FR) 2011.

Valtorta Maria, *Lessons on the Epistle of St. Paul to the Romans*, Centro Editoriale Valtortiano, Isola del Liri (FR) 2007.

Valtorta Maria, *The Little Notebooks*, Centro Editoriale Valtortiano, Isola del Liri (FR) 2022.

About the author

Father Ernesto Zucchini read *The Gospel* for the first time in 1969 (when the title was still *The Poem of the Man-God*) before starting the seminary. He lived his life reading profusely which, in fact, influenced all his subsequent training. Even if it appeared that he left [this Work] aside, in reality, it had remained silent in his heart until 2007 when – already a priest and Parish Priest – he was drawn to a new text by the Benedictine friends of Our Lady of the Trinity of Monte Monastero (Piacenza PC). From the first pages of the *Notebooks 1943* – which had been given to him years earlier – he already had a spiritual experience that touched him deeply. Therefore, he started studying it again and has not stopped since. He left the doctoral thesis he had started and replaced it with the one he is (still) writing on Maria Valtorta and her Work, wagering on a theological and scientific depth which, at that time, no one had yet explored (J. F. Lavère's discoveries came to light only in 2012). In 2008, he held his first conference in Massa near the Capuchins (almost putting himself to the test), which was a small yet large unexpected success and a turning point. Right after this, he was contacted by the future benefactor who asked him to bring life to the Foundation (despite some unexpected difficulties) and assume the role of President. During that same period, Father Ernesto Zucchini began to hold a monthly broadcast on Radio Maria which was aired uninterruptedly every first Friday at 12:30, and to celebrate Holy Mass in Viareggio every 12th of the month with the particular intention for the Church to recognize Maria Valtorta and the Work. Since then, he has never stopped reading, studying and deepening his knowledge of the person and writings of Maria Valtorta, and disseminating them through numerous initiatives such as annual conventions, in addition to conferences throughout Italy and abroad, and recently through new technology with newsletters and live streaming. Since 2021, he has adapted the week of Spiritual Exercises of Saint Ignatius of Loyola to make it a Valtorta Spiritual retreat. In Italian, he wrote the life of Maria Valtorta: *Heaven in a Room* (also translated and published in French) and *The Cathedral of Maria Valtorta: A guide to the work of the great mystic* (Fede & Cultura 2021), which is a natural progression of the present text.

www.ingramcontent.com/pod-product-compliance
Lightning Source LLC
Chambersburg PA
CBHW022003160426
43197CB00007B/247